UNDER THE SHADOW OF DEATH

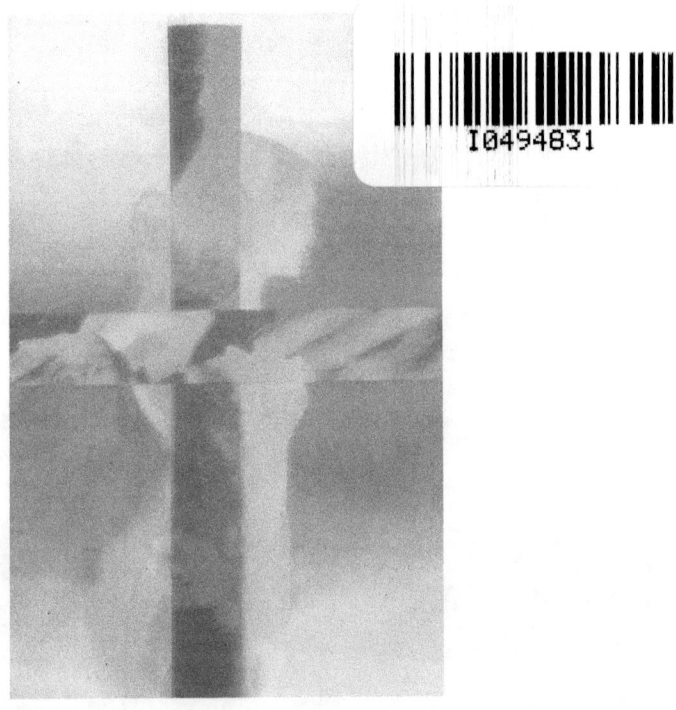

The Goddess On Crucifixtion

'I owe woman all my life,
I owe her this self which was born from a cry,'
'Woman opened my eyes,
Woman freed my soul,'

- Kahlil Gibran

ISBN: 1470112078

ISBN 13: 9781470112073

Library of Congress Control Number: 2012911928
CreateSpace Independent Publishing Platform
North Charleston, South Carolina

DEDICATION
TO
MALALA-YOUSAFZAI
AND
EVERY MOM

A fourteen years old student Leader who faced bullets of Taliban in their attempt to kill her. She has resolved to spread Female Education and transform Pakistan from Dark Ages to Modern Era.

FAMILY TREE (OF MAIN CHARACTERS)

Grand-Pa, SOHAN -had three issue-:

1-DEVA (Karmi's father) 2-BHANI- (Aunt) 3-Veeru (Uncle) He had the only child, Bholi

DEVA had two issues-: 1- KARMI (Wife of Subedar-Bhag) 2-MOHNA un-marr.

KARMI had three Issues-: 1-TARA 2-BALI (Twins) 3-UDHE 4-SATTI -Step daughter.

BHANI had four Issues -: 1-JEETI 2-MOHLI 4-SADHU 3-Surraina

INTRODUCTION

Sahib S. Gill is an author of four Books-: 1-Novel (Eng.) and 3-Short Story books (Hindi, Punjabi). Main theme of the Novel and Short Stories is the Woman. Academic Qualifications- Master in Economics and B.T. -Thirty five years' experience as Principal, lecturer in Economics, Psychology and English.

Hobby-Writing and Social Service: Built a Stadium and School Building at Daroli-Bhai; Punjab

Sahib Gill, sahibGill@gmail. com

ACKNOWLEDGEMENT

I am thankful to Dr. Jagjeevan Gill who worked as Editor voluntarily. Born in India and living in London/Canada she is familiar with the woman's life in the East and the West. In the third world countries Woman's life is not better than slave. Gender equality in the west is a far cry. I am grateful to the experienced Editor, Jennifer who worked hard on this Novel and made a sea change. I have no words to express thanks to a famous Indian Novelist Jaswant Kanwal and Dr. Jaswinder Singh, Dean, Punjabi University. They gave valuable guidance frequently. I am impressed by the excellent work of Create Space too.

ONE

Karmi woke up in the morning; she found that her husband, the subahdar Bhag Singh, was not in their bed. She looked hither and thither but could not find a trace of him anywhere in the house. The lamp was burning in the kitchen. The used tea utensils were lying scattered, just as he had left them after taking tea.

She thought, "He might have gone out to ease himself after taking tea."

Karmi's four year old son Tara got up, rubbing his eyes, came to his mother, and asked, "Mom! I do not see Dad, where is he? Her five year old step daughter, Satti, and twin daughter Bali came and they too asked, "Where is Dad?"

"He must be here; somewhere," She replied and started looking around again. As she stepped forward she saw a partly empty bottle of rum that had been rolled under the bed. She assumed that he was dead drunk after consuming so much drink; in his inebriated state he had gone to sleep without taking any of the delicacies prepared for him.

Karmi's house had witnessed a joyous occasion on the subahdar's joining his family after a long period of waiting but it was short lived. The grandparents came at dawn and asked the children, "Where is your mother, kids?" Thinking that their son might have told Karmi when he was coming back.

Karmi listened to her father-in-law speaking with the children; she came out of her room and replied, "He did not tell us anything while going, how could I come to know about his coming back?"

The parents got worried over their son's hurriedly departing, like a thief without telling anything.

They got tired of waiting day after day, but he failed to turn up. Karmi too had lost all hope of his returning. She wailed, "Like Sita,[1] my lifelong devotion to my husband has gone in vain." After some time she consoled herself: "In this male-dominated society, where even the goddess Sita was not spared, who cares about me, an insignificant figure? Even in the twentieth century a woman is treated like a pair of shoes[2] by her husband. He discards her when he wishes and gets a new one, but what is the fault of my children? They lost their Father the very next day of having him."

Her husband had been fighting for many years for India's freedom after a long service in the Army. Then he was taken a prisoner and kept at an unknown place. The people of his village were surprised to know that he turned up alive, especially when the relatives of all his missing colleagues had

---

1   wife of Lord Rama who was exiled by her husband

2   Insignificant thing

performed their last rites. Everyone came to see him and inquired about him on entering the house.

Karmi covered up his disappearance on one pretext or another for a long time. Ultimately, she too joined them in inquiring, "Where is he?"

People in the village had their own way of giving reasons for his self-exile. Someone said, "His wife had earned a bad name for him. Feeling ashamed, he left the village."

Another one said, "He did not attain the freedom. Instead he lost his job. This factor had upset him."

The creditors said, "His wife had run into heavy debts. Being unable to repay, he has gone into hiding."

Karmi felt very bad on hearing all those insinuations. Nobody condemned the subahdar for betraying his wife and children and ruining them.

She thought, "I have sacrificed my life for my husband. Nobody sympathized with me and gave credit for my sacrifice."

Tears flowed down her cheeks in the presence of her children, though she didn't want to show them. She cried, "O my God! For what sins are you punishing me?" Sometimes she cursed her husband too. "You have deserted me in midstream. It is not good on your part. How will I support your offspring?"

The children too felt sad on seeing the tears rolling down their mother's face.

All of a sudden black clouds had appeared on the western sky, and there was lightning and thundering again. The doors and windows were banging loudly. The frightened children had gotten into Karmi's lap. Then it started raining cats and dogs. To amuse her children, Karmi started relating a tale of birds, "There was a crow and a sparrow. They got together and sowed millet. The sparrow worked on raising crop, crow shirked work. When the crop was ready and harvested the crow took away the lion's share on one plea or another and left sparrow with a negligible share." Through this tale of the crow and the sparrow and other tales of birds and animals, she told them about male's high-handedness. She added, "Man is not only unfair to his wife, but he does not spare his daughter even. He kills the little one at birth."

Tara was a very intelligent child. He asked, "How did you escape, Mom? You were also someone's daughter."

She tried to dodge him. "My father was a social activist and opposed to all kinds of inhuman killings. Moreover, I survived to my bad luck. I owed some old debts of past lives to your father!"

Satti and Bali also joined him, "Tell us, Mom, how you survived."

She had to resume her tale of woes. "Our aunt Phino used to tell the story about me: As I was born, all types of efforts were made to kill me but they failed every time. Lastly *dhatura*[3] was put on my tongue; I survived that too. Ultimately the midwife filled the tub with water and tried to drown me. At that time she noticed a circular growth of hair on my occiput and told my mother, 'You are a wise lady, you will understand me. Just look at this circular hair growth. It indicates a male baby would follow her. She is a lucky baby. You should save her life.'

Mom said, 'What should we do with the circular growth of hair? A girl brings in a lot of responsibilities. We have to bring her up, educate her, marry her, and spend money through the nose. There are not enough yields from the fields. We cannot afford to bring up a girl as we are already head over ears in debt. We are doomed!' She directed the midwife to kill me.'

'If you do not want to save her, who am I to disobey you?' said the midwife. She was going to put me in the tub of water when Phino took me from the midwife. She looked behind my head closely. She too saw the circle of hair. She smiled happily and said to my mother, 'You are gone off your head, Bhabi.[4]

---

3   milk of a poisonous plant
4   sister-in-law

Don't kill your daughter. Look here. She has a circle of hair. You will give birth to a son next time. When he grows up, he will bring in good fortune. He will clear all the old and new debts. I advise you not to shut the door to your good luck.' Then all the members of the family stood in favor of saving me. All of them held me turn by turn. Everybody observed the hairy circle on the backside of my head and danced with joy. I survived by luck; hence I was christened Karmi (Lucky)."

"Then you are really lucky, Mom," said Tara.

"No, no! How I can be lucky? I was a small child when plague spread, and it devoured a large number of people within no time. It was so horrible that family after family and village after village were wiped out. My parents were doing the social service of cremation. They also got infected and died. I became an orphan with a little younger brother to look after, in this wide world."

"How did you survive the plague, when everybody died?" Tara put another question.

THREE

Karmi started relating the story of plague. "It was the month of October. The sowing season was in full swing. The people were quite healthy and working normally in the fields. They suddenly had some throat infection and died within hours. Village after village was emptied of human beings. It was very rare to see a fire burning in the hearth of any house. The people were struggling with death on an empty stomach.

"The hungry cattle bellowed, the dogs barked for food in the lanes; and the jackals howled in the periphery of the villages. It was a horrible scene.

"The dead bodies were stinking; the people did not stir out to cremate them for fear of infection. My father was a social worker. He was the first man who took the initiative and risked his life. He took his cousin, Phagan with him and started the cremations. They used to put the dead bodies in the bullock cart and drive toward the cremation ground. They sprinkled kerosene oil over the dead bodies for mass cremation since there was not enough firewood for individual cremation. Other people joined them in due course. They cremated a large number of bodies daily.

"It was to his bad luck that Phagan had a throat infection, and he too expired. There was strife over this issue in our family. Uncle Veeru opposed Father's doing the social service of cremation, 'You are bent upon dying with the dead, but you will kill us too. You will carry infection to our home. Uncle Phagan followed you and lost his life. Don't you like us living a happy life over here? Sit quietly at home; let the people cremate their own relatives. Why do you bother yourself for others?'

"Father explained his helplessness: 'Don't talk nonsense! Who doesn't want a happy house? We set up home to bring in happiness and joy. I work to protect you too from plague. Do you think I should not go to cremate Phagan? How can this be possible? He is my brother, my companion of joys and sorrows. He joined me on my request.'

"Uncle Veeru stuck to his stand, 'Phagan's own brothers are there; they can go to cremate him. You are not supposed to cremate all the dead in the village." Uncle Veeru did not want Father to go and get afflicted with plague. He was terribly afraid of plague after Phagan's death.

Mother intervened: "Karmi's father[5], Veeru is not giving you wrong advice. You should accept the counsel given by your own near and dear ones."

---

5   In Indian culture woman does not address her husband and his seniors by name out of respect.

"There is no such time when I did not listen to your advice. Just look at my helplessness. I am older than everyone in the fraternity. It is therefore my duty to lead. If I do not stand by them in this hour of need, who else will? The dead bodies are getting decomposed and stinking. If the bodies remained like that, the disease would spread all the more, wiping out everyone. Someone has to risk his life.'

"Yes, go ahead and risk your life, but why are you making the entire family the sacrificial goats? If you contract the disease, you would infect us also.' Mother also supported Veeru.

"Do not complain afterward that I did not tell you in time. I am leaving the house and going to the field with my family." Both the brothers were living together, and it was proper for Veeru to inform him before leaving.

Mother said, "Just listen to me, Karmi's father. Send your children with Veeru. Don't endanger the children's life by keeping them with us."

Father agreed and said to her, "You can also go to the field with the children. What will you do by staying with me?"

"Have you gone mad? I cannot go leaving you behind."

"Don't worry about me—think of the children. At least you will be able to bring up the children after me."

"You are more important to me than the children. That is why wives had been burning in the pyres of their husbands. In certain clans they are still burning."

"Leave aside burning with me. Take care of children."

"The husband-wife relationship is everlasting, even in the next life. I can't go away with Veeru."

"Alright, stay with me, and continue to be my companion of this life and the next one."

It was decided that Father and Mother would stay in the village to serve the people, and we, the kids, would go with Uncle to the fields.

Uncle sent the cattle with the farmhand, Bholu, to the fields. His wife, Nhami, and our cousin sister, Bholi of our age, got into the bullock cart. When we were made to get into the cart, we started crying. Though we were very young yet, we could understand what was happening all around. As we cried, mother too started sheding tears and my Dad felt sad. He turned his head to the other side and wept.

"We stopped crying for a while and sat down on one side. Our father engaged us in talking to divert our attention. When we stopped crying, Veeru drove the cart ahead. My younger brother, Mohna, shrieked once and got silent very soon. I started playing with Bholi. After an hour or so, we reached the farm. Within ten days or so we heard the news of our parents' death. Those who went out to the fields survived, and others who stayed back in the villages and towns were swallowed by plague." Karmi heaved a deep sigh while relating her story.

"Why have you sighed, Mom?" asked Tara.

"I recalled my dreadful past, my son. My childhood was lost in orphanage; and my youth marred by my husband. What a horrible life I have lived! O God, no Mom should live such a life."

FOUR

Most of the people died; those who survived came back to their homes in the towns and villages. Uncle Veeru also returned along with his family.

Nhami, aunt, was a very hard-hearted lady. She told Veeru the very first day, "I can't bear other people's burden. They are welcome to live with us, but they should earn their living. We cannot shoulder the responsibility of educating them."

Nhami did not like Karmi and Mohna. How could she think of giving them education? Her son, who was of Mohna's age, had died. An eccentric had poisoned her mind, 'Your son has been killed by your sister-in-law with the help of another eccentric' Veeru tried to make her understand, "You ran after charms and amulet. You did not get treatment from some physician. Your baby boy died due to your negligence." The illiterate woman did not understand the real cause of her son's death. So she put the orphan kids to a lot of trouble.

To start with, the children of both the brothers studied together, and their expenses were met out of the joint income of the family. Things changed after the plague. Nahmi became the be-all and end-all: her husband was henpecked.

"One day Uncle argued with her: 'They are like our Bholi. We should not withdraw them from school. Let them continue.'"

But Aunt did not relent "Do not compare our Bholi with the orphans, since we are alive to support her."

"Everything is going on very well; what do you expect them to do after leaving the school?" asked Uncle.

"Mohna will work as a cowboy and take care of the cattle, and Karmi should do the household chores. They are not kids now. They are grown up. Let them earn their own living. It is a joint family. If they keep going to school, who will work on their behalf? If you expect from me to do their job I would not. I am saying this frankly."

"You should withdraw Bholi also. Then the people would not blame for discriminating against them," said Veeru.

"Why should I withdraw Bholi? Her education will continue. We are here to work for her."

Karmi and Mohna's education came to an end, and they became slaves in their own home.

Aunt Nhami used to get up very early, and wake the kids too. Both of them used to sleep on the roof. Nhami started shouting at them very early in the morning to put them to work, "The sun has risen so high, get up…Oh, Mohna, death to you!" Mohna was in sound sleep and kept on sleeping. Karmi got up on the first call. The people in the neighborhood were fed up with Nhami's early-hours shouting.

One day Nhami lost her temper. She was going up the ladder and went on howling, "You mortal brat, get up! Flies are biting the cattle, making them restless;—you are sleeping unconcerned. May you die in your sleep! It is not so easy for me to milk the buffaloes. You are lying comfortably. Get up and take them to the pond! They will take bath and feel comfortable. It will be easy to milk them." Veeru, lying in the courtyard was listening to her grumbling, said, "Why are you disturbing the whole village? Let the people sleep for a while. They go to sleep after doing hard work the whole day and get tired. Make smoke by burning cow dung or dry grass, and the flies and mosquitoes will fly away. Let the child sleep too for some time."

Karmi came down after listening to her aunt's abuses. Mohna kept sleeping and took some more time to leave the bed. When he came down, Karmi stood there with a glass of half-churned curd for her brother. She said to him, "It is very sweet, just gulp it down. I churned it quickly for you so that you could take it. You should not go empty stomach."

Mohna took the cattle to the pond and returned after their bathing. Nhami had finished milking and instructed Mohna, "Take them for grazing now, as they don't graze when it gets hot." Veeru understood from her maligning behavior that Nhami was feeling vengeful toward his nephew and niece, particularly the boy. He questioned her, "Why are you so cruel to Mohna? He is just a small child; behave with him as your own son. How can he control cow and buffaloes at the same time? The cow walks fast like a doe, and the buffaloes walk majestically like an elephant. He can't control both! Tie a small log on the cow's neck. It will not let her run fast."

Nhami tried to tie a log to the cow's neck. The cow was restless. She gave a slight push to Nhami who fell flat on her face. Veeru laughed at her folly. She lost her temper and started abusing her husband: "This is my bad luck that I was married to a worthless fellow like you." Veeru brought a basket full of green fodder and emptied it before the cow. The cow started munching it. Veeru tied that piece of log to its neck without any problem.

Mohna untethered all the cattle. The cow was like an adolescent girl who didn't care for petty hurdles. As it was set free, it walked away very fast and entered Mita's field. He ran after it but failed to check her. The cow trampled the crop under its hooves. The buffaloes followed the cow, and the calves followed the buffaloes into the field. Mohna tried his best to drive the cattle out, but in vain. The cattle were beyond his control. He started crying helplessly. Then Mita appeared on the scene. Seeing his crop being destroyed, he lost his temper and started beating Mohna mercilessly. Mohna had been beaten beyond bearing—his nose started bleeding. Mita asked him the name of his father.

"Deva, sir," Mohna replied.

Knowing Deva's name, Mita felt sorry for punishing him too much. His behavior changed. He said, "It is not your fault. The real culprit is Veeru, your uncle, who sent you at such a minor age." He drove the cattle to Veeru's house. The house of the *sarpanch*, the head of the village council was on the way. He took him with him. On hearing the noise, some other spectators reached the scene. There was a good gathering. The Sarpanch admonished Veeru: "Your cattle destroyed an acre of Mita's crop. You must make good his loss. You sent an innocent child to graze the animals; he is not old enough to do such a rough job." Veeru shouted at his wife, "Come out and face the *panchayat, do not go on hiding.*

"I had tried to convince her not to send the boy to graze the cattle, but she did not listen to me…he was going to school all right…she had withdrawn him. I am at fault and I will make good the loss."

"He is agreeable, Mita, what do you want?" the Sarpanch asked the owner of the field.

"I am not out of the panchayat's purview. I will abide by your decision," Said Mita

After consultation with the members of the panchayat present there, the decision was announced: "Veeru Singh, you have caused the loss to the extent of two thousand rupees. You will have to pay this amount in the month of November. In case you fail to pay, you will have to pay an additional sum of one hundred rupees as fine for every month."

"Well done, noble Sarpanch. Justice should be like this. There is lot of corruption in the courts where everyone is out to fleece you. Even the leaves of the trees demand money. It takes a life span to get justice," said one of the old men standing nearby.

Nhami earned a bad name in the village. Everybody cursed her for maltreating the orphans. She stopped sending Mohna to graze the cattle, and instead he was asked to feed them at home. There was no change in her attitude and no relaxation in his work. She continued to awaken him early. He took the cattle out of the shed and put the fodder before them. Then he drew water from the well and made them drink. He used to get terribly tired. Blisters appeared on his hands while he was working to pull the buckets full of water. But what could he do? He did not have his parents sitting there to share his problem. After he had finished one duty he was directed to do another one. Karmi pitied his lot but could do nothing. She herself met with the same fate.

Nhami dismissed the lifelong maid and assigned her garbage job to Karmi. She took the plea that the maid was old enough and could not do good job of cleaning.

When Mohna got some time, he helped Karmi by filling the baskets with dung. Karmi carried the baskets to the garbage pile: One day she slipped and fell down. The basket full of dung mixed with urine emptied on her body. She sprained her foot too. Afraid of her aunt, she got up and resumed her work.

That day Veeru came from the fields to collect seed. He noted that Karmi was limping as she walked. He asked her, "Why are you limping, Karmi?" She kept quiet and did not say anything—instead she began to cry. Veeru was shocked to see the children doing the menial job of cleaning the cattle shed. He realized, "My wife is revengeful toward my brother's off-spring." He guessed that Karmi might have slipped while carrying the dung, and knew the reason for her crying. Her aunt was troubling her deliberately. Veeru said to his niece, "You, children, will not do this job any more. Do you understand? Let your aunt do it. Mohna should go with me to the fields. He will not stay at home any more."

Looking at his wife sitting with the neighbor he got annoyed and said angrily, "You should feel ashamed of putting the little girl to the arduous job. You have been gossiping with the veteran's wife since morning and the kids are put to hard jobs. Why are you so cruel to the innocent children? If no one else sees you, God is there to watch. Fear Him." Nhami was very clever. She went in and started preparing tea for her husband. "I am not going to take your tea, or whatever it is. Pour it on your head!" said Veeru. Then, taking the fertilizer and seed Veeru went back to the field. Nhami knew the ferocity of Veeru's anger. She thought it better to keep quiet. In order to please him she took tea with snacks for him and went to the field. Veeru took her aside and advised her, "Exceeding all limits of decency is not good for you. Do not be revengeful to the children."

Next day Karmi took his lunch to the field. Looking at her from a distance, Veeru thought it was Nhami and took it as his victory. He said to himself, "The woman is set right by admonishing on her folly, *otherwise she overpowers you.* She has come to her senses." But when Karmi drew near, his doubt was cleared. He said to her in surprise, "Why have *you* come today on behalf of Nhami? Let your Aunt do her job." Karmi replied, "She was busy at home, she sent me,"

"What big job does she have at hand? You are trying to cover up. A dog's tail may be kept in a bamboo flute for any length of time—its curve will not go."

Karmi returned after delivering the lunch to her uncle, Nhami was still gossiping with the veteran's wife. All the household chores were still waiting to be done. Flies had gathered over the used pots and pans. Nhami said to Karmi, "Kammo, first of all clean the utensils. I am just coming to help you." Karmi cleaned the pots and pans and arranged them in order on the shelf. Her aunt still was talking to the veteran's wife.

After finishing the job Karmi went to take a bath. She took soap cake, towel and her clean clothes.

Nhami, keeping a vigilant eye on Karmi, came to her and said, "Are you going to take bath now, girl?"

"Yes, Aunt, I could not take bath yesterday. Now I have finished my work and I should bathe," said she fearfully. "A bundle of dirty clothes have been lying soaked since yesterday. It will be better if you wash them before taking bath," said her aunt. Karmi went to the well and filled the trough with water. She washed and rinsed the clothes. She asked Mohna, "My dear brother, help me in wringing the clothes. My back has started aching. I am doing the hard jobs since morning. The work is still unfinished."

Her brother took pity on her, "You can relax. I will wring the clothes myself." "Without wringing by both of us, the water will not be drained," saying this, Karmi joined him. She too could not bear to see her brother doing jobs by himself for her.

Mohna had started going to the field with Veeru. The wheat crop was being given water for the first time. Water was drawn from the well by two Persian wheels, one revolved by a camel and the other by a pair of oxen. Blinders were put on the camel's eyes, and it walked by itself, but the oxen had to be driven manually. Mohna used to drive the oxen.

Whereas his aunt always howled at him at home, no one was there to abuse him in the fields. He was as free as birds. A month passed joyfully.

It is rightly said, 'Misfortune afflicts a poor man.' Mohna got up very early in the morning and went to the field. As he was in the seat driving the oxen, he dozed off and fell down. He suffered a serious head injury. He was bleeding too much. Luckily the oxen stopped there and then. The people working in the neighboring fields came to his rescue. The wound was bandaged tightly, and the bleeding stopped. Veeru was nowhere to be seen nearby. People were aware of his habits. They knew about his love affair in neighboring quarters. They guessed that he would be with his sweetheart. Immediately, a person was sent to inform him.

Ratna, his cousin, rebuked him. "You had put the little boy on the seat of beam and went away to enjoy yourself with your 'mother'. Had we not come in time, the boy would have met his end. You should have a sense of responsibility toward this child. He is expected to doze off at any time."

Veeru took ill of Rattan's remarks. Ratna understood, looking at him he said, "We have nothing to gain by checking you from going there. Go ahead, and enjoy yourself. If you have no sense of responsibility, you will not realize it at our advice. Now take the boy to the doctor, do not delay any more."

The boy was put in the cart and driven to the doctor. Hearing the name of a great social worker, Deva, the doctor took keen interest in the treatment of the boy.

No one relied on Veeru. As long as the doctor did not declare Mohna out of danger, all of them remained there. When they reached home, Karmi was sitting on the stool and taking her meals. As she saw her brother's forehead bandaged, her morsel got stuck in her throat. Seeing her sister, Mohna also got emotional and started crying.

The news of the boy's injury spread through the entire village like a wild fire. Everybody knew about Veeru: that he was addicted to drugs and had other wrongdoings. He discontinued the kids' education and was exploiting their labor. After Mohna's accident, people condemned him all the more.

After hearing the people's voice, Veeru got inimical toward Mohna. He rebuked him on one plea or the other. He stopped taking him to the field. Nhami also maltreated Mohna at home. It became quite difficult for him to live in that condition. He felt suffocated. If he was asked to do anything, he did; otherwise he kept moving about aimlessly. He did not talk to anyone. His aunt, Nhami, diagnosed that he had been possessed by some ghost.

A train going to Ganganagar passed near his village daily in the evening. Mohna used to go upstairs and watched it daily. One day, as he saw the train, it came to his mind, "My Dad's sister, Bhani, used to go by this train; why should I not go to her?" He started thinking of running away from the house. One day, he made up his mind to board the train. He knew that his aunt's village was a mile or so from Ganganagar. He could walk to the village from there, but he did not know at what time the train would arrive and which road lead to the village.

Mohna did not open his mind to anyone, not even to Karmi. He feared that his secret would be leaked. The next day, Veeru, along with his family, went to the field to pick millet. Mohna too went with them and worked in the morning. Pretending to have a headache, he left the field at midday. On reaching home, he filled a big platter with wheat and sold it at the shop to get money for paying the rail fare. That was usual with them. Whenever his aunt needed money, she sold wheat that way.

He went to the station an hour before the arrival of the train. Trains on the line generally ran late. The train was late by two hours that day. The passengers went away to the bus stop. He was left alone at the station. There was a dead silence there. The sun had set. He, being alone, felt like crying. Neither could he go back nor had he a way to board the train. Then chance helped him: he sighted an old couple who were carrying a tin. He stood up and went to them. He came to know that they had been blessed with a grandson. They were carrying a tin of *panjiri*[6] for their daughter on the birth of a son. They were going to the same village. So he had company up to his destination. It was dark when they reached the village.

His aunt Bhani was overjoyed to see him. She took him in her tight embrace and kissed him. She asked him, "How could you come alone, my boy?" "I have come with the old oil man of our village. His daughter has given birth to a son and he was bringing *panjiri* for her," answered Mohna. It was already very late at night, so they went to sleep without talking much.

Next day his aunt noticed the scar of a wound on his forehead. She got upset. She asked him to tell her how he had suffered the injury. She took him in her lap and made him relate the entire story. She inquired about Karmi also. Knowing that her nephew and niece were treated very badly she felt bad. She

---

6 Wheat flour fried in butter, mixed with dry fruit and sugar, is called 'Punjiri'. It is given as gift at the birth of first child by her parents.

heaved a deep sigh, and her eyes filled with tears, she started wailing for her late brother. "Oh, my dear brother, why have you gone making your children orphan?" Bhani's daughter *Jiti* brought in tea. Sipping tea, she continued talking about her parental home.

SIX

When Veeru returned after picking millet, Mohna was not at home. He thought he might have gone to play with some friends and would come back soon. After some time he checked up at those places, but could not find him there. Veeru was worried, and thought, "If he has died some accidental death, people would blame me and even accuse me of murdering the boy." Karmi too got worried about Mohna. "He is the only source of inspiration for me to live. Without him my life is hell. How do I pass the days without him, only I know?" She thought of many ominous things. She did not eat or drink and kept on crying.

Aunt Bhani, knowing about the maltreatment, was very upset. She took Mohna with her and set out for her parental home by jeep. As she reached there, Veeru was not at home. He had gone in search of the boy, and the atmosphere of mourning prevailed in the house. Karmi heaved a sigh of relief as she saw her brother. Veeru also returned in the afternoon. He was dumb founded on seeing his sister with Mohna. He respectfully touched her feet. Bhani did not respond, as she was very much annoyed with him.

When he went in and met his wife, she told him, "Your sister is in a very angry mood. I went to her with a glass of water, she refused to take it." As Veeru sat near his sister, she started rebuking him. Showing him Mohna's scar, she said, "You spared no effort to kill the boy. Only God has saved him. Shameless fellow! You should realize the fact that he is your brother's offspring, your own blood. You should have treated him as your own. What his father had done for you, you cannot repay him even in seven lives; you were of the age of this boy when our father died. Our brother Deva brought you up. He sent you to school. You played all the time in the village square and returned home at the closing time of the school. You did not let him know whether you had come from the school or after playing. You had no interest in studies. You beat one boy or got beaten by another. Every other day there was some complaint against you. When you did not mend your ways, he withdrew you from school and put you to work, but you did not change. "One day, when you tried to harness the oxen to the plow, someone sneezed and you abused him: 'Who is this bastard who has brought this bad omen?' On hearing the abuse, they ran after you to teach you a lesson. You saved yourself by hiding somewhere in the neighborhood. "You were sent to irrigate the field with the canal water. You created another problem there. You fought for the turn and hit the neighbor's head, causing a deep wound. The

police filed a case against you. It cost us the value of
one crop. The doctor and the police had to be bribed
to make our case strong. Brother made sure that you
were saved.

"You kept bad company and did nothing to con-
tribute to the family income. In spite of that, Deva
kept your equal share in the property he bought.
When he came to know that you were out of his control, he parted ways with you. He got you married
and gave you a separate house to live in and half
of the share of landed property. You did not attend
to farming. You wasted your time in going to fairs.
Sometimes you blamed your wife for infertility and
pressed upon your in-laws to marry you to their second daughter. You unnecessarily harassed them and
returned after getting insulted. Bholu was the farmhand. He worked for you. Agricultural expenses
exceeded your income. You could not make both
ends meet. You borrowed money from the commission agent. Ultimately he too refused to lend you
any more until the previous balance was clear. You
gave up farming and bought some pigeons. You fed
them with almonds and started betting. Most of the
time, you lost the game. Sometimes you went for
hunting and wasted many days and ignored agriculture. What evil was there that you did not indulge in?
When you lost most of your holding, you got a horse
carriage. The mare of your carriage was as stubborn
as you yourself. Hardly a month had passed when

you killed the mare by trying to thrust spices down her throat by force.

"Look at these children. What have you done to them? They are reduced to the position of orphans. They look underfed and overworked."

Veeru kept listening to his sister quietly, with his head down, and kept scratching the ground with his toe.

Then Bhani turned toward Nhami. "Have you forgotten the days when he was bent upon turning you out of the house, blaming you for not being able to bear a child, and compelled you to get your younger sister married to him? Bless these kids' father, who helped you to settle in this house. Then you gave birth to a girl followed by a son. And today, you dislike his children. Listen to me. I am not ignorant of such things. A daughter cannot forget her parents, even if she may be living far away, across seven seas. I get all the news in minute details. The way you have treated your brother's children can't be tolerated. Such type of maltreatment is not meted out to strangers even."

Bhani called the sarpanch and other kith and kin there and asserted, "I will not let my brother's children live here like this. I am taking them with me. If Veeru wants to keep the land belonging to the children, let him take it. He should deposit the annual rent to their account. He should make clear his mind right now what he wants to do."

The sarpanch reassured Bhani. "We are with you, sister. You are doing all the best for them. The children will be brought up properly under your good care."

Bhani did not stay for the night. She returned to Ganganagar with her niece and nephew. Her family rejoiced at the children joining them, and they looked after them in a very nice way. Bhani had two daughters and two sons. The daughters were elder to the sons. Suraina was the elder son and Sadhu, the younger one. Of the girls, Jiti was the elder and Molhi the younger one.

The boys went to college. The elder son lived like a lord. His going to college was just a pastime. He struggled for many years but failed to qualify BA. *Sadhu* was good at studies. He was doing law. Bhani's family was fond of educating the boys. As regards girls, their thinking was akin to those of orthodox landlords. Being educated, Bhani gave a little bit education to the girls. Jiti was married in a good family; her husband was a lawyer. Molhi, younger daughter of Bhani, was married to one of their relatives, an army officer. The daughters went to their respective homes at an early age.

SEVEN

Karmi and Mohna's education had come to standstill when they became orphan and had to live with their uncle Veeru. No school gave them admission at Ganganagar; they forgot everything whatever they had learned earlier. As a last resort, they were sent for education to the *gurdwara.*

Bhani's younger son, Sadhu[7] was a law Graduate, and of progressive thinking. He said, "If they were to be put for religious education, why were they brought over here? We have to prepare them for the betterment of their present life. Gurdwara is just for religious education. It is just possible that they may become fundamentalist like the ones in Pakistani Madrassas. Put them in school. We have a duty toward the offspring of our maternal uncle."

Sher Singh, *Sadhu's father*, said, "The teachers do not admit them. They are very weak in studies. They would not be able to cope with the syllabus and keep pace with the class."

"If they can't cope with their studies, then the teachers should work hard on them. It is their duty,

---

7 Karmi's cousin

as they get paid for teaching. I go and will talk to them," said Sadhu.

The next day he took both of them to Khalsa (Sikh) School in Ganganagar. The teachers started making lame excuses. *Sadhu* said, "Give them a test, and admit them to the class they are found fit for. And if you do not want to do that, let me know!" The children were given a test, and admitted, Karmi in sixth class, and Mohna in t fifth. Both of them lost a year in transition.

There was another advantage of putting them to school. Paul, the son of Paltoo, the potter living in their neighborhood, was also in the same school, so they got company. Paltoo's house was at a short distance. They had taken residential plot from Bhani. Paltoo Ram had two daughters and five sons. The two elder ones worked with their father as potters. The next two worked at the kiln. The fifth and the youngest one, Paul, went to school with Karmi and Mohna.

Paltoo Ram and his wife made pottery and sold it locally or carried it on the cart to other far-off places. In the harvesting season, they bartered with harvested crop and earned sufficient food grains for the year. It was beneficial for Bhani to have them in the neighborhood, as Paltoo's daughters helped her in household chores.

Paul too benefitted. He had no bicycle, and used to go on foot. On Karmi and Mohna's admission to school, Paul started riding with them on their bicycles: Karmi rode the cycle alone, while Mohna and Paul rode together and cycled in turns. One day Mohna was riding, and Paul sat behind him. The wind was blowing in the opposite direction. Mohna was finding it difficult to pull Paul. Karmi noticed it and took pity on her brother. She said to Paul, "Mohna is too young to pull you. You should join me."

Paul rode on her cycle: he was driving, and Karmi was sitting on the carrier. She enjoyed the ride with Paul. He took pleasure in pulling her. Coming and going together was fun for all three of them. They mixed together well. The feeling of high and low disappeared. At home, Karmi and Mohna did the homework together. In case of difficulty, they consulted each other and as such made good progress in their studies.

After finishing the home chores, Paul had been assigned the task of taking the goats out to graze. Earlier he used to take them to the canal side. Ever since Mohna and Karmi had come, he started grazing the goats in their fields.

On the following Sunday, he took out the goats to their fields for grazing before noon. It was quite hot that day. He felt thirsty. He went inside the house and met Karmi. He asked her for water. Instead of giving water, she brought out *sattu*[8]. Paul enjoyed the drink and drank to his fill. He failed to express thanks in

---

8   Fried Barley Flour mixed with Sweet water is used as cold drink

words but thanked her through his eyes. He gazed at Karmi with love. In response Karmi smiled a little and walked inside with a willowy gait.

Paul reclined under the nearby *neem*[9] tree and dozed off. Karmi came out after having a nap, and she saw that her "Ranjha" (legendary lover) was fast asleep under the neem tree, but with the passage of time the sun had come over him. Karmi felt the heat as if it was she herself who was facing the sun. She did not feel like awakening him. She went in and called the servant, who lifted the sleeping boy and put him on the cot under the shade.

The goats returned home after grazing to their fill. Seeing the goats without his son, Paltoo got worried. He ran here and there to look for him. At last he went to Bhani's farmhouse. As he went in, he found his son sleeping comfortably there. Paltoo abused him affectionately and awakened him, pulling his arm. "Wake up, you bastard. You are lying here as if it was your father's Bungalow." Bhani saw him and came out. She said, "*This is his house,* Paltoo. You could let him lie here. For me, Paul is just like my own kids. All children are alike.

"Make him a doctor, Paltoo Ram. Don't bother about money. I shall help you." Bhani was very good at heart in doing good deeds.

Paltoo Ram got inspired from Bhani's family and wanted to give high education to Paul. He too got

---

9   It has medicinal value.

inspiration, completed his school education with merit. Paul got admission to medical college in Bikaner under reserved quota[10].

In order to meet the expenses of his son's education, Paltoo took another kiln job on contract. His family too worked hard to make Paul a doctor. While Paul was doing M.B.B.S. Karmi joined college at Ganganagar. Paul often came to meet her on his way to Bikaner, and their love story continued. Mohna passed his tenth class and then gave up studies.

---

10 For low caste people quota was reserved in Professional school /colleges and in jobs too.

EIGHT

Bhani remained on the lookout for a suitable match for Karmi. She was very keen to get her married and settle her. In marrying off her daughters, Bhani had faced no problem. They had nearly two hundred acres of land and were a well-established family but difficulty came her way when she had to find a match for Karmi. She in the family of Aunt Bhani enjoyed all the privileges that Bhani's own kids enjoyed. She had been brought up in a landlord's family; people still regarded her as an orphan. Bhani looked for a family of her status and wanted to wipe out the stigma of orphanage with money.

Karmi felt insulted and often thought, "When these so-called Landlords regard me an orphan, below their status, Aunt should not talk of fixing my marriage with them. She should look for a boy of a working-class family who will give me equal respect."

'Love marriage is the real solution of low-and high-class problem.' But Karmi did not dare to reason with her aunt.

Paul came to know about this development, he asked Karmi, "Tell your aunt about our love. You are educated. You should express your mind freely. Even the illiterate girls are more daring than you. They express their decision boldly and do not retrace their step. For the sake of their love, they swim across the river on a mud pitcher[11]."

"You can talk to my aunt, Paul," replied Karmi. "You are a man and better educated."

Both of them could not muster enough courage to tell her aunt about their love. Meanwhile, her aunt settled her marriage with a widower, a big land lord, who belonged to a village near Abohar. His was a leading family of the village, owning one hundred and fifty acres of land. He put up a condition, "the girl will not do any job. She will look after the house and children." Bhani agreed.

Karmi could not challenge her aunt's decision, as she was under her obligation. Bhani had brought her up and given her motherly love. Preparations for her marriage started, and her education came to an end. She had to leave the college.

One day before marriage there was a sandstorm at night. It was pitch dark with zero visibility. The doors and windows were banging. They didn't know in the din and noise, when the dacoits broke open the rear door and entered the house.

The criminals drew the family together and ordered them to hand over all the jewelry and the cash.

---

11   He referred to a legendary love story of Sohni-Mahiwal

When they were about to run away with the booty, Sadhu fired at them with rifle and hit the *dacoit* carrying the suitcase, and he fell down. Sadhu ran downstairs to snatch the suitcase. Another dacoit fired at him, and the bullet hit his thigh. He fell there. Exchange of fire continued, and some pellets hit Karmi on her face. A bullet hit Bhani's husband. He died on the spot. The members of her family got busy taking care of the injured, and the dacoits escaped.

Bhani proved to be a wise lady. She sent a messenger to Karmi's would-be in-laws. The marriage was postponed indefinitely. Karmi cursed her fate sitting at home. "I do not know what sort of sins I have committed that this unfortunate event happened at the time of my marriage? Now with the scars on my face, no one will accept me. I am ruined and left to clean the plates in Aunt's house."

Bhani was aware of her agony. She made her sit near her and started consoling her. "Hardships confront the brave people, my child. Face them boldly. If you lose heart, you will get crushed under the mountain of hardships. Beauty is short-lived, whereas your virtues will last for life. You have all the virtues of a good wife. Your virtues will hide the scars at your face.

"I have told your husband-to-be about it. He said, 'It does not matter. This could happen to me also." Then Karmi gathered courage to express her heart,

"Aunt, I do not want to challenge your decision. I shall feel obliged if you, please, allow me to convey my views about my husband-to-be. I have come to know that this man is not only arrogant and greedy but also a drunkard. He does not need a wife, but a maid to serve him and rear his children. I want to be a wife and not a maid. It would be better if you look for a match from some family of my status. He will understand my problems better and treat me as equal."

Bhani could guess that Karmi was interested in someone else; she asked her, "If you have a boy in sight, let me know. There is no need to feel shy of telling the truth." Karmi mentioned Paul's name in an undertone and told her aunt, "He had sent his sister to me with the marriage proposal but I told her, 'Talk to my aunt.'" Karmi's childhood friend, Paul, was handsome and possessed good qualities. She was deeply in love with him, but she could not openly speak her mind to her aunt.

Bhani was possessed of the ghost of low caste; she was not prepared to marry her niece to a potter's son. She turned down the proposal flatly.

Karmi was stunned to hear her views. She said, "You have been teaching me against caste considerations all my life, and now you yourself are caught in the web of high and low castes. Words like *"potter's son"* do not sound well from you. You used to say, 'What is important is one's worth and not birth. One endowed with virtues is a good person, and even starving with such a 'husband' is not bad for a wife.' Has the stigma of his caste not been wiped out by his getting baptized and becoming Singh?[12] Is he still a potter? When the Tenth Guru baptized the Five Beloved Singhs, taking from different castes, he had put an end to the caste system and shown the path of equality and fraternity. He had advised people to come out of their wrong notions and not to waste their precious lives in the illusion of caste, color, or creed. They should foster love and friendship. He sacrificed his father, mother, four sons, and himself—the whole family—to achieve that mission. But it seems we are still suffering from the disease of high and low caste. It kept India slave for centuries. The ghost of high and low is still haunting us, rather more than ever. It means that we have failed to appreciate the teachings and sacrifices of *Guru Gobind Singh*. We built gurdwaras in his memory, fixed their photographs on the walls, printed calendars with photos, but we have forgotten the true spirit of equality and fraternity—the Guru's cherished mission. The gurdwaras became means to wrest state power and make money. By forgetting his mission we have buried the guru's mission in a deep ditch. The gurdwaras became 'Smadhees[13]' of the Guru's Mission.

---

12 Baptized Sikhs to make them Singhs (Lions) and made them capable to fight against the state terrorism of Muslim Kings and Hindu Rajas. He built a Formidable Secular Force.

13 Samadhee-It is a structure , may it be small of grave size or big like Tajmhal

"By misleading the people, the 'Dallas[14]', blood-suckers of the working class, became the rulers, and the true Sikhs remained the downtrodden outcasts. The Dallas brought the Sikhs back to the primitive stage of orthodoxy." Karmi opened her mind to her aunt very boldly.

Bhani was surprised to hear what her niece had told her. She said, "You are talking so well. But, my daughter, it is quite different from real life. The real awareness comes to the girls when they enter the life ahead.

"I will relate to you a happening of my youth— Jassi, a Jat girl, studied with me. She fell in love with a very handsome low-caste boy, *Channa*. He was tall, fair-complexioned, and had sharp features. He won *Jassi*'s heart.

"The ghost of love continued to possess *Jassi*. After some time, *Channa* became an officer. She told her parents about marrying him, but they did not agree. She went to the court and married the boy, Channa; Jassi loved, without her parents' consent. "She gave birth to a son. Her in-laws brought *panjiri*. Channa had gone on tour. Jassi did not let them enter the house. The neighbors reasoned with her. 'It is dark now; the night has set in. Open the door; they will stay for the night and leave in the morning.' Jassi was of a stubborn nature. She did not relent and sent them back. It was a dark and cold night. How

---

14 Guru Gobind Singh did not find 'Dallas' fit to be his true Singhs.

they suffered, no one knows. "Jassi gave birth to two daughters also Still Channa's caste irked Jassi. Ultimately, fed up with her behavior, he committed suicide.

"Now think for yourself, Karmi. You may also not get infatuated like Jassi. Even the noted people in society bow down before the caste considerations."

"Mt. Everest is not easy to conquer but your Karmi would do it. Paul too has the courage to confront the world of narrow thinkers. He has been brought up under your care and became a doctor." Karmi did not give up even when her aunt had said to her, "You, simple girl," said Bhani, "do not understand me. You seem to be under the spell of love. A few days back, Paul was grazing the goats and molding the pots for his father. So what if he has become a doctor! He has no property. Simple girls like you are led into a bad situation. All of them seem to be so very promising before marriage, but all this proves to be an illusion when married and faced with reality."

Karmi told her aunt what she aimed at. "He is a doctor and I am no less. I shall work hard to make equal contribution to the family income. There is no question of starving. Even if it comes to such a pass, it would be hundred times better than becoming the maid of a so-called landlord." "My child, I used to think like you. I have brought up Paul like my own son and educated him. But now, looking at what is happening in the real life, I feel shaky. The love marriage of Jassi and Channa failed. It broke my courage too. I have given my views. The final decision rests with you. I would arrange your marriage wherever you would like." It was up to Karmi to decide. She could choose a life of love over a life of slavery with feudal lord.

Karmi got lost. "If I save my love and marry Paul, Aunt will have to face humiliation. She would get a bad name in the society. She gave us shelter when we were in dire necessity of it. She is a goddess to me. I should stand by my aunt's commitment even though I have to sacrifice my love."

NINE

Karmi's marriage was fixed. Income from land in her and her brother's names had accumulated for many years that was withdrawn.

The songs appropriate to the occasion were sung. Young and exuberant girls sang and danced to the beat of a drum throughout the night.

The feeling of belonging to someone else made her happy she began to weave the dreams of entering into a new world.

The auspicious moment had come after waiting so long. The army band, was marching ahead of the marriage procession, followed by camels, horses, and chariots. It looked like the procession of a king. The number of those in the marriage party, including the attendants and servants, exceeded two hundred. Bhani got worried. It was agreed that the number of guests in the marriage party would be small. But those attending on them also numbered a hundred. As they were making arrangements for the additional members of the marriage party, an emissary of the bridegroom showed up and said, "*Sardar Jang Bahadur Singh Brar* has sent a message that drinks should be arranged in the community center at the time of the marriage party's arrival!"

When Karmi came to know about this message, she went to her aunt and said, "We have to deal with the arrogant people very sternly. It is not a marriage party but a swarm of locusts. They are demanding wine to be served to them, as if they have not seen it before. They won't behave well in the future." The hidden revolt against the landlords arose in Karmi's mind.

"I can understand what is in your mind, my daughter," said Bhani. "But it is not proper for us to return the marriage party. We will be blamed. And then no one would accept your hand. Let us forget this for the moment. That we will have to incur extra expenditure doesn't matter. Actually Bhani too feared the future, "I do not know what sort of fate is awaiting you, my daughter!"

Tears stood in Karmi's eyes on hearing what her aunt had said. She went in and cried on Sadhu's shoulder, who was sitting in bed with his leg in a plaster cast. There seemed to be no way out. Sadhu tried to get up angrily but could not move forward. Aunt's elder son had gotten dead drunk before the arrival of the marriage party. He was lying unconscious.

Next morning, before the *anand-karaj* (the Sikh marriage ceremony), a messenger came from *Jang Bahadur* to arrange a decorated mare and fifty rings to show at the time of ceremony. "Make sure that I do not lose my face among my fraternity. Make a show of it," the messenger said to Bhani. "We will not keep any item out of that."

Bhani again got upset on hearing the message. How could she arrange for this demand at the eleventh hour? She was convinced that Karmi was right, and said to herself, "They are not good people. We cannot expect such people to do anything positive."

She too was hesitant to marry off Karmi to such type of people. Consultations started in the family.

Jang Bahadur had conveyed his demand through the go-between also. When the first messenger did not return, he sent two more messengers, and when they too did not come back, he got upset. He himself went there, accompanied by his uncles, Karmi came to know about the arrival of the bridegroom in the *haveli* (mansion). She requested her aunt to show firmness: "Be brave, Aunt. Don't be lenient toward them on the issue of unreasonable demands."

Bhani, accompanied by the Sarpanch and other members of the panchayat, went to the haveli. She initiated the talk: "Honored guests, I had expressed my inability to meet your demand of giving a mare et cetera in dowry, the very next day after the *dacoity*."

"We, the Sidhu[15], have this old tradition. We are descendants of the Ruler *Maharaja Ala Singh*. Our prestige cannot be maintained without this formality," said Jung Bahadur's uncle. Hearing the name of

---

15 sub caste

the ruler Maharaja Ala Sing Bhani got furious. She said, "We are not *Shensi's*.[16]" We have solemnized so many marriages without taking any dowry. And our prestige has never been hit. Rather, our good-will gesture added another feather to our cap. People regard us as respectable lords "Madam, we all have our own customs and rituals. We have no right to change the customs of our *Sidhu clan*."

Bhani said, "There can't be a better dowry than giving away one's daughter! Who gives the daughter, gives everything. The daughter perpetuates the lineage of her husband. She may give birth to a national hero and make the family proud of that. The mare will not add to your prestige; rather, it reduces you to a menial position to do the job of cleaning its dung."

The bridegroom showed his true colors. "For me, the family position is more important than my wife. Once it is lost, it is lost forever. And who cares for the woman? The landlords can get any number of top-class women."

Bhani got enraged on hearing the haughty words of the bridegroom. She replied, "I have understood you now. You need a well-decorated mare and not a virtuous wife. The matter comes to an end between us. An animal needs an animal, and a human being needs a human being." With these words, Bhani went out.

"I have heard everything, Aunt, sitting in the adjoining room. I will not marry a man of perverted thinking," said Karmi firmly.

---

16 lower caste

Bhani went to the gurdwara immediately with the sarpanch and Mohna. The sarpanch called the members of the fraternity on the loud speaker: "Dear brethren, the marriage party is insisting on having a decorated mare and not agreeing to a simple marriage. It is the question of our prestige. I request you to send one member of each family to the gurdwara."

People holding swords, spears, and axes rushed to the gurdwara. The marriage party had also heard the sarpanch speaking through the mike. They got worried about saving their lives and quickly ran away.

Everyone in the village praised Karmi. She became the hero, challenging centuries old custom of Dowry. She had upheld the prestige of the village. She returned the marriage party without bride. Karmi taught a good lesson to the dowry seekers. Karmi's praise by one and all encouraged her to stand firmly and fight for the cause of women. When her girlfriends came to congratulate her, she advised them, "We have lived the life of a secondary citizen for a long time but now learn to live as an equal. Inculcate such qualities in you that a man of your choice may feel proud to seek your hand.

Sadhu applauded Karmi's stand, "Karmi, you did a marvelous job, and have got rid of the wrong people and saved yourself from mismatch.

"Their forefathers served the British rulers, collecting revenue for them and acting as their touts. They were rewarded with estates for rendering such services to them. They have traitors' blood in their veins. What sort of alliance can you have with these people? Your forefathers had sacrificed their lives for our motherland, in the service of people."

Karmi was happy at heart at the breakup, as she still loved Paul. She thought, "How nice it would be if Aunt still agrees to my marriage with Paul. Aunt *had* seen only the Sidhu's huge landed property but did not visualize their womenfolk's lives, they lived as *dasis*."[17]

Then Karmi said to her cousin, "Just broach the subject of my marriage with Paul; May be she agrees now."

Sadhu talked to his mother. "We are faced with a new problem, Mother. After turning away the marriage party, orthodox people do not like Karmi, as she broke with age-old tradition. Everyone is not so wise as to appreciate it. Why not talk to Dr. Paul now?"

"They do not match us in any way, my son. We are Jats, a high-caste community, and they are low caste potters. We live like kings in mansions. They are poor, living in shanties. We have mares neighing around. They have goats bleating and the asses braying."

Karmi was listening to them. She said, "All of us are descendants of the Rajputs, dear Aunt. Whatever profession our ancestors followed, it gradually became caste. Those who did farming became Jats, and those who revolved the potter's wheel became potters, and those who worked as blacksmiths, iron smiths became to be known so, et cetera. 'One does not become high by birth, but by worth.' On doing

---

17 slave like maid-servants

bad deeds one becomes bad and on doing good deeds, becomes good. Paul is a doctor. People salute him as a dignified person. So what if he comes from a potter's family? No one cares for my education. I am still not B.A. I cannot get a better match than Paul. Moreover I cannot be high by being merely a Jat."

"It is easy to talk like this, my daughter. If you are married in a potter's family, you won't spend even a single night there. What is common between them and us? If you marry in a lord's family, you will rule, and if you go to the potter's, you will stoke fuel in their furnace."

"My dear Aunt, a husband is like a god to a wife. You used to instill these noble ideas into my mind. Doing a job honestly is like worshiping, be it a potter's job or a landlord's work. It makes no difference. Never mind living in the potter's house—I would be happy to sleep with my husband even on a bed of thorns. "Even now I would consider it my good luck to marry Paul. If I go to a potter's family after my marriage, I will work, Paul too. Our children will not be potters. They will become engineers. They will not bake the cups of clay. They will make china pottery, cups, and saucers. They will not take tea in clay cups but in china cups and saucers. They will beat the so-called landlords in their status and living standard."

Sadhu disagreed with his mother's outdated thinking. He said, "Mom! Look at your Suraina. He is a dead drunkard. Will his in-laws be proud of him, that he is a Jat and their daughter is married to a landlord? One does not become great by having big landed property. One becomes big by inculcating the qualities of a big man. Most of the sons of these so-called landlords frequent the brothels and squander their money. They make no contribution to the family income, but when the time comes, they inherit the legacy of their parents and become moneyed people and thereby muscle men. With muscle power they capture state power. They do not have a dime's worth of wisdom. They are parasites on our society and spoiler of nation.

"Paul is a hundred times better than those ruffians. He has all the qualities of a decent person. What is the harm in asking him? If he does not agree, what would we lose?" His mother had no reply to that argument. She said, "It is up to you. If the girl so desires, why should I object?"

The next day Sadhu went to Paul's house to talk about the marriage proposal. Paul's family gave Sadhu a warm welcome. In the course of discussion, Sadhu asked, "What do you think now, about your marriage with Karmi, Paul?"

He replied angrily, "How can the potters match the Jats now? I have not become someone else today. I am a potter even today. Having been rejected by the landlords, now Karmi has sent you to me!"

"Paul, I have come to you because of your love for Karmi. You like Karmi, and she likes you. She turned back the marriage party for your sake. The dowry was an excuse only. We were not paupers. We were in a position to meet their demand for a mare in dowry."

"*Now* you are talking of our love. Why did not she think of this in the first instance when I asked her? What is the use of coming now, when it is too late? If Karmi had true love for me, she would not have refused me at the first instance. Even Aunt would have agreed in the course of time."

"Karmi could not challenge my Mom's decision. She is like her own mother. It was not easy for her to go against her wishes. The way she pleaded for marriage with you before my mother, only I know."

As they were talking, Paltoo Ram came there, puffing at his *hookah,*[18] *said,* "Now it is below our dignity to accept this proposal. People would say that the potter has been won over by money and accepted the girl rejected by the landlords. It is an insult to us." Meanwhile Lado also came in. Addressing Paltoo Ram, she said, "You have lost your head, puffing at the *hubble-bubble*[19]. After centuries, luck is going to smile at us, and now arrogance has overpowered you! You are creating hurdles in the matrimonial alliance with Karmi. Paul must have done some very good deeds, that Mother goddess has come to our house to write our good luck. Under the spell of tobacco, you are turning it down. It is still time. Let us avail of the

---

18 Hookah is rough tough tool of smoking tobacco.
19 Mini hookah

opportunity, make good of it. Else you will continue turning the wheel all your life."

Paul said, "Why are you after Dad, Mom? He is absolutely right in turning down the marriage proposal. They have come to regard us as low caste. If they are big people they are at their own place. We are in no way less than anyone. We earn an honest living."

"You are talking like this because you have got education and become a doctor. Just ask me, who has gone bald carrying the basketful of pots on my head and selling them from house to house. Becoming a doctor has made you go off your head. You cannot find a girl like Karmi and a family like theirs. If you ask me truly, they have made you a doctor. The '*sardars*[20]' of such a high standing have come with the marriage proposal; it is a matter of great honor for us. You should be happy."

Paul said, "This proposal is not for potter, Paltoo's, son; it is for my medical degree. Had they not been possessed by the ego of Jat, they would not have declined our proposal then. They still have the feeling of high and low in their mind. They will always keep us under their subjugation. I cannot accept that kind of life."

---

20   Sikh landlords are called Sardars

Bhani had divided her property among her sons and
her daughters were married off in good families.
But she was always worried about Karmi. Turning
away the marriage party proved a curse for Karmi.
Nobody was accepting her for marriage. For most
of the people she was an orphan, and for others she
would not prove to be an adjustable wife. Karmi also
felt badly, believing that she would be dependent on
others for life. Sometimes she painfully remembered
renowned saint Sheikh Farid's couplet:

O God don't make me sit at others' door

If you want me to sit like this, take away my life.

Mohna also thought like his sister. One day he
said to Karmi, "How long would we continue to live
in Aunt's house in this position? If we go back to our
village, people would know us as Deva's offspring.
Though our father is not alive yet his good name
survives. People remember him for his good deeds.
Here, in our aunt's family, we are considered out sid-
ers. So long as we are here, neither one will accept
you for marriage, nor would I be able to get married.
Let's go back to native village and take back our
land from uncle Veeru. We will fight for our right, if

need be. Giving up our right is not renunciation but cowardice."

Karmi was very happy to hear Mohna's views. She said to him, "I had considered you a little boy, but there is a lot of weight in your arguments. You are right. We are good for nothing here. We should move back to our native place. After the demise of our aunt, we will have no right to stay here too. Her property would be divided among her sons. They would not let us stay even for a night; it will be good for us to leave this place during our aunt's life-time."

They were still thinking on these lines that Bhani had a heart attack. Everything was upset. She was taken to Ganganagar Hospital immediately. She was kept in the emergency ward for two days and a week in the private ward. She had gotten very weak. In her worsening condition, how could Karmi request for permission to let them go? It was the time to save her life. Karmi had to exert herself day and night to nurse her aunt. She massaged her and helped her to walk a little. Everyone was concerned with Bhani's life, but no one had that much time to serve her. In about a month's time or so, Bhani was able to walk and eat normally.

Finding an opportune time, Karmi sought her aunt's permission to go. Her aunt got upset and got lost in thoughts: "If Karmi goes away, who will look after me?" When Bhani felt a little better, she expressed her wish: "I wanted to give you a send-off in my life time. But time does not wait for anybody. I failed miserably in my mission –to marry you. The time has come for me to leave. Only God knows when I shall be given a send-off for the next world. How would I pay off your debt? Just call Suraina and Sadhu too."

Both the brothers came there. Bhani had already prepared her will; she took it out and handed it over to them. There were three copies. Sadhu read it out. Aunt had willed one tenth of her property in favor of Karmi. Sadhu agreed, but Suraina objected to that will and talked nonsense to his mother.

Seeing that her son had challenged her decision, Bhani's condition took a bad turn. She was taken to the hospital. Karmi went with her to look after her. Tears rolled down Karmi's cheeks as she looked at her aunt's condition. She started crying and said, "I do not need property; give it to Suraina and Sadhu. I need your love. I am not taking a single dime from this house. You are my mother in the real sense. I want a long life for you. I would not go leaving you in this condition. Let Mohna go if he so desires."

On Karmi's refusal to accept her share in the property, Bhani found some consolation. She recovered from her son's attack and felt better.

Karmi worried. "Luck did not favor me. No match could be found for me in Aunt's lifetime. Who would find one after she is gone? Nobody would pay a huge dowry for me!"

Aunt Bhani got well and was discharged. She had no time to make changes in her will. One day Suraina came home dead drunk. He created a fuss. He shouted at his mother, "Who are you to give away my father's property to Karmi?" Hearing this rebuke, Bhani lost her nerve. She again suffered a heart attack during the night. She was taken to a hospital and given oxygen and medicine. The attack was severe, and no medicine worked. She breathed her last at daybreak.

After the last prayers in Bhani's memory, the worldly affairs became the subject of discussion. Karmi made it clear in the presence of all near and dear ones: "My aunt regarded me as her daughter. She had included my name in her will. But I don't want to take anything out of this house. A sister needs the love of her brothers." With those words, she tore off the copy of the will and said, "Dear brothers, I am leaving along with Mohna. I beg your permission to go to our ancestral village."

Sadhu reasoned with his brother: "Karmi surrendered her share in the will and made a big sacrifice. She gave proof of her sisterly love for us. Now we should give her suitable gifts besides mother's assets already given to her."

The entire family gave Karmi and Mohna a hearty send-off. Sadhu drove them in his jeep to their village.

PART II

After declining Karmi's marriage proposal, Paul repented: "I was unnecessarily arrogant. If they called me the son of a potter, what was wrong in that? It is the truth. Even if Karmi's aunt meant to insult me, I should not mind that for the sake of love. Karmi kept on fighting up to the last moment to protect her love, and she succeeded in breaking all the shackles. Karmi's aunt too ultimately surrendered to her will. So I should not have turned down the proposal on false prestige. It was my defeat. I lost everything in this defeat."

It was a childhood love, a very deep love, indeed. He could not drive Karmi out of his mind. He realized that life was nothing without her; as the time passed, he missed her all the more. He started losing interest in everything, even bathing and taking meals, and he spent sleepless nights.

One day Paltoo said to him, "Why are you so mad for Karmi, my son? You will get a far better match. You are a Doctor."

"Dad, do not go on advising me unnecessarily. I have already suffered on account of your ill advice and spoiled my life."

Paul did not like to do anything and kept himself confined to bed all the time. If he took a sleeping pill, he had some sleep; otherwise, he twisted and turned throughout the night. After some time, even the pills did not have any effect. Sleeplessness disturbed his mind, and he acted like a mad man. In the beginning he remained silent, but later he started crying. He used to leave the house and walk about aimlessly without talking to anybody.

Paltoo was convinced that his son had really turned mad. He discussed his problem with Paul's maternal uncle. "Paul seems to have lost his senses. He is always saying 'Kammo, Kammo'... I am of the opinion we should take him to some hospital."

Both of them took Paul to the mental hospital, Amritsar, where Dr.Vidya-Sagar, a renowned doctor, diagnosed and admitted him. Electric shocks were given for a week or so, and the treatment continued for a month. Paul recovered and was discharged from the hospital.

The doctor advised his parents to get him married immediately to prevent the recurrence of the problem.

His maternal uncle was an educated and a wise man. He put in an advertisement in the matrimonial columns. Since the boy was a doctor, they received many offers. One of them was from a retired *Tehsildar*.[21] He had sent a photo of the girl too. Moreover, she was the only issue of her parents.

---

21   Revenue officer having the powers of Magistate

After reading the letter, the maternal uncle said, "I think this proposal is worth considering. Look at the photograph and show it to the boy also. It is a well-to-do family and that too from our own community. The girl is more beautiful than Karmi. I think this alliance will suit him." Paul also liked the girl. His family considered it a great boon to have a matrimonial alliance with a Tehsildar's family.

When they went to see the girl, she had just returned from the beauty parlor. She looked very charming, and the jewelry added to her beauty. From her appearance, she looked like a film actress. Paul was so impressed he forgot even to ask about her educational qualifications. She was only matriculate.

The boy appeared to be happy with the choice of the girl; his parents agreed to the marriage. They had an eye on her father's money. "She is the daughter of a rich man; he would give us a very big dowry. From potters, we would become lords."

The marriage was performed with great pomp and show. The bungalow next door to his in-laws was given to Paul, and the dowry could hardly be accommodated in the new house. Five lakhs rupees were given in cash.

When the bridegroom came with his bride to her doorstep, Lado tried to perform the welcome ceremony by moving a jug of water around the heads of the wedding couple. The bride jumped at the very sight of her mother-in-law. Paltoo did not dare to give his blessing and sat behind on the cot. After the ceremony Paul settled with his in-laws and forgot about his parental family.

Too much money turned Paul's head. He forgot everyone—his parents, brothers and sisters, and other relatives. He went on a honeymoon to Kashmir and spent a month there. Then they went to Agra, Goya and other places of tourist attractions. When they returned after traveling, dinner parties started in their honor. His evenings became colorful. He enjoyed life and forgot about medical practice too.

THIRTEEN

One day Paltoo had a horrible dream. He got up early in the morning. His wife, Lado, brought in tea for him. As he was sipping the tea, he said to Lado, "Paul has been married for six months, but he has never come to visit us. How is he living, we do not know. Today I had a bad dream. It disturbed my sleep early in the morning." Paltoo stopped sipping his tea, placed the glass aside, and started relating his dream to her: "Paul again had a fit, and he went on talking…. Last time he used to be quiet, but this time he is saying 'Kammo' 'Kammo' continuously.

"He had been cured properly and got married. He was perfectly normal, and was leading a happy life. What has gone wrong now? Perhaps he might have stopped taking medicine. Then…." On hearing Paltoo Ram's sad story, Lado too got upset. She could not take her tea. She placed her glass on the ground, covered her face with her head cover, and started crying.

Paltoo Ram said, "What would you gain by crying like this? I will go myself to enquire about him."

"No, I will not let you go alone. You may say something that may offend our new relatives. I will go with you."

They started preparing for the visit. The sky was overcast with clouds, and it looked like rain would soon come. Paltoo Ram took his bath and put on new clothes: a white muslin dhoti[22]; a snow-white shirt; and a red laced turban. He was ready. It had started drizzling. He got hold of a plastic bag, folded it into a pointed cap, and put it on his head. He looked very funny. Lado looked at him and said, "What a joker you have become! Throw away this cap. We are going to visit our son's in-laws. This bag does not look nice on your head. You can cover your head with a towel, if necessary."

Lado wrapped a Sari[23] with red dove prints around it. Paltoo threw away the bag and took a cotton shawl out of his wooden box. Both of them stepped out of their house. They had not yet crossed the canal, five hundred yards away, when it started raining. Paltoo wrapped the shawl around Lado and himself. It was lightning and thundering. They stood there under a tree in panic. Paltoo said, "One hurdle or the other is coming our way today, which is quite ominous. Let's hope all goes well."

As soon as the rain stopped, they moved ahead. At ten o'clock they knocked at their son's door. They

---

22 Two and half meter long a piece of cloth, wrapped around the loin. One end passing between the legs is tugged behind in Rajisthan.

23 Rajsthan is a state in India situated in the west part.

had gone there for the first time, and Paltoo was quite nervous at the gate of the big bungalow. He could not find the button to ring the bell. No one came out even after continuous knocking for some time. Then some passer-by guided them to press the button on the gate, he did it. The bell rang in the house next door. After five minutes, their son's mother-in-law came out frowning, and said with contempt, as if they were beggars, "Sahib is taking rest. Come after some time."

"We want to see Pala," said Paltoo Ram meekly.

"He is also not in," and saying this, she shut the door. "It seems she has not recognized us, Lado!" Paltoo Ram tried to reassure his wife. But she knew about her attitude—that she had scant regard for them. She suppressed her anger within herself. They were dead tired, as they had reached their in-laws after getting drenched in the rain. It was impossible for them to go back. They were feeling thirsty, and their bodies ached too. They saw no drinking water tap nearby.

Paltoo heaved a deep sigh and said, "Hi Ram…,"[24] and turned back. Lado followed him. As they were returning, they saw an old man sitting in the doorway of his house and reading a newspaper. Wishing the retiree "Good morning," Paltoo sat down on the floor close to his chair. His wife sat down by the side of her husband.

---

24   O God

"Where have you come from, Chaudhary (SIR)?"

"We have come to meet Sahib," replied Paltoo.

"Had you some business with him?" asked the old man, turning his face from the newspaper.

"Our son is married to his daughter! He was not in, and so we turned back."

"You could have waited for a while and taken tea there."

"We could have if somebody had asked us to. She just banged the door on seeing us, as if we were lepers."

"This is quite usual with the 'big people.' They cannot stand the body odor of a common man." The old man served them cold water, and thereafter he brought tea for them. Then he said, "My dear Choudhry, consider this house as your own. There stands the cot. Spread it and relax till your son comes."

After keeping silent for some time, the old man said, "The doctor keeps lying down all day long; perhaps he is not feeling well."

"I do not know," said Paltoo Ram, and hung his head down in worry. They got sick of waiting after an hour or so. Paltoo said, "We had better leave now. We do not know when he will come back," and they stepped back out on the road.

Next day the old man saw Dr. Paul going in the lane and called him. "Doctor, your father and mother had come to see you. They waited for you and sat here for a long time. Your father did not seem to be well; he had difficulty in walking and used a stick to support himself."

"My in-laws were at home; they should have gone in and waited there. I would have come in the meantime." Paul tried to cover up their maltreatment at the hands of his in-laws.

"Your mother-in-law simply told them, 'You are not in,' and shut the door. They could have gone in if someone had invited them in and asked them to sit and wait."

Paul got worried. He went home and said to his wife, "My father is not keeping good health. We have to go to the village just now." Lacchi did not want to go with him. She unnecessarily took a lot of time to get ready. It was quite dark when they reached their ancestral home. Paul met the members of his family but Lacchi went in and sat on the cot. She did not wish anybody as they were strangers to her. She considered the shanty as a poor potter's house and not that of her in-laws.

A puppy saw her, came close to seek her love and started licking her feet. Instead of caressing it in return, she kicked it with force and threw him away. The puppy ran away yelping. She disliked everything in the house and frowned. She got fed up sitting there, and the wrinkles on her brow deepened. Looking at her furrowed brow, every one avoided her and kept away.

Paul went to his father, who was lying in the bed. On seeing his son, Paltoo felt very happy.

"Do you have any health problem, Dad?" Paul asked him as he sat down on the cot. "My whole body is aching, my son." Paltoo could not restrain his tears and started complaining. "I had married my son in the hope that our daughter-in-law would come and bring with her all the joys of life. But whatever happiness was there in this house, had gone away. Instead we have to go after you to seek happiness. Ever since you have been married, it is only today that you have thought of visiting your ailing father. Your wife is sitting far away like my boss and behaving as if every one of us is untouchable." Paul did not like what his father had said. He frowned, stood up, and moved toward his mother. "Is everything all right, Mom—you had gone to visit me?"

"We had gone there to see you, my son."

"If you had gone there, you could have waited for me in our house. I would have come eventually."

"We could have gone in and waited if anyone had asked us to come in, but your mother in-law dealt with us very rudely and shut the door on us." His mother tried to vent her feelings. "You have forgotten us after your marriage and behave as if you belong to your in-laws only. So much time has elapsed after your marriage, and still your marriage bills are not paid. Who will pay them? The creditors keep pestering us.

"You should pay them."

"What have you left with us to pay them?

Paul said to his mother, "Have you not spent money on the marriages of my other brothers and sisters? I am also a member of this family."

His mother was shocked to hear her son's reply. She said, "We have made you a doctor. Your brothers could not be educated. Just calculate how much we have spent on your education. How did we afford that money?"

"I also worked myself. Just calculate my earnings too."

"Cursed be your birth! We had thought that since our son had become a doctor, he would raise the walls with gold and we would get rid of the potter's label. Our son has become a doctor, but our potter's label could not be got rid of. We have become poorer than ever before. You cannot stand our odor. Instead of paying for the expenses incurred on your education you have made us pay the marriage bills too. What a worthy son you have proved yourself!"

Lacchi was listening to what they were saying to each other. When she could no longer tolerate what the parents were cursing, she shouted, "Have you met with your parents? Let's go now. You had been missing them for so long. Have you embraced them to your satisfaction?" With these words she stepped out and moved to the car. The doctor followed her.

FOURTEEN

Next day Paltoo had a heart attack. He was writhing in pain. Lado sent her son Bhoori toward Paul. He was not at home. His wife said, "He has gone to play golf. I will let him know when he comes back."

She did not ask her brother-in-law to sit and wait. Paul returned very late at night; Lacchi was asleep at that time. Next morning she told him, "Your father is ill. A person had come to call you." Although she knew his elder brother, she termed him as a messenger. "Get ready, let us go," Paul told her. "You can go; I have no business to do there."

Karmi's cousin Sadhu was their neighbor. As soon as he learned about Paltoo Ram's severe pain in the chest, he took him to the civil hospital in his car. No one was there—neither doctor nor nurse. Sadhu sent someone to inform them in their residence quarters. The nurse came all alone. Someone told that Doctor would be available in his clinic.

She put the patient on the stretcher with Sadhu's help and carried him inside. Oxygen was not in stock. She could not do anything in the absence of the doctor except to give Paltoo two tablets of pain-killer. The patient was groaning in pain. The emergency doctor was not there although the 'Board of Emergency-ward' was hanging there.

When Paul reached, his father had expired, and his mother was crying. She cursed him: "You wretched fellow, you could have come in time to save your father's life. He died calling you, *'My son!'* ... *'My son!'*"

Paul felt very bad. He stopped going to his in-laws. He was so much annoyed with Lacchi that he asked her to make a decision: "If you do not share our grief I shall not share yours. If you want to live with me sever all relations with your parents."

She kept mum and gave no decision.

This caused turmoil in their house, and they abused each other and kept on dogfighting. One day Lacchi left the house spitting venom like a snake. Paul thought, "She is trying to scare me. She will come back. She had acted like this earlier too."

He waited for a while. She did not return. He got worried and ran after her. But she could not be found anywhere. Then he went toward the canal. He saw there was a crowd gathered near the waterfall, and he went to the spot where the people were watching the dead body stuck in the fall. Paul found that the dead body was that of his wife.

His father-in-law filed a case of murder against Paul, and he was sentenced to life.

FIFTEEN

On leaving Bhani's house, Karmi and Mohna became refugees for the second time. With her brother she went to her uncle's house. She did not want that her uncle and his family know that there was any ill feeling in her mind. They too gave them due respect, and even her aunt looked after them very well.

Bholi had finished her education, and got married too. She had not yet gone to her in-laws. This made Karmi and Mohna to enjoy their stay with her.

One day Karmi broached the subject of land. But her uncle ignored her request. She told Mohna, "Getting land from Uncle is not so easy task as we had thought. It is not sensible to fight with a bad person. Let us have a foothold first, and then we will deal with this matter. Instead of idling away your time, Mohna, you can start the business of buying and selling bullocks. One can make a beginning in a small way. Buy just one bullock in the first round, and after selling it go to *Nagaur*[25], as the bullocks of Nagaur are a great attraction for our people. There would be a sizable profit. You will gradually gain

---

25   Place famous for oxen

experience in buying and selling, and then you can expand the business."

"I can do business, but where is the money?" Mohna expressed his problem. "Do not worry about the money. Leave it to me." Her aunt Bhani had given Karmi her savings before dying. She wanted her brother to start business with that money.

In a very short time, Karmi established harmonious relations with her kith and kin.

She went to the house of her uncle Phagan, who had been very close to her father. His son, Rattan, treated her like his own sister and gave her a warm welcome. He said, "How fortunate to see my sister after a long time!" Though they lived with their uncle, their inward affinity was more with Rattan, who, besides farming, had been engaged in cattle trading from the very beginning.

Karmi said to him affectionately, "Dear brother, I want Mohna to do some work. If you deem it proper, he can join your business."

"It would be a great pleasure for me if I can be of any service to you. I have a great regard for your father." Then Rattan said to Mohna, who was sitting near him, "Is it of your liking, my boy? You will have to do lot of running about. It is not an easy job."

"It is OK, brother," replied Mohna.

They went to Nagaur in the first trip and selected the cattle from various houses. The market was held once a month. There was the risk of being cheated in the market. It was not so when buying from the houses, as they could satisfy themselves by examining the cattle again and again. They could also inquire around the neighborhood before finalizing the deal.

They saw that two grown-up calves could be bought for the price of one bullock and hence could earn a good profit this way. Mohna bought two, and Rattan bought four calves. The Nagaur calves were in great demand, and many people came to have a look at them. The mere name of Nagaur doubled their profit. The calves of that place were rated high as those were of high pedigree. They look good when they were yoked to the chariot, they had their own attraction. In those days a chariot was a prestigious vehicle, very much used in marriages and other festive occasions. Mohna's business flourished, and Karmi was very happy.

Karmi was fed up sitting idle. She started her own business in a favorable location in the village. The village was quite far away from the town, and no one wanted to travel that far. They preferred to buy ready-made clothes locally from Karmi. She made good profit in this business. However, Mohna's earning depended largely on his hard work. He had to be away from home for months in severe cold or exhausting heat, and Karmi worried a lot till he came back.

She counseled her brother. "Your business cannot be done single-handedly. Join me in the business of a

cloth merchant. When the two of us are in one business, our income would also be doubled and could
run into hundreds thousands."

But Mohna had the foolhardy mind of a Jat. He
said, "I do not like tailoring work—it is a menial job. I
will do farming whenever I am in a position to do so."

"You are mad," said his sister. "You do not want
to do a business that pays, but remain on the beaten
track of your forefathers. Farming is a losing business, and you will be ruined."

After a year, Mohna too came to his senses. He
joined his sister and both of them started earning
very well.

Mohna could not maintain accounts and could not
run the shop without Karmi's help. Karmi engage
Bholi as an assistant. Karmi went to the town and
placed orders for the cloth, which was shipped to their
shop. Bholi and Mohna managed to run the business
in her absence. Bholi maintained the daily accounts.
Within a year or so they had a roaring business.

When Veeru found out that the children mixed up
so well with one another, he too changed his attitude.
He vacated Karmi's house, which was very close
to her shop, and they set up a shop for ready-made
clothes here. These clothes were in great demand at
that time, and Karmi succeeded in this business so
well that she expanded further.

She formed a cooperative society, borrowed
money, and stocked her shop with the ready-made

clothes. Instead of purchasing these clothes from town, she got them stitched locally, by the girls otherwise sitting idle in villages. They did it on a contract basis. It proved to be cheaper. The girls stitched clothes sitting at home and charged much less. The sale of ready-made clothes exceeded the sale of cloth. Karmi's house was quite spacious, so she established a tailoring and embroidery school. She engaged two technical hands from Kashmir who specialized in their jobs. By dint of her hard work, Karmi turned her village into a local market.

As their business was well established, a matrimonial proposal came for Mohna. Karmi was very happy. "With God's grace, luck has smiled on us," said she to herself. Mohna was not at home. Such proposals were always expected.

Karmi talked to Mohna about this. He was happy inwardly but did not say yes. He thought, "My sister is an epitome of renunciation. In order to see me married, she is going to sacrifice her life. If I get married before her marriage, she would remain unmarried for life." Thinking of her sacrifice, he touched her feet and said, "Sister, you are great! You always think of me and do everything that builds me, making your own sacrifice even. Please keep in mind that I am not such a mean person that I shall accept any proposal for marriage. First, I shall give you a hearty send-off as a bride in the palanquin."

They loved each other so much that they sacrificed for each other.

All the boys and girls of Karmi's age had been married. Since Mohna was not accepting any proposal, after a year or so, offers for him too stopped coming.

SIXTEEN

Bhani's daughter, *Molhi*, expired, leaving behind two daughters. Her husband was a subahdar; He faced the problem of looking after his daughters. His two months' leave came to an end. After him there was no provision for Baby-sitting. He left the girls with his sister-in-law, Jitaan, and joined his duty.

How could *Jitaan* take care of so many children? She had three of her own kids, and now two more had come. She had to do her household chores also. She got sick of them in a month or so.

In the hour of dire necessity, she remembered her sister, Karmi, who was still unmarried.

She left her children at her parent's house, and, accompanied by *Sadhu*, she went to *Thikri-wala-Native village of Karmi*-to prepare Karmi's mind for marriage.

Karmi received *Jitaan* and *Sadhu* quite warmly. *Jitaan* told her that their deceased sister *Molhi* had been very worried about Karmi's marriage. "Who is there to find a match for you? Your parents died long ago. Our mother looked after your interests; she too passed away." Then she had asked me to find a suitable match for you. I have a proposal for you. I think our brother-in-law would not be a bad match for you. He is a nice man and the family is quite affluent. You will be all-in-all and sister's children would be better looked after. If he marries another woman, she would not treat them as her own."

Karmi listened to her but she was not happy with the proposal. The subahdar was an old man with daughters to look after. Karmi considered Jitaan selfish, as she seemed to be looking after her own interests. "She had never thought of me earlier," thought Karmi, "but now when the necessity arises she pretends to show sisterly love." She gave no response to Jitaan's proposal.

Then Jitaan asked her bluntly, "Why do you look crestfallen, girl? Say something!" Even then Karmi kept quiet and did not utter a word. She kept her head lowered as usual.

Karmi was lost in thoughts of her debacle in the first marriage. She had a feeling of getting cheated again. She started thinking, "I had escaped becoming a wife for husband and babysitter for her children at that time. Now Jitaan has come to trap me in a similar case. No one cares for me. She is here just to serve the interests of her widower relative. She thought me suitable to serve him, bear children for him, and do babysitting for Mohli's daughters. She noticed all the good qualities of becoming a 'dasi' in me. But she did not notice all the drawbacks in this man while matching me. She should have given weightage to my plus points, find a boy of my age. There is not a single trait in the subahdar to qualify me. I am a virgin and making an honorable living. If I am married to this man, I shall lose my independent life."

As the discussion was going on, Sadhu also came in, limping with the support of a stick. Mohna too was with him.

"Let's have a hot cup of tea with snacks, Kammo," said Sadhu affectionately.

Sadhu sent Karmi to the kitchen and started talking about her matrimony,

"What does Karmi say?"

"She says nothing," replied Jitaan. "She does not seem to have liked the proposal. Her face tells the story. Had she agreed, I would have been free of the heavy burden, and the girls could have been brought up properly."

Sadhu endorsed what Jitaan had proposed for Karmi. "It is good for her too. Brother-in-law is a subahdar. He has a sizable land holding also. What more does she need? "What do you say, my young friend? What is your opinion?" He turned toward Mohna and asked him.

"Whatever you purpose for her cannot be wrong, dear brother." Mohna could not say no to the older cousin.

Karmi was in the kitchen preparing tea. She was also giving vent to her feelings. "If my mother were alive today, I could have bemoaned my lot before her. O my mother, you gave me birth but left me to rot. You took no pity on me. To whom should I relate my tale of woe? Who would listen to my painful story? Why do not these people let me live my life? Every time they want me to get hitched to an old man. I am after all a daughter of someone; I too have some aspirations. How would this old man think of my yearnings? For him, I will be only a maid and a babysitter for his children." She continued unburdening her mind as she prepared tea.

Then she felt as if her mother had spoken to her from somewhere. It was not her mother in the kitchen, but her inner voice: "Do not lose heart, my child. You are not alone to suffer this agony. Many girls like you have their aspirations trampled underfoot—one is hitched to a blind man, another to a leper (bartered for monetary benefits). Just look at them who cannot get married for want of dowry. They rot for no fault of their own. The poor girls smolder like a wet dung cake throughout their lives. The society regards them as cursed rather they become the subject of hatred in the society. No one has human feelings for them. Be realistic, my daughter; my darling. Just feel the pulse of time, and agree to the proposal without creating a fuss."

Karmi brought in tea with sweet balls of milk paste. Sadhu laughed and said to Jitaan, "Karmi has brought sweet balls for us, so happy is she. You say she disagreed." Karmi lowered her eyes shyly. "Mad girl…

one should not feel shy. Of course, there are so many deceptions, but there is nothing to worry about with this liaison. What could we do earlier when we were cheated? We would not find a better place. A subahdar's position is not an ordinary one. Wherever he goes in Cantonment area, the soldiers stand at attention. You will become a subahdarni[26] sitting at home. Because of you, Mohna would also get enrolled in the army."

Then Sadhu turned to Jitaan and said, "Arrange for the marriage immediately, sister. It is now your responsibility."

Everyone was happy at the matrimonial settlement. Karmi had agreed, but there was no bloom on her face. She considered it a mismatch. But when she recalled her mother's words, she felt relieved. She smiled a little, turning her face to the other side.

The subahdar was overjoyed to learn that his marriage had been settled with karmi- a very intelligent and wise girl, beautiful with sharp features. **It is very hard to find such a match. The daughters got a mother, and the subahdar a new bride.**

He ordered the orderly to serve him rum. He turned on the gramophone. He drank and danced. He kept singing and dancing all alone. He did not stop drinking till he was dead drunk. He did not know when he had dozed off and went to sleep without taking his dinner.

---

26   Wife of subahdar is called Subahdarni in Indian Language.

SEVENTEEN

The date for Karmi's marriage was fixed. She entrusted her business to Mohna and Bholi and was free of her responsibilities on her parent's side.

When the girls tried to splash henna on her palms, she felt very shy and said, "Is this my age to be hennaed like this? Everything looks nice at the proper age. My days of making love and joys had been spent in shedding tears. I do not like these customs and rituals now. I have told sister that four or five persons of near relationship should come and take me with them after the marriage *ceremony. It should be simple.*" Karmi emphasized the last words because she was not in favor of Pomp and show of Marriage Palaces.

Karmi went from her parental home to her in-law's house.

It was the first auspicious night of their marriage. Bhag was busy drinking with his friends till midnight. Then he entered his wife's room carrying with him a packet of sugar bubble. When he reached his room Karmi was lying in their bed, she looked as she was sleeping." He stopped close to her and lost in thoughts, "I am late, it will be bad on my part to disturb her," thinking of manners he came out and had a peg of rum, and then another one.... He did not know when he reclined to one side. He came to senses when orderly awakened him and placed the tray of tea near him. He carried the tray to his *Memsahib*.[27] Karmi felt shy on seeing the subahdar standing in front of her and holding the tray. She lowered her head. She repented. "For him this was the night of bliss. He might have come with so many aspirations to my room. I acted foolishly in order to get better of him. I should not have acted the way I did. Just see how the army men are so enthusiastic about serving their wives!"

She said to her husband, "I had a headache. You should be considerate to me. You forgot me and got busy with drinking.... I don't know in whose room you had gone to sleep?" Karmi said this with a smile and blamed him. Bhag felt ashamed and lowered his eyes. Really thinking himself at fault, he apologized. "I will give no cause for complaint in future, ma'am." He accepted his mistake without having made it.

They were invited to a dinner next Sunday by a junior officer. All the officers' wives were seen wearing saris. Karmi was born and brought up in a village. She did not know how to wrap the sari around her. The subahdar brought another officer's wife to teach her how to dress in a *sari*. The subahdar ironed his clothes for the party and ironed Karmi's too. He

---

27   honorific for an officer's wife
      Ma'am

felt very happy serving Karmi. Afterward he went into the bathroom and dyed his hair.

When they got ready to leave he noticed strands of gray hair on Karmi's head. This caused him tension. "The lock of gray hair does not look nice."

"Everyone's hair turns gray with age; what is the harm if I have some as well?" said Karmi.

"Just wait, ma'am, I will set it right." Saying this, he went in. He brought the shoe polish brush and dabbed it with black polish and blackened her gray hair. Then he said, "Go in, darling, and look into the mirror. How beautiful you look now!"

She went into the bathroom and looked in the mirror. Her hair had turned black, but the smell of boot polish was nauseating. She came out with a sullen face, but how could she tell her husband, "You have made me a laughing stock"? She tried to smile to please him and said, "You have done wonders. There is no gray hair to be seen." The subahdar walked majestically with his new family.

Jitaan came to meet with the newlywed couple and stayed on for the night. Karmi asked her about the family photograph lying on the shelf. "I cannot find Molhi standing with the subahdar, sister. Who is this woman standing with him?"

Ever since Karmi had come to live with him, she tried to inquire about the woman with him in the photograph but did not have the courage to ask.

"Do not you know her?" Jitaan laughed and expressed her surprise at what Karmi had asked her. Then she said to herself, "How innocent is this girl! She is not aware of brother-in-law's first marriage. For her only Mohli was his first wife, as if he was very young. She does not know how old he is. He rose from the rank of a soldier to a subahdar. He could not be a young man."

"Had I known, why should have I asked you?" Karmi showed her annoyance at Jitaan's laughter. Jitaan finally stopped laughing and told Karmi, "This woman is his first wife."

Karmi was shocked to hear this. She thought to herself, "My eyes have opened today. How much has the absence of my mother cost me? Had she been alive, she would have certainly thought twice about the suitability of the match. Jitaan is concerned with Mohli's girls only. She did not bother about me. You may have hundreds of relatives, but none becomes your own. All of them have their own vested interests. What to talk of his being a matching partner? He is on the last leg of his life; he is of my father's age! How many more years will he live? One day I would be made to weep for him. He would leave behind two daughters of his first wife, and I would also have some. How would I look after the herd of kids all alone?"

Jitaan went away and left Kanti and Satti with Karmi who got them admitted in the Cantonment school. Kanti could have been in the second class, but because of her mother's death, she had lost one year. She was admitted to the first grade again. The school was a long distance away from home. The problem of sending the girls to school and bringing them back cropped up. The subahdar suggested to her to call Mohna. She agreed. She already wanted to do that. With Mohna's arrival the problem of taking the children to school and back was solved. Karmi had company, and she did not feel the loneliness.

A month had not yet passed Kanti fell ill. She was taken to the military hospital. The doctor gave her medicine for two days but the fever still persisted. Some people said that she was going to have smallpox; others said it was TB. Her condition worsened with every passing day, and ultimately she expired. Only Satti was left behind. She kept Karmi busy. An affectionate mother-daughter relationship developed between them. The girl felt as if she had gotten her own mother.

The New Year day was celebrated in the Cantonment. Others had just one or two drinks, but the Subahdar drank excessively. He kept performing 'Bhangra' (Punjabi folk dance). Everybody followed him to stand up and dance with him. As the subahdar was fully drunk, he became unsteady. When Karmi saw that he was about to stumble, she controlled him. Because of her, the subahdar continued to dance till very late at night. Everybody laughed when he collapsed. Karmi felt small; she left the stage and occupied a back seat.

EIGHTEEN

Mohna got fed up living in Karmi's house. As he had nothing to do the whole day, time became a drag for him. He often thought, "It is rightly said that a brother living in his sister's house is like a dog. How should I tell her that I want to go back? Keeping my inner feeling suppressed would not help."

One day he mustered enough courage to say, "Sister, I want to go back to the village. I will take possession of land if I go there. Nobody gives any importance to application by army personnel. Uncle bribes the clerk with ten rupees and the application is thrown in the wastepaper basket. In their eyes his high rank has no value. Corrupt people have no regards for his services to the Nation. I cannot give up my ancestral property like this. If we had some other means to earn our livelihood we could suspend our pursuit to get our property. But now it is difficult to forego it."

"Then what is the way open to us?" asked Karmi. "Will you fight? I will not allow you to do that. You may starve or have very little, but do not fight. It is bad to fight with a bad person. He is like a wild animal."

"I will abide by your decision. I will not pick a fight. I will run the shop in partnership with cousin-sister Bholi. I will earn my living. I should be able to stand on my own feet. It does not look proper to continue to be a burden on you."

"Do you have any discomfort living here?"

"No, sister, I do not have."

"Alright, then, keep staying on. I love you more than the land. Human life has no value in our country. They kill a person for a small sum of money. We listen to such horrible stories daily. You cannot expect anything reasonable from Uncle. You might have heard of Pritu, the milk seller in our village. His parents had died when he was very young. His maternal uncles took him to our village. Regarding him as their sister's offspring, they brought him up. When he grew up he started selling milk. He earned handsomely. One day something strange struck him. He declared, 'I am going back to my native village. I will do farming there. Why should my kinsmen thrive on my land?'

"They tried to change his decision but in vain. His native village was situated near the border in Amritsar District, where no law of the land prevails. The police are not to prevent the crime but to cover it up. The rival party arranged his disappearance within days of his arrival. His case was declared untraceable."

Mohna too was determined to get his property back from Veeru. After a long discussion, Karmi convinced him to file a suit in the court. She went with him. When they reached their village they found themselves in a strange position. The village folk feared Veeru, a wrongdoer. No one was prepared to be a witness against him. Karmi and Mohna had to hire professional witnesses. After wasting precious time and money for years, Mohna realized that there was no justice in the courts. The judiciary was equally corrupt. One had to buy justice, and that was not within his reach.

NINETEEN

Karmi got pregnant. Subahdar was happy at heart but worried too. His two wives had already died at the time of childbirth. He thought that in Karmi's case, the situation was the same. He could do nothing to save her life except for praying to God. He had to send her to his village, they had already overstayed in Army Quarters. Before leaving, he took her to the military hospital for a checkup. The X-ray report showed that they were going to have twins. The problem was more serious for Karmi. 'There are no maternity centers in villages where she could go for delivery. And if there is one, there is no staff, and if staff is there, there is no medicine. For pregnant women life is always at risk.

Karmi was worried herself lest she should meet the fate of the subahdar's ex-wives. As the expected date of delivery approached, her stress intensified.

It was customary to give birth to the first baby in the parental home. *Sadhu, Karmi's cousin*, took her to his village. Karmi heaved a sigh of relief. Sadhu was educated, and he understood the problem. He got Karmi admitted to Civil Hospital Ganganagar. She gave birth to twins—a boy and a girl. The girl was named Bali and the boy, Tara. Karmi was discharged from the hospital after three days.

Sadhu was relating to Karmi, "Had Mohli been in hospital, her life too could be saved. The subahdar sent her to his native place. An illiterate midwife attended to her delivery. She cut the umbilical cord with an unclean knife, which caused infection. The midwife had no knowledge to cure the infection. Her ignorance took Mohli's life. There is an acute poverty in the villages—people cannot afford to pay the expenses of maternity hospitals. Their illiteracy aggravates the problem. People who are well off also leave their wives on nature, thus a lot of women die without maternity care. They waste a huge amount on religious functions, on the celebrations of marriages and other social functions. If they do not have money, they take loans, as it is a matter of social prestige for them. They spend little on the delivery of their wives and leave them on luck. If she dies, it is she who loses her life, and it is her parents who lose their daughter, but the husband has nothing to lose. He gets a new wife with the award of dowry."

Once the worry of pregnancy and delivery was over, Karmi discussed another problem with her brother. "We can barely manage with my husband's salary now. What would we do after his retirement? There is no home or hearth. The ancestral home is in a dilapidated condition, and that is not worth living in. Where would we go to settle?"

The subahdar had overheard her talk with her brother. He tried to console her, "My darling! I have to shoulder so many responsibilities. I went home, replaced the roof, and had to incur lots of expenses on the marriage of my niece. The buffalo had died; I had to buy a new one for my parents. There is still time to retirement. We will see to it when I go on pension. Why do you worry unnecessarily now?"

The next day Sadhu was boosting Karmi's courage. "It is not only you who is financially tight. It is a national problem. Poverty is a punishment for slavery. The British rulers do not consider the slaves as equal. We are destined to serve our masters. That is why you are debarred from your husband's promotion to commission, it is meant for your masters only."

Karmi said, "May be we are slaves, but we have the same life as that of a masters and the same duty. So the right too should be the same. We should fight for rights and equality. Even the mother does not feed her baby unless it cries."

Sadhu made his point clear. "In fact, our people are not aware of their rights. Religion has dominated our life. Early in the morning the *Maulvi*[28] starts crowing, and the Muslims indulge in offering prayer. The Pundits start ringing the bells, the Hindus sit in for worship. The Sikhs have become more fanatic than the other two. Intoxicated with religion, we do not

---

28 Muslim Priest

mind if we are not treated as human beings. We have become used to the life of a slave. We have been fighting in the name of religion for centuries.

; the British rulers are taking advantage of our religious weakness."

Karmi started blaming her husband and other Indian Army officers-J.C.O. - for not making the Indian Army conscious of their rights. As they were talking loudly, their neighbor, Naib (Junior) Subahdar Kehar, came in. He was quite friendly with them. As he entered the house he said to Karmi, "What wrong has my brother done that you are frowning at him?"

"There are a hundred and one problems in the house. What should I tell you and what should I not?" Karmi tried to dodge him intelligently.

"Tell me if there is anything that I can do for you."

Karmi could not restrain herself—she said, "Your brother is going to retire. We hardly make both ends meet in these days, what shall we do when proceed on pension? But even the monetary angle is not so important. I worry about the mind-set of the Indian army—you are in the forefront in the battlefield to fight and die for the cause of the British. When it comes to promotion, only the white men are pro-moted. Your promotion stops at the rank of subah-dar. You people do not dare to question this type of discrimination. It is a grave injustice. Just see: your brother has been stuck up at the subahdar's rank for such a long time. Had he been commissioned, he would have drawn a handsome pension, much more than that he would get now."

Sadhu interrupted. "He is, after all, a subahdar. He should draw such a decent salary that he should be able to live a decent life. You work for the government, and when you need money, you have to raise loans. Is this justified? Britain is ruling half the world with your help. When the question of awarding a commission arises, the black color stands in your way."

Subahdar too spoke his mind. "This discrimination will not last long. The Indian Army is sick of the maltreatment meted out to them. One day they will revolt against the tyranny of the rulers. Our forefathers had already shown the way in 1857; fighting first war of independence."

TWENTY

The subahdar rejoined his unit in Malaysia. Karmi's concerns always occupied his mind: "There is no hearth or home to go to ..."

Sadhu's reply to her had left an indelible impression on his mind. "You are discriminated against because you are slave. You are debarred from commission because you are slave...."

The subahdar began to actively inculcate the idea of independence in the minds of his fellow Officers and soldiers. He thought that slavery was the root cause of discrimination in pay and promotions. He developed relations with the Indian revolutionaries like Ras-Behari-Bose and Pritam Singh in Malaysia.

Indian soldiers generally came in contact with the Indians settled in Southeast Asia. The desire to become free had become stronger with the passage of time.

The meeting between the Indian soldiers and the Indian immigrants was like the confluence of *the Ganges and the Jumna*, and it proved to be a great source of strength to the freedom movement.

Japan too had realized their rising power and regarded the Indian prisoners of war as equal to their soldiers.

Ras-Behari-Bose had founded the Indian Independence League by enrolling the Indians settled in south-east Asian countries. Almost all the Indian immigrants in Southeast Asia had been organized to fight for freedom.

Captain Mohan Singh read the pulse of Indian immigrants and convened a mammoth conference at Bangkok. It was resolved to raise the Indian National Army. Capt. Mohan Singh was given the rank of lieutenant general and designated as commander-in-chief.

General Fujiwara of Japan freed the prisoners of war to join Indian National Army (INA). The strength of INA increased from two thousand five hundred to forty-five thousand.

Netaji Subhash Chander Bose was watching new development. He took over the command of INA from Gen. Mohan Singh. The Japanese accepted their demand of full freedom. The government of free India was set up on 21 October 1943 at an unknown place. M. K. Kiani was made the commander-in-chief.

After the Japanese had conquered Burma, the secretariat of the Azad, Hind Fauj, was moved to 51 University Avenue, Rangoon, on 7th January 1944.

After the establishment of their own government, the enthusiasm among the Indian National Army rose very high.

The Indians settled abroad, started donating liberally, and rendered all kinds of help. The women raised a Jhansi brigade.

Netaji gave the slogan-: "March to Delhi." It enthused the spirit of "do or die" **in the Indian National Army for Independence.**

On 13 April 1945, the Foundation Day of the Sikhs (the Baisakhi Day), the INA attacked Kohima, the capital of Manipur in India. That was the first step of the March to Delhi. The Japanese sent two divisions of their army for attack on Kohima in support of I.N.A.

The battle of Kohima was the most horrible, compared to the other battles of the World War II.

As the INA was advancing, Gandhiji got unnerved and gave the statement, "You should be under no misapprehension that you would be accorded a warm welcome on reaching India..."

This declaration of Gandhiji raised suspicion in the minds of the Indian people. Instead of cooperating, they opposed rather fought against INA. Gandhiji's statement proved to be a boon to the Britishers and Fatal Blow to I.N.A. and Japanese Armed Forces.

Japan was no longer in a position to help I.N.A. Her own forces were starving for want of rations.

In order to overcome the worsening situation, Netaji left for Russia to seek their help. His plane was shot down while flying over the city of Tepi on 18 August 1945. The news about the death of Netaji Sobhash Chander Bose spread like wildfire all over the world and the media covered it. Gandhi ji and his Congress Party did not utter a single word of condolence. It made their intentions clear-to whom they supported- National Liberation Forces of India or the Britishers.

After Netaji, what to talk of ammunition, even Ration was not supplied to Azad Hind. The valiant soldiers continued to fight on empty stomachs. They had taken positions in far-off places and distant hills, and they fired once in a while. When hunger tormented them, they raised slogans—Long Live India! Long live Neta ji Subhash Chander Bose! The enemy retaliated by showering bullets on them, and they were silenced forever.

Those, who survived, were made prisoners of war. For fear of public uprising, they were detained at unknown places for a long period. But nobody was given any information about INA detainees— they were supposed to be dead.

TWENTY-ONE

The supply of ration to the families of the Indian National Army was stopped. Whatever little money they had, had been spent. They were starving. Their children demanded food. It became all the more difficult for pregnant women like Karmi.

It was a question of the survival and maintenance of the families of INA. They got no solace from anywhere; rather, they were ordered to vacate their quarters. The British government continued to perpetrate cruelty on the freedom fighters' and their families. All India Congress was expected to come forward for their rescue as it was a National Party but they including Gandhi ji continued to tolerate the atrocities committed on them. They should have come forward for the maintenance of the families of INA.

Time passed, and there was no news from the subahdar and his compatriots. When Congress Party failed to sopport them, they had to borrow or take loan for their maintenance.

Shera and other moneylenders came again and again to demand the money that Karmi's family had borrowed from time to time for their daily expenses when I.N.A. was not paid their salaries or aid was delivered to them from any compatriot body.

Long time had passed, people had lost all hope of the subahdar being alive, and so the moneylenders got restless for their money.

Though the *Azad Hind Fauj* had lost the war, yet Karmi's fighting continued all the seven days of the week, and three hundred and sixty-five days of the year.

The close relatives asked Karmi, "Do the dead ever come back? Perform the last rites of your husband and remarry."

Karmi firmly answered, "He will certainly come. I will not be unfaithful to my husband who has gone to fight for our freedom."

Hundreds of patriots were missing. Their families were starving, paying the price of freedom.

Karmi was rather in a worse situation than ever before. She was pregnant, and delivery was due at any time, but she did not have a dime. One day when she had no other way out, she said to her aged mother-in-law, "I have started having birth pangs, mother. What to do, and where should I go?"

"What are you talking about, my daughter? The poor people too bear children? I shall call Gulabo, the midwife. She charges forty Pound of wheat and a suit, that I would manage myself.

"Go right now and call her, Mom."

Mother went and brought with her the old midwife.

With the sickle in her hand, she was ready for delivering the baby. Karmi, looking at the rusted sickle, shouted at her, "*No!* Do not use it; you will kill me with it."

"I have been doing this job for decades. There has never been a complication. The mothers come out of the confinement hale and hearty. I don't understand what else you expect from me."

"Boil the sickle in hot water," Karmi instructed the midwife.

After boiling the sickle as directed, the midwife asked her, "Is it OK now?"

"Now wash your hands properly with soap."

After an hour or so, the male child was born safe and sound. He was named Udhe.

The menial lady tied the wreath on the main gate and received her tip. Looking at the auspicious leaves of *neem tree* the whole village rejoiced. Bards, eunuchs, and others came to congratulate them. They sang and danced. Her mother-in-law gave a plateful of grain to everyone.

Karmi gave good news to her husband after Udhe's birth, and then another letter—but none was answered. The subahdar's regiment had revolted and joined INA. The mail was not delivered to that unit.

Her father-in-law drank to his fill and sat down in the main square of the village. The people congratulated him and asked for drinks.

He replied, "I do wish to give you a crate full of rum, but I am sorry, my son has not come, pray for him, he may be alright and come soon." Tears rolled down his cheeks as he spoke those words.

Master Kehr, sitting close by, broke his heart by giving bad news: "Nobody can say anything. The war that INA fought at Kohima was a decisive battle. God knows if anybody survived."

An elderly man noticed that the subahdar's father was disheartened. He was shedding tears. He contradicted Kehr, "Subedar is a National Hero. He is fighting to break the chains of slavery and liberate the Nation. He will come with flying colors."

After the defeat those who survived were detained at unknown places, proceedings were launched against them. The case continued for years. A decision had to be taken, keeping in view the reaction and strength of the Indian people.

As the case was lingering on, discontentment against the British rulers spread in the civil as well as in the army. There were signs of revolt. The Union Jack was burned in the cantonments at various places. The British government realized that punishing prisoners would cost them much. In view of the prevailing situation, the freedom fighters were released.

Though they had been acquitted by the British government but the Indian national government did not withdraw their cases. The government refused to count their past services. They were sent to their villages to rot in their old age, without pension. People everywhere resented this. As the national government faced criticism and earned a bad name, they played the game of giving "tamrapatras" (inscribed copper plates). Very few freedom fighters accepted the tamrapatras, considering that an insult to them and their fellow Martyrs.

The patriots of Azaad Hind Fauj still entertained high hopes that the public would erect gates to welcome them with flower wreaths when they would go to their native places after their release. On the contrary, their kith and kin, considering them dead, had performed their last rites.

If the British government had kept their families in the dark, it was the foremost duty of the national government to inform their families whether they were dead or alive. If dead, they should have been honored and their families rehabilitated, but the party in power showed opportunism accepting Partition and betrayed the Nation as usual. The national government was in a hurry to rule. They took the wooden slippers of the Vice-Roy of India to the 'throne' as the insignia of British King and started ruling.

TWENTY-TWO

It is just possible that India and its people might forget the valiant fighters of Azaad Hind Fauj but Karmi could not. She was living in the hope that her husband was alive. He would come one day. While waiting for him, she had been worshiping all the gods and goddesses and praying for her husband's well-being.

One day Bapu[29] broke the news early in the morning. "Congratulations, my child, Bhag is coming!" He had brought sugar bubbles from the shop and distributed them among people while coming home.

Karmi's joy knew no bounds as she heard about the return of her husband. She felt as if she was flying high in the skies. She tidied up the house, giving it a fresh coat of mud and cow dung. She drew pictures of peacocks and peahens on the walls. The house bore a new look. A day before his arrival, she feasted the children of the clan. She also brought sweets to distribute, and mud lamps to make light. She soaked them in water and made them ready to be lit at night. As the sun set, the entire house brightened up with

---

29   respectful term for father-in-law or father

illuminations. Then she put the lamps in a brass plate and went out to place them in the *gurdwara,* the terrace of the well, and the matees (memorials of the martyrs).

Grandma Bhago met her on the way. Karmi touched the feet of the old lady. In return, Granny prayed for her to be blessed with a long and a happy married life.

More ladies met Karmi on the way. They were surprised to see her carrying mud lamps and said, "Diwali[30] is after many days, but you are carrying the lamps today—you are doing something unusual" "No, not I, but the people usually do something unusual. They don't celebrate Diwali, but ape others. If you ask them 'Why do you celebrate Diwali?' they don't know. They simply say, 'to celebrate the return of Rama[31] after his exile.' They do as the Romans do—Ram is just a mystery. I am celebrating the true Diwali. My 'Ram' is coming home after waging the war for freedom of the country. He is my husband, he is also my Ram; he is my 'Rahim'[32] too. Today, it is both *Diwa*li and *Eid*[33] for me!"

The subahdar returned home. He was surprised to see Karmi celebrating Diwali in advance. She felt overjoyed, as if she had attained something very special. She touched her husband's feet. He embraced her joyfully and kissed her forehead.

---

30 festival of lights
31 Ram: Hindu god
32 Muslim god
33 Muslim festival

Laughing, she said, "Please, Let me pour some oil[34]first and perform the welcome ceremony."

She poured oil on both sides of the doorstep, then picked up dust from the ground under her husband's feet and touched it to her forehead. She did everything in keeping with the auspicious occasion. Udhe also came in, jumping with joy, followed by the other children. Karmi lifted Udhe and handed him over to her husband, saying, "Here is the new gift—of your own flesh and blood." Bhag held the child to his chest, caressed it, and then something came to his mind. He frowned and said ruefully, "You never told me about the birth of this gift. You could at least have dropped a simple postcard. Such good news would have increased my life span by ten years. I stopped short of asking you, 'Whose child is he?' "

"Ask the 56 APO why they did not deliver mail to you! I have been writing one letter after another and sending them to this address—it is just possible you might have joined the INA in the meanwhile."

Karmi got busy with her work. Subahdar took a bath and went to bed for rest. All sorts of thoughts were passing through his mind. "How can this boy be mine? I had gone to war long ago. He was born after I had left; I wonder with whom she had been in the bed." And to remove his doubt, he tried to recall the year in which he had come on leave. Since he was agitated, he even forgot the year, not to speak of

---

34   a welcome ceremony

remembering the date and month. He was thinking, "Perhaps it was five years back, but the boy does not seem to be five years old. He looks younger, he can't be mine. It seems she has been making merry with someone." He abused her. "The bastard.... She considered me dead. She is doing this and that just to fool me."

He started perspiring. He threw away his blanket and started shouting, "Where are you? Come here…. Don't go in hiding now."

He looked around but did not find her anywhere. Then he thought, "She would have gone out to ease herself. Let her come back. I will teach her a good lesson."

He started searching his diary but did not find it. He did not remember where he had kept it. Then he said to himself, "Possibly I have left it in the Center."

He had kept a bottle of rum in his bag before leaving his detention center. He took it out, uncorked it, and put to his mouth impatiently. He drank in one swallow as much as he could. This inebriated him. He lost his senses and didn't know where he was lying.

Karmi had cooked chicken and prepared many other delicacies. He didn't touch them. She tried to awaken him, but he was not in a fit state to eat a meal. His mouth was wide open, his eyes were blood red.

She got unnerved. "What has happened to him? He was quite well and had been talking and playing with the children."

She had been gone for a short while in the neighborhood and could not understand what had happened to him in the meantime.

"It was my fault," she thought. "I shouldn't have taken so much time. How long could he have waited for me? An idle brain is a devil's workshop. He may have started drinking. I had just gone to the shopkeeper to borrow some money. It took me lot of time there."

Subedar woke up in the small hours of morning. He had calmed down a bit. The effect of rum had gone.

Then he came to his senses. "I have tried to dig my own grave. Without consulting the diary, nothing can be said definitely. It is just possible that I am mistaken. The boy may be mine. Thank God she was not at home; otherwise she would have plucked my hair. A woman cannot bear a false allegation on her character. Like Lord Rama, I too was going to shut out my '*Sita*' under suspicion. Lord Rama did it on washer man's labeling allegation against his wife with reference to *Sita's character*[35]. I am a beast...a soldier's mind is emptied of all wisdom; otherwise, who would leave his family behind and go away to fight the war? Have the rulers themselves ever gone to the war? Why should they go? The mercenaries like me become easily available to them. We just

---

35 A washer man passed remarks against his wife that he was not Lord Rama who will excuse her-: Lord Rama's Sita was kidnapped by Rawna, King of Sri Lanka, King of Sri Lanka; Rama had to wage war against him to get his wife back. The washer man said to his wife, "Do not consider me Ram who excused his wife..."

go on fighting like dogs for nothing…What have I gained? I hardly know my children and my children do not know me. Is the army service of any use to me? In the name of discipline I lost my own balance of mind. I would have erroneously killed my wife, "I had gone off my head fighting the whole of my life, and now I am suspecting my wife. The goddess, that she is, has given me sons—precious pearls. What would have been apt for me was to feel obliged to her for life. I haven't given any credit to her. Man is a beast compared to woman. Of course both of them possess animal instincts, but man has gotten more dominant. I would have destroyed my family in an instant. Almighty has saved it. What a great lady she is! She never minds that I am an old man, a mismatch for her. She is always happy, as if she has gotten the most suitable match. She works like a loyal slave, caring little for her food or clothes. She faced all kinds of hardships in her life during my absence. Have I given her any credit for that? No. I am a fool of the first water! I did not realize the greatness of a woman for a man. It is a precious gift of nature. Had I been there in her place at home, and she had been in the army, I would have taken full advantage of her absence; I would have found new pastures every day. Do the soldiers ever restrain in any way? They go to the brothel, then bring home a 'gift' for their wives and destroy the whole family. Then they bemoan their lot. I must thank my stars that I have been saved of all this. If one has a wife, she should be like Karmi! It is quite ironic that I haven't brought anything for the children. I have come back after such a long time. I should have brought something special for her and her children! But she didn't let anyone know of this; instead she got sweets for me and gave them to the children as if I had brought them. How happy has she felt on my return! She has celebrated Diwali and valued me as Lord Rama. What sort of a man am I? I proved myself a mean person."

The subahdar gave up lethargy, stepped out, passed urine, and had a wash. Then he looked at the stars and observed that it was very early and dawn was a while away. The morning star had not yet risen; the cock had not crowed. He thought, "I should awaken Karmi in the small hours of the morning." Then he changed his mind. "Let her sleep. She had been running about the whole day and must be tired. There is no problem of making tea. I should prepare it myself."

He lighted the lamp in the kitchen and put on the kettle to boil water for preparing tea. The light from the kitchen fell outside on Karmi's back and Udhe's face.

He could properly examine the face and features of the boy. He looked at him minutely, thinking, "His features do not resemble our family, or his complexion.... Perhaps she has concocted the story

127

of writing letters to me after his birth. The wise men say, 'A woman and a mare belong to the one who rides it.' I was sitting in the trenches. I did not know whether I would die or survive. It was enough that she had been my wife. When a long time had passed and nothing was known about me, it was bound to happen, considering the circumstances, a widow can live as a widow, but the people do not let her. Some paramour of her beauty would have sprung in the neighborhood. The swindlers are more after beauty than gold or silver. This was also the story of a beautiful woman related to Jagga. Jagga's brother Autar was very old. His wife was quite young. She had three children and still looked like a frolicsome filly. She was seduced by a young lover. Their affair continued. He visited her at night. Then he started coming in the daytime also.

One day Autar came to meet him and stayed on for the night. He related his tale of woe. 'My dear brother, your sister-in-law has gone astray. Kaila of the mafia gang has seduced her. She has gone so far ahead in her affair that she does not care for me these days. I am worried about my life…. She can get me eliminated…anytime. Do something for me."

Who can save the man whose life partner comes to the point of getting him killed? Hardly ten days had passed when he was killed His body was stuffed in a gunny bag and buried at the river side. The police covered up the crime after taking bribe.

"I am also old and my wife is still young; it is just possible that it may so happen with me that had happened with Jagga's brother. My wife may consider me a hindrance in her way and…I would not die the death of Autar! But I have never observed a bad streak in her, nor have I heard a man coming to her. It is just possible my suspicion is unfounded. Udhe might be my son. Is it justified in any way to hang her because of a mere suspicion? No way, It is better that I myself should quit before any such rumor gets afloat. If I start quarrelling, it may be, she herself go away with the child. In that situation shall I be able to look after the rest of the family? No…."

The subahdar had his tea and said to him, "What is the use of living a wretched life of suspicion? It is better to renounce the home and hearth and go away to a secluded place to recite His Name. This is why the sages retired to the caves of hills for peace of mind."

He picked up his bag with a heavy heart. While stepping out, he looked at his daughters in turn and then at Tara. As it was a time of departure, he got emotional. Tears flowed and it became difficult to leave the house…He took courage, blew a flying kiss and tiptoed out. He turned to the side room, where his parents were sleeping. He thought of having a glimpse of them before going away.

They heard their son's footsteps and woke up. His mother said, "We have been awaiting your return so very eagerly, my son. And now you are ready to go away. You had no time to sit with us even for a while."

"No, Mom!—how can I forget you? I owe my life to you. You are like God to me. I am so unlucky that I am not destined to serve you. I have left behind some important documents. I am going to retrieve those from the records," with these words, he departed.

TWENTY-THREE

Sadhu came to know about the subahdar's self-exile. He reached Karmi's village. He was the only nearest relative of Karmi who could help her in such circumstances. He launched his campaign for the search of her husband. He visited all the places of his interest-: The Sikh and Hindu Temples-'Hazoor Sahib' Gurdwara in the south to 'Hardwar' in the Himalaya hills in the north but failed to find him anywhere. He felt very sad. He observed his sister was under acute depression. He could not bear to see her in that condition. In order to divert her attention, he said in a lighter vein, "Karmi, Gautam Buddha had also done like this. He had renounced his royal status, wife, and son and became an ascetic. He suffered throughout his life in search of truth about the life and death circle. Ultimately he attained enlightenment and achieved the position of Buddha. The subahdar has also renounced everything and became ascetic. Let us see what position does he gain?"

Karmi reacted angrily. "No, he will not attain any position. I know him very closely. He lacks the qualities of Lord Buddha. He should have strong willpower like him. He had raised the flag of the INA, fought valiantly, and advanced toward Delhi. When they reached Kohima and minarets of the Red Fort of Delhi were in sight, they laid down arms.

"He returned empty-handed. He had very high position in INA. If he was a man of some worth, he should have fought bravely till his mission was achieved. Independence remained confined to air-conditioned bungalows. Instead of becoming ascetic, he should have resumed his struggle to achieve independence for all, but being afraid of death, he became an ascetic. It is escapism. Of course Gautam Buddha had left his wife, the palace, and the king-dom too. What has your brother-in-law left for us? Only abject poverty! We fill our belly in the morning and are worried for the evening meal. I have about half a dozen children to bring up, and, in addition to them, his old parents to be cared for. Had he been a brave man, he would have discharged his respon-sibilities. Renunciation of the world is for the cow-ards who accept defeat. The husbands do show such type of cowardice but the wives do not. Though I am a woman, I will not run away from the respon-sibilities of a family life.... I faced all odds of life when he was waging a war of independence. I shall continue my 'war of independence'; let the INA lay down arms but I will not. I shall bring up the chil-dren, educate them, and also serve his parents to the best of my ability. The sad part of this incident is that he should have told my fault before deserting me. I was his duly wedded wife and not bought from the market. Marriage is a solemn pact, which he should have adhered to."

Karmi continued, boiling with rage and fury. Then she realized that her way of condemnation would have a bad effect on her children. They too would hold their father guilty and curse him. They would talk ill of him and get alienated one day. Sowing seeds of hatred will have bad repercussions on both sides. Moreover, an Indian woman is not supposed to talk ill of her husband, as it earns a bad name for her and her parental family. Karmi changed her stance and said, "I would not let this happen. This would mean my own defeat. After all, this is my family: he is my husband and father of my kids. He can err, being a human being, but the relationship should not be brought to an end so soon."

Time was passing on; months and years passed, but Karmi still hoped that subahdar would come one day. She was sitting when something came to her mind. She said to Satti, "My child, put this ladder against the shelf. We usually place important articles like money there. He might have left some money or letter or the like there before leaving. He was not the one to go away like this in a cowardly manner."

Satti started cleaning the shelf. As she was doing this, she found her father's diary. There were some papers in the diary, with a five-rupee note. That was the only legacy of the subahdar.

Satti picked up the diary and handed it over to her mother. Karmi leafed through the diary. Her heart had started galloping. She checked and rechecked but found no message, she felt lost.

TWENTY-FOUR

After the subahdar had appeared and disappeared suddenly, all kinds of rumors spread in the village. The creditors started pestering Karmi.

The buffalo had been bought from a moneylender, Sher, a long time back, and he had not been paid yet. He came to know that the subahdar had lost his job. Sher insisted on being paid immediately. Karmi could find no way to clear his debt. Four hundred rupees had been borrowed, and interest thereon worked out to another four hundred, totaling eight hundred. The moneylender insisted, "You should pay me now."

Karmi made her position clear. "He had come, no doubt, but due to some urgent piece of work, he had to go back."

"When is he coming back?" asked Sher.

"He did not tell me."

"You have been making excuses for a long time. I will not go today without taking my money. I do not know about his coming and going. You have borrowed money from me—it is up to you to return it."

For Karmi, it was a bolt from the blue. She had just a small canal-irrigated land on the highway and had three crops annually. It gave regular income, and was a mainstay of her family. She was making both ends meet and educating her children. Sher was pressing her to mortgage that fertile piece. The other land was un-irrigated, hardly of any use.

Sher emphatically reiterated his demand again and again. As a last resort, he untethered the buffalo and cow. He tried to drive them to his place. While going, he said, "These two animals are against the interest on the principal amount—the principle is still outstanding."

"I understand the buffalo being taken away against interest," said Karmi, "but taking cow in addition to it is high-handedness. It cannot be tolerated."

She stepped ahead and tried to snatch the chains of the buffalo and the cow from his hand. Sher held the chains tightly. As they were grappling, Tara came out, followed by the girls. Sher fell down in the struggle and received bruises. Feeling ashamed, he said, "If not the two, at least give me my buffalo. I will not leave it."

He went away, taking with him the buffalo. Karmi had to yield something to save her skin.

Next day the shopkeeper showed up with his account book and called through the window, "Subahdar sir!" Karmi recognized his voice. She was stunned on hearing him. She had hardly tackled one creditor and the other had appeared, adding to her worries. She had been buying groceries on credit for years, and a huge amount had become due. He was charging a higher price for everything taken on credit and added five percent interest on that. Scared by Sher, Karmi rushed out on the first call and sent him back; she assured him, that he would be paid before the end of month.

TWENTY-FIVE

After attending to household chores, Karmi turned toward Udhe. When she tried to feed him, she touched his body and found that he had a very high temperature. She had no money for his treatment. Udhe was her life and soul. She could not bear it even if he had a headache. He was lying exhausted with fever. Her father-in-law was doing something close by. She called him loudly, *"Dad!"*

She had never shrieked like that, ever. "What is the matter, Karmi? Is it OK?' he asked her, "Udhe is running very high temperature. His body is burning hot. He is taking labored breaths."

Karmi's father-in-law came and felt his grandchild's pulse. It was really very fast. They hired a rickshaw and took Udhe to the doctor.

The doctor examined him. The baby was in a critical condition. He was admitted. It was a case of diphtheria. He inserted in his mouth an instrument shaped like a Hubble bubble and started sending steam to the throat. That process continued for hours. The doctor also gave an injection for diphtheria. The inflammation inside started subsiding, and Udhe's breathing became easier.

He was discharged after two days. When the doctor asked for payment, her father-in-law had no money to pay the bill. Karmi felt ashamed.

She thought, "We have managed today somehow, but for how long? If someone else falls sick, what would we do? We should have some source of income, to meet emergencies. We would not be able to deal with it every time without doing some kind of work."

She made up her mind to set up a dairy farm. She had her land where she could grow maize and some sort of fodder.

She raised a loan from the bank and bought two cows of good stock. She got a secondhand cart with a male buffalo calf for carrying fodder home.

Tara volunteered to bring fodder from the field and to chafe it. Sisters helped him. Karmi fed the animals. All of them worked as a team.

After paying the bank installments they saved some money. Their dairy business became a success.

But Tara's education had come to suffer. He had to give lot of time to the cows. He got tired doing the hard work. His sisters saw his plight. They said to their mom, "Why are you spoiling Tara's life on cattle rearing? Engage some worker, or we should do the job. Send him to school regularly." "Oh, you are right! I am doing injustice with the innocent lad. I should myself see his interest. We should hire someone. He should be sent to school regularly." Karmi agreed.

Karmi had learned from experience that she couldn't afford to hire a servant. She started doing the job cooperatively with her daughters. They all went to the field very early and carried fodder on their heads and chafed it also.

Tara was sent to school regularly, but his work with the cattle had cost him much. He had missed lessons and lagged behind the class. Then he started missing class and joined the company of the street boys. He was sent to school from home, but he did not reach there; instead, he went to bathe in the ponds or played in the street.

Karmi was startled when she received a complaint from his teacher: "Your son is going astray, madam." Karmi went to school and scolded the boy in front of his teachers. Tara felt insulted. He retorted, "I am not going to be a deputy commissioner after getting education—I am leaving the school."

When Tara and his mother reached home, Karmi said to him affectionately, "You had never talked in this way ever, my son; what has gone wrong with you today?"

"What could have happened to me? Nothing—the year is going to be over, and I have not yet got all the books. I can't do the schoolwork. I lagged behind other kids in studies.

"I feel ashamed when I am beaten with cane. How could I face the other students then? One day I will have to do farming, so why should I not start it right now?"

Tara was right. How could he do regular work without books?

The number of the cattle heads increased. The girls too found it difficult to cope with the work.

Karmi had engaged a young boy of a nearby poor family. She somehow bought books for Tara and asked him, "If you find English a tough subject, should I arrange for tuition?"

Tara had realized his mistake. He said, "How will you go on arranging for tuition in every subject, Mom? I am weak in mathematics too."

Tara was fully aware of the financial position of the family. Taking his books, he started going to Bansa, the son of a trader family. Bansa was very good at studies. Tara asked for help wherever he found himself stuck. They studied sitting together at the shop and did their homework regularly. In the course of time, he was able to make up the deficiency and was doing well in all the subjects.

In spite of that, the class teacher had made it difficult for Tara to continue in the school. The English teacher unduly pressed him to take tuition from him. The teachers corruptly engaged students in tuitions, accepting families' payments but teaching nothing new.

Tara found him in a difficult position. Like him, five other students could not afford tuition. Their names were struck off the school rolls, making false entries of their absence. They were turned out of the school. Considering it a matter of shame, Karmi did not go to the school to complain. She had very high hopes for her son. She was expecting that after completing his education, he would shoulder her responsibilities. On Tara's debacle in getting education Karmi felt doomed.

Tara's other classmates got admitted to Dev Samaj[36] School and saved a year. Karmi did not allow him to join that school. She objected, "They don't believe in God. I don't want you to be an atheist."

Tara was raddarless, a man of nowhere. He passed his time in the company of spoiled kids.

---

36 Dev-Smaj is a sect that believes in Science and not in any super power

PART III

Karmi had put Tara in Khalsa School to make him a good Sikh, but he could not become a good Sikh; he turned out to be a fanatic. He started hating other faiths and thus distanced himself from humanity.

In Hindu and Muslim schools also, fanaticism was injected, and in the name of religion, seeds of hatred were sown, which resulted in the bloodshed of 1947. Lava had erupted and Holy[37] was played with human blood. Hundreds of thousands of lives were lost, women were raped and murdered, and many more were rendered homeless. There was heavy loss of property due to uncontrolled looting and arson. The same kind of fanaticism possessed Tara. He told his mother, "The boys in the village are going to Amritsar to bathe in the holy water on the occasion of the *Bhadon Masya*[38]. May I also go with them?"

"Only very old people go there, as they have nothing else to do," replied Karmi. "Your full-moon night or moonless night is in your school, in your studies, and in your home."

---

37 a Hindu festival of colors

38 Moonless night that falls in sixth month after harvesting Summer crops

"Ghuka, Ginder, Binder, all of them are going. There is no examination this year. May I join them, Mother?"

"They are not good people. I don't like you to be in their company. Moreover, the prevailing conditions are not good; riots are rampant in the country. Trains full of dead bodies are coming from and going to Pakistan."

Tara did not agree and was bent upon going with his teenager friends. Karmi, noticing that he was going astray, had become terribly upset.

As they were discussing this, the other boys, with whom he wanted to go, also turned up. Ghuka said, "Let him come with us, aunt. We will have a holy dip on the occasion of Masya and serve the congregation. It will be both an outing and a virtuous deed." Karmi knew that even if she did not permit him, he would not stop, so she agreed reluctantly.

Looking at them carrying swords, Karmi said, "You are going there, boys, for a holy dip. Why are you carrying swords?"

"The Singhs look Marshal with weapons. Sometimes we have to face an enemy," Ghuka replied arrogantly."

"How would you locate an enemy," Karmi asked him.

Ghuka had no reply.' He stood fumbling. When he could not find proper answer he just said, "The Muslims are our enemies."

"You have been given false notions about other religions in schools," retorted Karmi. "No religion is bad but perverted knowledge about the teaching of other religions is bad. It misleads you. This is what has harmed the country. One becomes an enemy of the people by doing so. You do something wrong under misconception and become enemy yourself.

"You become a good person by doing something good. The Sikhs pray for everyone's well-being and 'do good for all' is the mission before them; they are therefore good people. So it is bad to take sword with you."

Binder was a clever boy. He said, "Our sword is for our safety and not for killing. We will use it only in self-defense."

"This does sound logical. All right, carry the swords with you, but do not use them for killing others."

Karmi allowed Tara to go to Amritsar, but his company with Ghuka worried her a lot. She thought, "They are a family of evildoers; they have been killing and looting the innocent people. Ghuka is again carrying the sword. I cannot hope of any good deed from Tara while he is in his company. God save him!" A horrible future appeared before her eyes. She lay down in bed as she felt upset.

Bali saw her mother lying in bed. She could guess that she was worried about Tara. She gave her water to drink and asked her, "What has happened, Mom? You do not lie down like this."

"I aimed at giving Tara a good education and making him the mainstay of my life. Today it is clear from Ghuka and company that Tara has lost his way. He has dashed all my hopes."

Bali consoled her. "You should not lose heart over this matter. We, both the sisters, will fulfill your dreams and become the mainstay of your life. Daughters are no less than sons."

The trains were running between Lahore and Delhi carrying refugees displaced by the communal riots. People boarded and alighted and no one checked them. The refugees were traveling from place to place in search of some refuge, but these teenagers were adding to their woes by causing an undue rush to the trains.

An old man then took the courage to ask Tara and his friends, "Where are you going, young boys?"

"To bathe in the holy water on the occasion of Masya[39]," said Tara, with a sense of pride.

"No Masya or Punya is better than serving your parents, my dear sons. In such a big crowd, you are putting yourself to discomfort and causing discomfort to others too. You are going to bathe on the occasion of Masya—why are you carrying the swords?" The boys had no reply. They started ridiculing the old man and moved away.

The shrieking train, full of refugees coming from Pakistan, reached the platform. It was overcrowded, as other passenger trains had been canceled. People were boarding the special trains meant for refugees. The trains ran from Delhi to Lahore and from Lahore to Delhi, one after the other, packed to capacity. No one alighted from the train, but there were many trying to board it. Wherever they found some room, they rushed in. The boys were changing compartments at every other station. Tara tried to hold the window bar to get on to the roof. But his hand was drenched in the vomit of a pregnant lady. The other boys followed him, and they too got splashed. Instead of showing sympathy for the pregnant lady, they frowned at her. She was fully exhausted. She said, once or twice, "Water...water...oh." The Singhs, instead of getting her water, pushed her into the dirty water and occupied her seat.

The refugees had come from far-off places. They were extremely fatigued. They looked at one another but didn't like to talk. They were without food and water for many days. They were all old. It appeared that the young and able-bodied had been killed in Pakistan.

The trains had been running, and when stopped, did not move for hours. The boys reached Amritsar after two days.

They stayed in the Inn for a day or so. Tara saw that no one was keen to bathe because of Masya or to serve the refugees. When he saw *Modan,* he understood what type of people gathered there in the inn.

A hundred scoundrels made one *Modan*. He had kidnapped a woman, a mother of three children. They had been living in Tara's village. He was a drug peddler. It was not understood why the government was kind to *Modan.* He had made for himself an important place in the inn among the volunteers. At night such persons went to the Muslim blocks and indulged in killing and looting. If they came across a young woman, they pounced upon her and gave her their "refuge." They went to the Golden Temple in the morning to seek forgiveness.

While circumambulating, Binder, a boy with Tara, pinched a girl and disappeared in the crowd. His companions were caught, and thrashed by the devotees. The sins of his companions' made their intention clear.

Tara questioned him: "What had I promised to Mom? I should think it over again before moving forward?"

He said to Ghuka, "You should feel ashamed. What promise had you made to Mom before leaving? I will not be a part of your activities." The blood of a good mother flowed in Tara's veins. It overpowered him.

Ghuka growled. "Go away from here! We can't become black sheep. The Muslas are killing Hindus and Sikhs and sending trains this side full of dead bodies. You too wear bangles...."

Tara heard the curt reply. He was neither willing to go with them nor able to return. He cursed himself. "I should feel ashamed of myself. How would I show my face to mother? I had come here to dip in the holy water of the Golden Temple and serve the distressed and thereby perform the duty of a good Sikh."

Some other boys also revolted along with Tara. They were Tara's neighbors in his village. They had vowed to go to Tarn Taran, Town, on the occasion. Tara went along with them to Tarn Taran. They bathed at the sacred place at night, offered the holy pudding, and boarded the train for Ferozepore Cantt. Before their train reached Ferozepore, the connecting trains for other stations had already left. Instead of sitting at the station, they went to see the bazaar. They had seen such a place for the first time. Tara was awe struck at the dazzling lights of the red light area. The prostitutes were sitting like new brides waiting for their grooms for the first night. Most of them were afflicted with deadly diseases. Their skeletons, outlined under their shirts, were telling the whole story. Their cheeks were hollowed inward and their eyeballs were jutting out. Tara felt nauseated looking at them. He turned his face to the other side. ,

He stopped there and found it difficult to move ahead. One boy pulled his arm, and the others pushed him from behind. But he did not budge and stood his ground.

They argued with him. "You, simpleton, rascal, this is also like bathing in the holy water of Golden temple on the occasion of *Masya.* One should not go back empty-handed. How would you render your account in the court of Dharamraj"?[40]Tara felt disappointed in the company of these boys also. He refused to go ahead. Some boys supported him: "If he does not want to go, don't force him. It is not compulsory. We are ourselves feeling ashamed. We too will not go with you." Tara was thinking, "I couldn't understand these people, they meant something different by taking holy dip on Masya."

Tara recalled what the old man on the train platform had said to them.

On reaching home, he touched his mother's feet. Karmi felt very happy at seeing the change in him.

When Tara related the 'story of Masya', his mother said, "No one heeds the advice given—the fish returns only after licking the stone. It is good that you have licked the stone so soon. You will not falter in the future."

His mother's influence ultimately made a difference.

TWENTY-SEVEN

Next day Tara went to his classmates to get some books. He came to know that Matriculation examination was to be held in September. He told his mother about the good news. She said, "My prayers have been heard by Almighty—what can be better than this, my son!

"I need some money for admission. The D.C. of Ludhiana has made special arrangements for conducting the examination," said Tara.

"I will borrow from the milkman; don't worry about money."

Tara evinced great interest in his studies. Sometimes he walked two and a half miles to go to a friend's village to seek help.

Karmi sent Tara with Sadhu to Ludhiana. Because of the riots, all the trains and buses had been canceled. They got ready and went to the roadside to wait for a car or a truck. After waiting for a vehicle for the first quarter of the night, they returned home. Next morning they again waited for a long time. They saw a car coming from the Pakistan side and heaved a sigh of relief. Sadhu said, "Take hold of your luggage and stand up. It seems we will get a lift. Just see, the car."

He raised his arms and stood in the middle of the road, facing the car nearing them. The car owner was a good person. He stopped the car and asked them to get in.

As soon as they occupied their seats in the car, they started talking about the riots in Lahore. The car owner had himself initiated the talk. "The situation is very bad in Lahore. I have saved my life with great difficulty. I had gone out on a business trip. My family has been trapped, as they were inside the city. I called different quarters, but no one listened to me. There is a great turmoil. The police ordered me to go away and save my life. They are instigating and providing all kinds of help to the antisocial elements to kill our people. Taking you for looters, I was thinking of going ahead, and then it came to my mind that this is our own country. There will be no looters here! As I saw your turbans, I was reassured. I thought that you needed my help and I stopped the car."

When the driver came to know that Tara was going for the examination, he left them at the Center. Sadhu wanted to pay him. The man said, "'No, I cannot accept your money. I have got a chance, by the grace of God to help you."

The riots in Ludhiana had become more violent than those in Lahore. The city police superintendent, Husain Ali, was himself raising the fury. Any road he passed through, he filled with dead bodies. The boys saw the bodies groaning in pain.

The looters were moving freely in the garb of the Singhs', raising slogans, wielding naked swords, killing whosoever crossed their path. They searched the vehicles going to the bus station and the railway station and stripped the passengers. If they found any person appeared to be a Muslim, they killed him on the spot. They took no pity even on babies held to their flanks by their mothers.

The examination center was in Arya School. The principal was himself trapped while escorting the boys to the Center... The rioters stopped his car on the way. The Muslim boys were taken out.

The Center superintendent did not allow Tara to sit in the examination as he was from a different district. He directed him to take DC's permission. His uncle somehow managed to send the boy in and he himself went to the DC's office. Per chance, the examination started late and meanwhile, Sadhu had returned with the permission.

While one hurdle was removed, another sprang up. The rebel superintendent of police reached there to blow up the Center. A policeman was about to throw a hand grenade when Sadhu, standing nearby, struck his arm with his crutch. The grenade fell down in the jeep itself. The jeep was blown up and Sadhu Singh got injured. He was taken to the hospital, and, after receiving first aid, he was discharged.

After the blast, the DC cancelled the examination. The uncle and nephew's return to the village was not safe at that time. If they set out for the journey, they would be killed, and if they stayed on, the risk was no less. By chance, they had company who were going to Jagraon Town. They hired a taxi. The driver was an army man who had come to help his son to take the examination. They reached the station safely. When they were removing their luggage from the taxi, two Sardars, holding naked swords, rushed to them. "We want to search you," they ordered. "Search for what? We are returning from the examination center," Sadhu Singh pleaded.

"The Sardars can go, but the shaved one will be searched," said the 'Sardar' twisting his moustache.

"We are all Sikhs; none of us is a Muslim. I swear by God," said Sadhu

But they searched them and finding the circumcisions of their companion and his son severed their heads. Then they turned to Sadhu. "The traitors like you betray us," their leader said. "Put him to death too."

Tara started crying. The Sardar took pity on him. Their leader said, "Go away, and don't tell a lie in future."

It was midnight when they reached home. They knocked at the outer door. Karmi heaved a sigh of relief as she heard the knock. She rushed to open the door. Seeing them safe and sound she was reassured.

She took Tara in her embrace and forgot to ask about her brother's well-being. When she learned about his narrow escape, she said, "Let the education go to hell. I will not send the boy anywhere anymore."

TWENTY-EIGHT

Karmi had not met with her brother for a long time. Although he was old enough, for her, he was still a child. She said to Sadhu, "If you could stay on for a couple of days more, brother, I could go to Mohna. I have not seen him for a long time. The girls will do the cooking together. Another thing: I may stay for some more days you need not worry."

Next day, Karmi left quite early. The whole day was spent in traveling. Mohna was doing his cooking when she reached. She noted, embracing him, that he was running high temperature. Karmi made him leave the cooking. "You are having a high fever. Go in and take rest. I will do the cooking."

Mohna had a morsel or two and said, "I have no appetite." Karmi also did not feel like eating. Her mood was upset. She took few bites. They continued talking till late at night. Karmi said, "You have sacrificed your life in my service. Had you been married in time while living in your place, you would have had a family. The door would have been open for me to come. One candle lights another one."

"Had I agreed to marry before your marriage, you would have remained a virgin. One of us had to. My remaining unmarried is not considered so bad in our society."

The other day Karmi, accompanied by Mohna, went to see her cousin, Bholi. Her uncle was also at the shop. As they were talking about one thing or the other, Karmi said, "It seems, Bholi, that you are still not married." Bholi kept quiet, as she did not want to discuss her private life in the presence of her father

She led them to her house. On the way she told Karmi, "My Dad got me married a man from Canada, with the intention of going abroad but it proved to be a vacation marriage. A month or so were spent on honeymoon, and while going back he left a wrong address and wrong telephone number. We had no detailed knowledge about him. He was concerned with money only. Dad met his demand for two hundred thousand rupees. He had to mortgage his land to raise the money. He thought that the boy had come from Canada, and our family would also go there. It turned out to be a deception. We tried to contact him on phone but the call never went through. We wrote letters that never reached him as the address too was not correct. I went to the embassy and cried a lot. No purpose was served by crying, as the embassy did not issue the visa. Ultimately I have reconciled to my fate. I am neither a married woman nor a virgin. You know my Dad; he takes a heavy dose of opium and is lost in his own thoughts. He is unconcerned with anything else. My life is ruined. Nobody is there to help me in resettlement. Sister, it is you who created this job for me and made my career."

Karmi said, "You must have heard about the scandal at Jagraon town. A very big gang has been nabbed. They were engaged in arranging marriages with the people coming from abroad. They pose as NRIs and marry the girls and boys in India. They hire the bride/ bridegroom as the case may be. The marriage is performed with great pomp and show. They charge two hundred thousand rupees in advance and the rest two days before the marriage ceremony. The parents of girls are caught in their web. They sell their lands or whatever they own and fulfill their demands. They send off their loving daughters in the palanquin with all the joys. The attraction for Canada or America traps them. They have no fear of being cheated."

Bholi said, "I have met with the same fate. My husband went away after the marriage. There has been no clue left thereafter. No one bothers about girls getting exploited. Both the state and the society consider it normal incidents."

Karmi stood up to return, but her aunt did not let her go without taking tea.

Veeru also came in. Looking at Mohna lying down with fever, he did not remove his shoes and instead went away to call the hakim[41]. He gave Mohna med-

---

41 Primitive Indian treatment

icine for three days. The medication continued, but the fever did not go down. Veeru suspected small-pox. He brought a sorcerer, who treated Mohna. The sorcerer held the neem twigs and chanted as he moved the twigs around his head, and then blew at his face. He continued to do so for a week. This also did not work. Karmi could not go back, leaving her brother behind in that state of health.

Bholi told her, "Dad has given up farming. He now sits at the shop. I am also helped in this way. Earlier the youngsters came to the shop and made a nuisance of them. No one comes when Dad is there, as they fear a beating with the shoe."

"You have become a very wise lady, Bholi."

"All this is due to you, sister. I learned all these things working with you. You have put me in a heavenly position. Dad would have ruined me by keeping me indoors. What wonder has he done last time by marrying me off to a stranger without having a go-between?"

Judging the mood of the family, Karmi broached the subject of land. "Tell Uncle to leave the land. Then we can think of marrying Mohna also. Land is a symbol of status for Jats. No proposal for marriage is received without land. This will help him settle down and have his meals prepared for him by his wife."

Bholi called her father and said, "If we are not going to do farming, let us give back Mohna's land to him."

"Do as you like, my child. Who am I to stop you?"

Veeru was thus able to please his daughter as well as his niece.

Entrusting her own business to Bholi, Karmi had won over the entire family. Bholi herself was educated. Her parents had also changed with the times. What a human being can do for a fellow human being, money cannot do. The land and property are like a heap of earth without one's own people. The land had not given them anything compared to what Karmi had gifted them. This helped Bholi to earn her living. The uncle and the aunt too had come to their senses. Karmi amply proved that love is mightier than sword.

Many days had passed since Karmi had left her house. Mohna's condition worsened day by day. Karmi returned home, taking Mohna with her in his sick condition. They reached the village in the evening facing all the odds. Sadhu also got worried on looking at Mohna. They took him to the hospital. All tests were done, but no disease could be diagnosed. Vomiting and diarrhea increased with every passing day and he died of de-hydration.

Mohna's passing away was an unbearable blow for Karmi. She was in high spirits because of him. His death caused her irreparable loss. Life had become quite burdensome for her without her brother.

The business of dairy farming suffered during Karmi's long absence. The cattle could not be fed properly. Grain and cottonseed could not be mixed with chaff. The cows yielded little milk. The buffalo too dried up. The old ones ran out of milk, and the new ones could not be bought. The cost of maintaining dry cattle made the business a losing game.

There was no money to replace the uneconomical cattle heads. The repayment of bank installments was overdue, and there was no possibility of raising fresh loans from the banks. People were passing through hard days due to crop failure. Borrowing money from the private moneylender was not economical. The lenders had raised the rate of interest very much. When they sat down for the evening meal, Karmi told her family members about the problem of the dairy that had failed and asked for their advice.

Without thinking, Tara said, "Take a loan from the bank and buy cows of Jersey breed. We cannot do without dairy."

Karmi reasoned with him. "The bank installments have yet to be paid. We can't get a new loan. The moneylender charges a very high rate of interest. After paying so much, nothing would be left for us. Why should we struggle to fill others' coffers? Instead of suffering losses, it is better not to do such business. Whatever loss has been suffered can't be helped. Let us not incur any more of it."

The matter came up again for discussion after a few days. How long should we sit like this my son? Instead of sitting idle, let us start the cloth-merchant business again. I can also start a sewing and knitting school. If you join me, we can make it a success. You can help by bringing stocks from the city."

"I do not like this business," said Tara very clearly.

"You know, my son, this business pays quite well. We don't have to invest our own money. If you think this is the work of weavers, I will not do it."

They failed to take any decision.

As they were on the subject, their maternal uncle came in. He said, "What has happened, Karmi, you look so sad?"

"Your nephew has made me very unhappy. Since the three of them are grown up, I thought of putting them to work, but he thinks all this is below his dignity. If he had to do a decent and high quality work, he should have studied properly, and done B.T. a teaching course. The teachers are in great demand. If he had obtained high marks, he could have got admission on merit. He did not pay proper attention to his studies. He was in bad company of spoiled kids of the village. Once or twice he tried to distill wine. It is good that he did not succeed. He did not study properly and wasted time in the company of Ghukka. His father remained away from home, his absence and my leniency, spoiled him."

Sadhu said, "You are not solely to be blamed. The school also is responsible. He was in school for ten years. He learned nothing from there. The teachers did not do the duty of a Guru. It was Khalsa School where instead of teaching them, they made them learn stanzas of the prayer by memorizing them and when they did that, they made them learn *another part of Guru Granth Sahib (Holy book of Sikhs).* The schools are to make them worldly wise. Gurdwaras are meant for prayers.

"They did not teach the students what was useful in life and told them everything that went on spoiling their careers. They instilled into them venom in the name of religion, and they distanced themselves from good society. Had they learned to love others, the circle of their associates would have widened, and they would have learned a lot more.

"The uneducated sons of the carpenters have done better than Tara. They did not depend solely on the school teaching. Along with education, they learned the profession of their forefathers and now they are able to earn their living. They have set up their own workshops and play a pivotal role in our economy. The sons of the farmers and their farmhands have remained blank as they were. They have nothing to do. As an idle brain is Devil's workshop they were misled by the I.S.I Of Pakistan that involved them in subversive activities, against their own mother-land.

"Neither Maharaja Ranjit Singh was educated, nor had Akbar gone to any school. The credit for their success goes to their Gurus. The term *guru* includes parents, teachers, and one's company and environment. Either one can prove to be asset to make pupil great. The education of a child begins even before its birth and it continues till death. The four walls of the building are not called school. A school is the name of all the sources that provide education. Tara did not receive all this in his school.

"The real fault lies in our basic structure, which cannot be changed by Tara. It is not even within your and my power. It is in the hands of the leaders who run the government. The system of education is not in accordance with the needs of the time. Education imparted today is of no use to the child in real life. So the child takes no interest in studies and regards the school a prison. What will he gain from a place that he hates? It is mere wastage of the golden age of learning. The British government, during Macaulay's time, keeping in view their own requirement, prepared the syllabi to produce clerks. Centuries have gone by, everything changed, but the system of education has not changed. Still Clerks are produced, Education needs a radical change. Other countries are reaching the moon and stars, and we are living in the bullock cart age. The vested interest in the government formulated wrong policies, which have created numerous problems for the generations to come; still we claim 'India is shining.' "The Chinese won freedom two years later. They molded the educational system in accordance with the changed needs of science and technology, and they have left the world behind. Our leaders are busy filling their coffers and putting their sons and daughters, into the seats of power. Nobody bothers about the country."

Then Sadhu said to Tara, "It is no use blaming the leaders and the schools. You should act courageously. Though you do not have your father to support you, it doesn't matter. You have got six acres of land. God has given you a brain and two hands. What is there that you cannot do, if you have the will to do it? Do not sit down in despair. Study hard and do something."

Uncle's advice fell flat on him. Next day Tara went to attend some function in Ghukka's house. He had invited the entire village, as he had to present a pouch of a hundred thousand rupees to his party leader.

When he returned, his mother advised affectionately to make him realize his mistake. "It seems what your maternal uncle has said had no effect on you. You have proved to be a stone. A drop of water may or may not fall on a stone; it makes no difference to it. You neglected your work and went to attend the function. Let him do anything he likes but neglecting your work will not help."

Tara kept quiet and did not react in any way. Karmi kept giving vent to her pent-up feelings. "In fact, it is my fault, Tara. You are not in the wrong. I had been giving you whatever you demanded right from your childhood. You thought, 'My father is a subahdar. I can spend as much as I wish.' But the subahdar did not have extra income! We could barely make both ends meet with his honestly earned salary. Meager salaries were paid during the British rule. You should be proud of your father. He was a great veteran. He fought for Freedom; the war came to an end. When comparative peace prevailed in 1946, the veteran prisoners were released and given railway tickets to go home, empty-handed. I am still happy. His life has been saved. How many were they in number, who had survived out of hundreds of thousands? Thus he returned home. As no salary was received, debts piled up and heavy interest multiplied. The hope that your father would come with lots of money was dashed. Can you imagine my position?"

"The loss at the dairy further worsened the economic conditions. We are caught in a very bad situation. You are not a child now, Tara. What should be done is now in your hands. It is for you either to value the sacrifices made by your father and save his boat, or sink it. I cannot do anything by myself alone. I am broken now."

His mother's advice had the desired effect. Tara owned his mistake. He said, "I had not understood your suffering and sacrifices. In addition to that, had I realized what Father had done for the country to get freedom, I would have been a different person."

TWENTY-NINE

As she heard the decision of the court, Karmi saw a ray of hope in hard days. She said to Tara, "The highest court in India has given its verdict in favor of Azad Hind Fauj. It has ordered the central government to pay the soldiers fighting under the command of INA all their dues, count their past service, and grant them due pension. The teacher of our village has told me this today. We will get a lot of money. May God bless him with good sense?"

Tara expressed his views. "Let us go, Mom, and look for him. All of our problems are solved." "No, I will not go, my son. If he has behaved as if he had no concern for us, why should we run after him to search for him? Going after his money is an insult to me. I am his wife, not a keep. If we have not starved till now, we will survive hereafter too. I am confident of myself; as they say; God helps those who help themselves. Money follows the courageous just as air follows the fan. Even the mountains bow before the valiant fighters, the seas give them way. When Napoleon was going to invade Austria— then Germany—he was told, 'Sir, the Alps happen to be on the way; how would you cross them?' He answered, 'I would consider that there are no Alps there.' Napoleon did not let anyone feel that when they crossed it. We are in no way less than Napoleon.

"You are right, Mom. We should have confidence in ourselves. We should not thrive on the laurels of our ancestors."

Tara followed his mother in her footsteps. He made up his mind to complete his education and went to some of his class fellows. He got some new information that those students, who could not sit in the September examination, could join the next class. "I will now seek admission to the eleventh class in the college," he thought.

Karmi was very happy to hear Tara's news. She said, "Resume your studies, my son. Don't worry about the money. I would not let you suffer for want of money."

Tara got admitted to the eleventh class. Karmi heaved a sigh of relief when her son started the journey of his life on the right path.

Satti gave another suggestion. "I will take care of the shop. Let Bali also resume her studies. Both of them can go together and come back together. She too would make her life." Karmi accepted her daughter's suggestion. Udhe got into the eighth class. He was sent to his aunt to Amritsar to study. Karmi went to the shop to help Satti. They expanded their business after six months or so. The Sewing and knitting School was reopened. Income started pouring in.

After joining college Tara realized, "It is not possible to pay a big amount of fee every month. Why should I not do some tutoring on the side?" There were many coaching academies in the city. Tara taught there for two hours and earned thirty rupees, which was enough to pay his college fee. His mother's burden was lightened.

Tara was a student who had come from a village. His mother was not so well off. He spent money with utmost care. He took his meals at home and had his next meal when he returned. He wore simple dress. His only expense was on his books and notebooks. Bali was thrifty from the very beginning.

The city boys and girls dressed very well. They started calling him 'Giyani.' One day their first period was free. Sitting idle, they started making Tara their first-year fool. A boy named Kikkar said, "We have heard, Giyani that you sing very well. Why don't you sing a song for us? "

"No, I don't sing. Who has told you so?"

"We are saying so. You will have to sing. Or serve us with tea along with half a pond of sweets"

The old students generally teased the newcomers. They had caught Tara that day.

Tara was silent. He could neither sing nor afford tea and sweets. His pocket was empty. The other boys also joined them, asking him to sing or give tea. Tara was on the point of crying.

After a few days, there was another free period. There were some boys who sympathized with him. They said, "You look like a cowboy, with your disheveled beard. Keep it in good condition. Improve your looks, which are now rustic, like that of the villagers—that is why the boys tease you. You are in the college, so look like a collegiate."

Tara faced another problem: he could not understand lectures in English. He thought, "I don't follow anything. I come here blank and go back blank. Mother had sold the valuable necklace, a symbol of her marriage, for my sake. I should do something to justify that."

Tara started preparing notes from that day onward. As the professor gave lectures, Tara took notes. He learned the notes by heart at home. When the professor asked questions the next day, Tara was able to answer on the basis of what he had learned, though he could not explain fluently. The professors felt very happy and the boys applauded him. Gradually he was able to understand the lectures. And in due course, he also started giving good replies in English.

Karanjia's weekly paper was brought out from Bombay. It was generally read by the professors. Tara also bought a copy of that paper. He liked Karanjia's exposing the misdeeds of the government. Then he started reading other standard magazines like the Time also read the leftist literature coming from Russia. At the end of the first year, Tara came out with flying colors. The boys who had regarded him as a rustic villager started respecting him. He began to be counted among the bright students by dint of his hard work and sane thinking. He took part in college functions also.

The college foundation day was celebrated and Dr. Mathura Das, the famous eye surgeon and founder of the college, presided over the function.

Tara spoke on education in India. He had read many books and magazines on the subject; his speech was well prepared.

The stage was managed by a senior student. Noted speakers were called. New boys were not allowed to come near the stage. Tara sent his name to speak on the occasion. Considering him a new one, his chit was kept aside. The president noted this and whispered to the stage secretary, "Give a chance to the newcomers also, my friend."

The stage secretary could not refuse him, so he called Tara when people had started leaving their seats and the function was about to conclude. Tara spoke so well that he was clapped and cheered, and those who were about to leave stuck to their seats. Tara came to be regarded as one of the good speakers from then on. The recognition of his performance encouraged him.

The teachers of the old school were also present in the function, including Master Billa. Tara greeted him. He turned his face to the other side.

The headmaster noticed his rude behavior. He said to him, "Gentleman, you should respond to the boy's greetings. He is the same Tara whom you had struck off the roll."

Tara also thought of writing for the magazine. He wrote a story and showed it to the English professor, K. L. Kapoor, who was one of the top story-writers. He laughed after reading Tara's story. "You have develop yourself as writer also; it is good. But you should know that the publishers do not reward writers duly and instead take away the whole cake. So many great writers have starved or committed suicide due to poverty."

"One does not become a writer for money, sir."

Taking note of Tara's enthusiasm, Kapoor advised him to read more literature.

With experience, Tara learned another thing: Merely reading literature would not make him a good writer. One becomes a good writer with experiences. Tara started writing the stories of his life. In course of time, he began to be counted among good writers in the college.

A large number of students failed in the twelfth class. Surprisingly, Tara got through. He was feeling as if he had reached the grand trunk road after passing through very uneven terrain.

THIRTY

As Satti was growing up, Karmi started worrying about her marriage. "Had her own mother been alive, she would have married her when she could. But in my case, the position is quite different. If something untoward happens, people would not spare me and blame, 'Being the stepmother, she is more interested in getting work rather than in marrying her." She looked for a suitable match all the time. Wherever she found some possibility, she went there with her father-in-law.

Everybody wanted the celebration of marriage with great pomp and show. Karmi got worried over such questions. She said to her father-in-law, "People never demanded openly like this in the past. There is no contentment now, no patience. They frankly ask, 'What will you give us in marriage?' They want to bargain as she is a property, not a human being. They look for royal grandeur. Ever since the marriages have started taking place in 'marriage palaces,' it has become more difficult for a poor person to marry off his daughter. There is not enough land left with the agriculturists and no other source of income. For fear of such open demand for dowry, people kill their daughters in the womb. The female specie is in a danger zone. The law is there, but nobody cares about it, as it was passed not for implementation but to keep in the museum of files. The Government ministers in power themselves make it a big show, they spend in millions."

Dad said, "The girl would get old while you keep looking for 'a suitable match'. Living in the world, one has to follow the worldly ways. If the required expenditure has to be incurred, we will sell a piece of land. That would help us to marry off our daughter."

"An acre of land will not do, Dad. The entire land will have to be sold if the girl has to be given a befitting send-off. Old times are gone when marriages could be performed with little expense. We have to cut our coat according to our cloth. Aping the world would be ruinous for us. We should look for a boy of the working-class family earning their living by toiling hard."

Karmi had told her relatives and well-wishers to look for a suitable match.

Her aunt Nhami suggested a boy living *in Bhucho*- 'The boy is matriculate, quite handsome, and a *good* player. He is a hard working boy. The farming is entirely dependent on him. Their landholding is small: only two acres come to his share at the time of division. They do some farming on a contract basis also. They get a good yield. An acre or so has been purchased too'.

'The girl should be well versed and beautiful,' is the boy's demand. Satti has all these qualities'.

Karmi went to have a look at the boy and accepted the proposal. It was also decided that the marriage party would comprise only five members, and that the bride will be taken only in the dress that she was wearing at the time of the marriage ceremony. They were not giving her any jewelry. The boy's side may or may not give any jewelry gift.

The boy and his parents came to their place to see the girl and approved her. When the subject of dowry came up for discussion, the boy said, "Money can be earned by hard toil. It is spent as it is earned. It is virtue of the girl that matters much." Karmi was very happy to know the boy's views. Everything was decided, and the date of marriage was fixed.

As they returned home, the boy's father Baghel Singh said, "You did so much haste in taking a decision. We should have consulted our kith and kin before agreeing to the proposal. After they had agreed with us, only then we should have communicated our decision.

"We have been joining others' marriage parties throughout our life. Now is the time to invite them to join our marriage party. How would we manage with just five members? Can we leave behind your sister and her husband? I have only one daughter. I can't break off with her. We have been giving *gifts* and cash contributions, and now, when the time has come to get back that money, we gave up the old system. This is the first marriage in our family with the grace of God. We have to celebrate it with all the joys. Who knows how much of our life span is left? How can it be possible to perform the marriage in secret, without informing anyone? You have not done the right thing. You can go with your friends and bring in the bride. I will wait for you here."

"Dad, when we went to see the girl, you were with us. At that time you kept quiet. Now you are raising the question of your prestige. Only two days are left now. How can we back out of the decision now?"

The father felt bad and compelled them to fall in line with him. Their messenger reached the girl's residence. He placed before Karmi a letter written in broken Punjabi. Karmi got unnerved on reading the letter.

Karmi called the girl to prepare tea for the messenger. "Bali—I don't know where this girl has disappeared; she was here just now. Be seated, brother, and I will prepare tea for you."

Tara returned from college. The girls had gone to prepare feed for the cattle. They also returned. They discussed the matter inside in an undertone. Then they decided to meet the aunt Nhami, a go-between. They told the messenger, "Please, inform them that such important decisions cannot be taken without meeting personally. We will fix a new date for the marriage after meeting them."

Tara suspected her aunt. "Have you forgotten Aunt's bent of mind, Mom? She is quite an expert in duplicity. Only this would have come out of what she had recommended. What can you expect from the people who settled the matter and now have chosen to back out? We have lost nothing at this moment. And if we go ahead with solemnizing the marriage, the girl will be driven in veritable hell. I would suggest that we should refuse to marry the girl. They will come to beg, just mark my word. Aunt will also come to her senses."

Satti was listening to everything as she sat with her head lowered. "Nothing would be gained by starting a quarrel now. Rather, it would be our loss. Let us solemnize the marriage in a spirit of amity. A break-off at this stage would bring bad name to us. People would do all sorts of talking. Some would say, 'The girl was not of good character'; another one would say, 'They had no money for the marriage.' Let us call the boy's parents at your aunt's place. We should have a face-to-face talk."

Mother and son went to Nhami. Veeru was also called from the shop. They discussed the matter among themselves. After reaching a consensus, they sent a messenger to call the boy's parents.

Aunt showed her anger to the boys' family in the first instance, "Why did you send the messenger without consulting me? Had you lost faith in me so soon? You have put the girl's side into worry. Such things should be settled beforehand. Now you have thought of the kith and kin. Just tell me: can't your prestige be saved without a marriage party?"

Baghel explained his helplessness. "I misunderstood my relatives, thinking that they would agree to what I asked them to do, but no one listened to me. Whosoever was requested to stay at home and not to join the marriage party, got annoyed. Even our daughter and son-in-law do not agree."

"I tell you again that girl's father is not here. Her mother has to arrange the marriage of modest standard. Who will look after the marriage party? If you come to think of the girl, she is endowed with all the best qualities. You can't find such a virtuous and beautiful girl."

Baghel said, "We are helpless, dear sister. That is why we had sent the messenger."

Karmi suggested, "You can draw up a list of important members of the marriage party. What is the use of collecting all and sundry?"

"What you have said, it has great weight." The boy's mother expressed her agreement with the girl's mother. Baghel had to agree. The boy's mother scored out the names of mere acquaintances. Only ten to twelve names remained at the end. The date of marriage was fixed.

THIRTY-ONE

When Tara returned from college, he found that
Karmi was lying in bed and round patches of wheat
dough paste had been stuck on her temples. Tara
asked her, "Why are you lying down in this way,
Mom? "I have a very severe headache, my son."
Tara knew what ailed her. She was worried about
the marriage and it was not headache or anything
else, really. Though the date had been fixed, no
arrangements for money could be made. Tara ran to
the shop and brought two tablets of aspirin and gave
them to her with water. Then she had tea and got up
to resume her work.

Karmi talked about the money for the marriage.
"The maternal family will meet the expenses on
clothes, et cetera. They have conveyed this to us.
Things would have been different had her father
been here. We have to make the rest of the arrangements. We have to bear the expenses on the celebration of marriage, three or four dresses for Satti, and
at least one ornament of very light weight. For all
this, we would need about two thousand rupees. We
will have to arrange this money."

The mere mention of an ornament made Tara upset. He said, "Do not mention about the ornament. You will revive the dead issue. If we start ordering ornaments, the matter will not end with one only. We had made it clear that Sati's in-laws would give jewelry to the bride."

"My son has become wiser after going to college. I had got mad really, I was going to revive it. Go and call your grandparents and both the girls." All the members of the family got together to discuss the arrangements for marriage. The problem of money was placed before Dad. He said straightway, "I can put my thumb impression, you can raise loan against the property or sell it. The land is yours, and the rest of the property too, I am simply the patron. I wish Bhag were here to give her a send-off. Now you people have to do that job."

Karmi said to Satti, "Forget it that your father is not here. Whatever you want to have, come with us and buy it. The jewelry will be given by the boy's side; this has been decided." Satti shrank within herself, feeling shy, but said nothing. Karmi sent Tara to call Sher, the moneylender.

She said to him, "What do we owe you from last time, brother? "You owe me twelve hundred rupees, including interest." Sher had made the calculation up-to-date before leaving his house. He had taken away the buffalo against the interest due. The net amount payable, therefore, was eight hundred. "Please add another two thousand to the amount," said Karmi to him. "We need money. You can go to the court with Dad and have a pro-note deed signed.

"No, I won't do this. What have I gained by putting everything in writing last time? I got nothing but your bitterness .I tried to take away the buffalo as a last resort and incurred your wrath."

"What else do you want? You can tell me," Karmi said most humbly. "I will deduct the past dues from the new amount. If it is acceptable to you, get the money; otherwise, no new lending until you clear the last account." Sher was taking undue advantage of their helplessness. "It would mean that only the past due would be adjusted, and hardly a hundred or two hundred would be paid to us, which would not serve any purpose." Tara, being educated, understood the moneylender's clever game.

"We can mortgage our land. Will that satisfy you?" Dad said.

Sher made it clear, "One thousand rupees for an acre is the prevalent mortgage rate. It should be acceptable to you."

Tara ruled out the proposal for a mortgage. "It would be a costly bargain for us. We have to mortgage three acres. We would lose a lot of income by giving you three acres."

Bapu reminded him of his past obligation towards him. "One should not become so selfish. Sometimes some consideration should be shown to someone.

Please remember that I have been giving you money even without interest."

Sher relented. "All right, uncle, I will do as you say."

Dad tried to clinch the issue. "An acre of land at the rate of three thousand per acre will be mortgaged. Do you agree?"

Dad tried to settle the issue. Sher was clever. He said, "The land would be one situated at the highway." It was fertile and under irrigation. The income from an acre was equal to that of three acres of other land. "In that case you would like to starve us. You are such a calculating person and pose as if you are granting us a big concession." Dad was not willing to part with that land. "Let the matter be decided, Dad. Do as he says. He helps us whenever we are in need." In view of the impending marriage, Money lender's condition was accepted.

Both the sides agreed to mortgage the land as desired by Sher.

"You had got quite hasty, Karmi. You could have allowed me to do some plain speaking. You do not know how these people suck our blood in the profession of moneylending. The families, which are uprooted by them, never return to their normal position. This chap had been taking money without paying interest. And now he did not show any consideration and charged interest at five per cent. Law does not permit more than one per cent."

"An elephant is very costly for a dime sometimes, and at other times it is dam cheap for a lakh of rupees. We need money today for the marriage. Any rate is cheap today." The marriage was solemnized in a very simple way. Satti went to her own house.

THIRTY-TWO

One day, Karmi said to Tara, "When a Jat's land is mortgaged, his prestige suffers. We have to get it released somehow or the other. Labha (Sati's husband) is also of the view that we should resume farming, and he would help us in plowing and sowing with his tractor."

Tara already was extremely busy with his college education, and did two hours' tuition work besides household duties.

He told her plainly, "Where is the time with me for farming? Farming is not child's play. One has to toil the whole day. The farmers turn recluse, fearing the hardship of work. The farmhands run away, leaving their share. I have no time for farming."

"We are not doing it for fun, but because of compulsion. The land under irrigation is mortgaged. It is a major loss to us. It was yielding three crops. We won't be able to make our both ends meet without taking it back."

Tara agreed with his mother. Along with his education, he started doing farming. He engaged a worker. The new relatives helped in plowing and sowing. But the sad state of affairs was that the land under irrigation was very small, which could be used for agriculture—and the rest was without the provision of irrigation. If it rained, a mustard crop could be had; otherwise, even the expenses incurred were not covered.

One acre was used for fodder and the remaining two for cotton. They sowed good seed, having bought it from the university shop. After every hoeing, the field was irrigated and fertilizer put to it, but still the cotton crop was not good. They consulted the university experts. They found that microbes had attacked the crop. Even after spraying insecticide twice, the microbes were not dead. The insecticide was adulterated.

Anyhow, nature helped the farmers: a few days of bright sun killed the microbes.

Thereafter, hoeing and watering was very effective, and good prospects of the crop were noticed. The entire family was very happy.

But to their bad luck, then caterpillars attacked the crop and destroyed the pods. They tried their best, but the caterpillars could not be destroyed. The insecticide undoubtedly was adulterated and least effective.

A complaint was made to the sub-divisional magistrate, but it had no effect. The matter was reported in the newspapers but no action was taken. Nobody cared about the poor farmers. The manufacturing company had already bribed the minister. Tara's complaint got mingled with dust.

There were no buyers for the caterpillar-affected cotton. Later on, wheat was sown in the entire land. The microbes attacked the wheat crop also. They had a poor yield from wheat crop too. The financial year was over. Even the expenses incurred on farming were not covered.

How much income could they have from five or six acres? Farming on a small holding is always more expensive. The elders say, "A mighty one eats the buffalo and a weak fellow is eaten by the buffalo."

A few months elapsed. The examinations were over. Tutoring work was also not available. The problem of paying the fee cropped up. Tara talked to his class fellow, Kikkar. "Our crop failed this time. We cannot get money from the commission agent or village moneylender. The cotton was damaged by caterpillars. The defective chemical had no effect on those insects. Last time, the seed that we got was adulterated. Every year our debt burden is increasing. We had a paddy crop on the land taken on rent, but there was no buyer for that. It remained lying in the open for a long period. The stray cattle destroyed more than one third of it. The rest turned black because of heavy rains. We had disposed it off at half the price to the minister. He collected a lot of stock at half rate and passed it on to the government agency on full price. It is the minister who is obliged to fetch the full price for farmer's product but he himself buys at half the rate. It is the minister who is to protect the farmer from adulteration in seed, fertilizer, and crop medicine. But the businessman is doing all kinds of adulteration under the patronage of ministers and their henchmen. What is the alternative left to the farmer, other than committing suicide? Death is better than living a life of ignominy. We even could not meet the expenses selling at half the price. This time, paying the fee is a problem for me. What should I do? Can you lend me some money to pay the fee?"

Kikkar said, "We too had to sell it at half the price. The farmers fail to return the money of the commission Agent. They are unhappy at their own place. If the producer suffers, it affects the whole market ultimately. My parents have raised their hands, saying, "We can't pay your fee. Give up your studies and work with us." I would suggest you to see the principal. If he grants you full fee concession, I too might get the benefit," said Kikkar.

Tara met the principal, who granted him half-fee concession. The other half he managed to pay somehow.

THIRTY-THREE

The Gandhian slogan- "The land will be distributed among the tillers and the black money among the needy people"- remained hanging in the air. The distribution of surplus land was never taken up seriously; just the eyewash was done to befool the electorate. The government did not distribute surplus land—above seventeen and half acres- among the farmers. It could help in increasing the output. Under the pressure of the landlord lobby, nothing was done. Government framed laws only to hoodwink the people. The surplus land with the big landlords turned barren without utilizing it. There was no yield out of that. It led to a serious food crisis. Prices rose sky-high and famine-like conditions prevailed. The leaders started going abroad with a begging bowl. They had to buy grain at the sellers' rate and on the stringent conditions stipulated by the sellers.

The state governments could not undertake the job of distributing surplus land, but did some minor reforms.

The small farmers too had some land that was too scattered in small pieces around the village. They could not install tube-wells for the supply of water, nor could they work a tractor or harvester. The state governments had to undertake consolidation to make it feasible for mechanized farming.

The work started first in Karmi's village. The entire village got together and formed a consolidation committee. A scheme to bring the farmers' land at one place was formulated. All the land of a farmer was to be consolidated at his largest tract—and if the largest tract had gone to some other farmer, then around the second-largest tract. Had the consolidation been on this principle, it would have been better, and all the small pieces of a farmer's land could have been consolidated at one place. "Might is right" became the principle. The wealthy farmers, who could exert pressure or grease the palm of the revenue officers, managed to get fertile tracts of land, and the poor quality land came to the share of the weaker farmers. The big farmers became bigger, and the small ones got smaller.

After her husband had turned an ascetic, Karmi had got into untold suffering. The consolidation department added to her miseries. Her largest tract had the well and was situated at the highway. It was a fertile land, which helped them to make both ends meet. It was devoured by Tehsildar's mare. Subahdar's nephew, Nikka, grabbed Karmi's rightful place by giving his mare to the Tehsildar. Karmi was given his barren land.

Nikka had been brought up by Subahdar. He did not get education and idled away his time and had taken to bad ways. After Subahdar's joining the army, Nikka became a puppet in the hands of Karmi's opponents like Shinder, the Blue Party leader. She had become the leader of the masses and had eclipsed him. Shinder had got inimical towards Karmi.

Karmi obtained the power of attorney from her father-in-law for fighting against high-handedness in regard to consolidation. Wherever she had to go, she went there with Tara. A few outings opened her eyes. The Tehsildar would not have cared for her prayers. Therefore, she went to the chief minister directly. This irked Nikka. He turned belligerent.

More than land, Karmi got worried about the security of her family. Nikka often came to their house, dead drunk, and knocked the door violently, trying to force his entry. Karmi used to get panicky. One night, there was terrible knocking at the door. The children began to shriek. They went upstairs in fear. The door gave way in a few minutes. It was a bull after the buffalo. Karmi heaved a sigh of relief that the calamity ended with the bull. Nikka was no less. He could be expected to do any harm to karmi and her family. Karmi remained more vigilant. .

Other small farmers had also been wronged in the process of consolidation. Their fertile lands under irrigation were allotted to the influential farmers, and their barren land was given to the poor ones.

They had raised hue and cry in front of the subordinate officers. No one listened to them and gave them only false assurances. Karmi organized the farmers under the common flag of a united front.

The consolidation department was under the control of the Chief Minister. Karmi got their thumb impressions on an application. When the chief minister came on tour, they handed over the application to him. Karmi told him about the corruption in the consolidation work. "Sir, there is no principle or law. The Tehsildar, who had been bribed, allotted good lands to the influential farmers and barren lands to us." Others also gave a vent to their anger.

The chief minister cancelled the consolidation of their village and suspended the Tehsildar. A new Tehsildar was posted in his place. But the new one too was hardly honest. The second exercise was also futile. The farmers were back to protest in square one. They did not get justice. One of the aggrieved farmers committed suicide. The United Front took out the procession taking the dead body with them. The media highlighted the farmers' march. It shook the government.

Ultimately the government had to bow before them. A new Tehsildar took over. He acted wisely. He constituted a consolidation committee to redistribute land. A member from every locality was taken in the committee. Karmi was made the head. The entire distribution was done under the supervision of the committee.

Karmi struggled for eight to ten years, but full justice still eluded the Farmers. The lawbreakers were not punished: The rich landlords occupying fertile land became richer. The law-abiding poor farmers suffered: as their income dwindled. They got poorer. If the tiller of the land suffers, the whole country is a loser.

Karmi got half the land at the well, while the other half was across the railway line. They toiled hard to carry the yield across the railway line. The expenditure involved was more than the income out of that land. Those who had tractors drove them over the lines. Once a landlord's tractor was stuck in the line, and it was time for the train to pass. Everyone was trembling with fear. By chance, another tractor reached there. The tractor was tow-chained and pulled out—a serious accident was averted.

This incident made them safety-conscious: the need for a railway level crossing was felt. But the passage across the line was not feasible for an individual. Only the panchayat was entitled to do.

THIRTY-FOUR

The barren land of Karmi yielded no income; whenever there was some rain in time, there had been sowing of crop; generally, it did not rain in time. Neither the government agency nor any cooperative Agency gave money for improvement in agriculture.

Karmi was hit hard all the more. She said to Tara, "If you take initiative, we can set up a co-operative society in the village. The society gives loans for six months for farming. We would get adequate money for farming, and repay after the harvest. In this way the entire village will benefit, and so would we."

Tara liked the suggestion. He met the villagers. With whomsoever he talked, agreed with his proposal. One after the other, the entire village became members of the cooperative society. A few rich landlords too opted, but the people were not willing to include them. They feared their dominance. They would get benefit from the society at the cost of the poor and the needy. The very purpose of forming the cooperative society would be defeated.

After the cooperative society was formed, money was arranged from the society. They bought the inputs for farming on cash payment. They got genuine fertilizers and genuine insecticides. They could do timely sowing, timely use of fertilizers and spraying on crop. All this helped in doubling the yield.

Karmi continued to save some money from farming income somehow. She took some loan from the society, and had a bore done in the first year and the tube-well installed the next year. Her barren land was brought under irrigation. It started giving two bumper crops in a year. She repaid the loan in installments regularly.

Karmi observed that some farmers were misusing the loan amount. They took loan for farming but spent it on marriages or religious functions. By doing so, they did not have good crops, and failed to repay the loan. The society in turn could not repay to the bank and became a defaulter. No further loan facility could be had. All the members of the society ran into difficulty.

Karmi, being the president, stopped paying cash to the members. The loan was given in the form of seed, fertilizers, and insecticides, and cash for payment to the labor. The misuse of loans stopped.

In the course of time, the wealthy farmers, through a political approach, also became members. Through their influence they got needy inputs from the society on a priority basis, and once again poor farmers were left high and dry. By the time the new stocks arrived, the small farmers were late in sowing, using fertilizers as well as spraying insecticides.

Their labor was the same, expenditure was the same, but their yield was reduced drastically. Then they came under the debts of the commission agents. The cooperative movement was sacrificed at the altar of politics.

Karmi made an alternative arrangement. She enrolled the small farmers as members of the Land Mortgage Bank. Dad also got enrolled. They got an alternative source of finance. After raising loans from the bank, the mortgaged lands were released. Tractors were purchased. Karmi bought a small Russian tractor. It was used for plowing, sowing, and for drawing water from the bore. Their income doubled. They had a paddy crop followed by wheat. Their land was freed, and they lived comfortably.

Karmi did another good deed for the un-employed women. She set up a cooperative society to finance cottage industry for them. She herself became its member. The women started knitting and embroidery work on woolen shawls, scarves and lady suits. Some did the weaving of carpets at home. Supplying raw material and marketing their product was done by *Khadi Bhandar (stores)* aided by government. The women got employment and earned money. They began to be respected in their families.

Karmi had brought in a revolution. She was able to do what the government could not do in thirty years. She became a leader, doing voluntary service to the weaker sections of society.

In view of her social service, the villagers decided to make her the village Sarpanch. They went to her, the old Sarpanch said, 'Ever since you have come here, you have brought a sea change in the village. I do not have good eyesight and good health to serve the people. I would request you to take over the charge as Sarpanch."

Karmi replied, "I am all alone, with onerous responsibilities. How can I shoulder this? Whatever service I can render, I am doing it without being a sarpanch."

The villagers returned disappointed. Tara met them on the way. He was a young blood, after listening to them, he said, "I also think that she should do it. I will do the running about. But her becoming a sarpanch would be of any use only if the entire panchayat works with a sense of service."

The people of the village returned with Tara. He said to his mother, "If the village is bestowing on you an honor, you should accept it and honor them in return."

'If you lend a helping hand, what objection can I have?'

As soon as Karmi gave her consent, the village panchayat was formed unanimously. Nikka opposed her, but the people snubbed him and made him fall in line.

THIRTY-FIVE

First of all, Karmi paid attention to provide a passage over the railway line, as it was in the interest of the entire village. A resolution was passed unanimously. Karmi submitted an application to the concerned railway authority. They rejected it, as accidents had started taking place at the level crossing. Government had stopped building new level crossings. Sanction of level crossing gates entailed huge expenditure. It was difficult for the village to bear this. Three years' salary of the gatekeeper and the cost of the gate were to be deposited in advance.

Karmi put up a new proposal, "You cannot approve a new passage...All right; you can restore the old passage, which is not in use."

They agreed to transfer the old level crossing. Karmi did the running about and offered an old passage for inspection. Only the level crossing was there, with no approach-way on either side. The Tehsildar was shown the site and requested to report accordingly.

Approval was received. The passage was provided over the lines. Hundreds of acres of land lying uncultivated became cultivable. The farmers had the bores done and installed the tube-wells. The land turned into gold. The economic condition of the people improved a lot, for which Karmi got the credit.

The farmers could not do with farming alone. There was the need to have some side business to supplement their income. They had some heads of cattle, but they were not of good breed. The milk they yielded was sufficient only for family use. The farmers were not in a position to buy more cattle. The bank managers were demanding their 'fees' for sanctioning loan with subsidy. If the farmers took out loans, middlemen ate up the subsidy—thus they had to pay full price for the animal. The milk-selling proved to be a costly business.

Karmi met with D.C. but he had to satisfy the minister by giving him his monthly 'quota': he had to present to him an attaché case full of currency notes every month. The subsidy went into the minister's pocket, and farmers were left bemoaning their lot.

Karmi tried to remedy the situation but in vain. She convened the meeting of the United Front. The people of the entire area were very unhappy at the hands of the Deputy Commissioner It was decided to lay siege to his office. A week's notice was served. A copy of the passed resolution was issued to the media. The notice unnerved D.C. and other Officers concerned.

Before the end of the week, subsidies began to be disbursed for buying cows and buffalos. Both the D.C. and the bank manager were transferred. Everybody got money for buying one or two Jersey cows. They had got surplus milk, but then there was the problem of marketing it.

The milkmen kept different jugs for measuring the quantity of milk. They used the bigger jug while buying from the farmer and the smaller one while selling. Karmi conducted a raid and caught them. They were fined. They swore to behave properly in the future.

Nestle company set up Dairy Plant in that area because of availability of milk. The business of milk-production started. Thousands of people got jobs. The people gave credit to Karmi for her sane leadership.

The panchayat settled disputes in the village. People did not have to go to the police station or the courts. If anybody went there, he returned disappointed. People had realized that the police did not settle but created the disputes. If the government machinery was corrupt, one could not expect justice. People followed Karmi's lead of truth and sincerity. They noticed revolutionary changes in their daily life and felt happy.

Karmi had set apart one day a week to go with the people to different offices and helped them in getting their work done. In this way their cases were expedited.

The panchayat arranged to purchase all the implements needed for farming. The farmers did not have to spend money individually. They charged very reasonable fees for hiring implements: just enough to meet the cost of repairing the tools and replacement thereof. A member was entrusted with the duty of giving and taking back the implements. The panchayat charged five rupees extra, which helped in paying the official on duty for his services.

One of the panchayat members objected to the dirty water flowing into the village pond. He complained that dirty water flowed into the taps and those who drank it fell sick. The animals were also dying. Mosquitoes had started breeding on water.

It was a reasonable complaint. The solution lay in building the sewerage system. Karmi moved a resolution demanding from the government the grant for sewerage. It was unanimously passed. A panchayat member was made responsible for the project. He suggested the demarcation of pond because; the people living in the area were encroaching upon the land meant for pond.

Karmi moved the application for demarcation. The qanungo (revenue official) visited the village, and in a week's time, the demarcation was done and the work of raising the boundary wall was started.

At the insistence of the panchayat, the health department started the work for repairing the taps.

Two big wells were dug up for collecting dirty water. It was filtered in one well and then went into the other. They sold that water which became a source of income.

Besides sewerage, the project of fisheries was undertaken. The villagers used their tractors for social service in excavating and building banks on all four sides of tanks. Those who did not have the tractors paid the labor charges. Thanks to the initiative of the village people, the tanks were prepared in a month's time, and filled with canal water.

A contract was given for two thousand rupees.

The villagers started getting fish at a very cheaper rate.

The dirty water began to be used purposefully; the mosquito breeding that caused malaria stopped. Clean water flowed through the taps. But so long as the sewerage was not built, the plan for fish remained incomplete. It could collapse any time during rains as they did not afford the Brick Work.

Grant for the construction of sewerage was not approved. Months passed in waiting. The financial year came to close on March 31st, but the grant was not sanctioned.

Karmi went to see the D.C. many times, but he was not available. One day a lawyer told her, that D.C. usually did not sit in his office. He had set up his office at his residence. He attended to important work there. The people came and returned disappointed. Deputy Commissioner's executive powers were exercised by the minister. The minister made money for doing the job—he issued coupons. The D.C. attended to the work of coupon holders, and others went empty-handed.

How could the panchayat manage to buy coupons? There were no funds to bribe the minister to get the grant sanctioned. Karmi requested the local M.L.A. to get the Grant from Minister.

He assured her but in fact he did nothing. She went with a panchayat member to press upon the MLA. She asked him to get the grant sanctioned from D.C. as the case was in D.C.'s office. It was submitted nearly a year back. The required amount was also deposited.

"Give me the reminder. I will have it approved. You can go back if you want."

The villagers waited, but no letter of sanction reached them. The financial year was over without sanction.

It rained heavily that washed away the embankments. The tanks got filled with dirty water. The fish seed was washed away. All the money and labor of the villagers got wasted.

Karmi thought, "When government itself creates hurdles in development work, what positive result will come out. Still the chief minister boasts, 'I am serving the people, not ruling them.'"

THIRTY-SEVEN

Water had been a big problem for the farmers of North India. There were floods during monsoon and droughts in winter. To solve this problem, the government of India decided to construct Bhakra Dam on the river Sutlej. It was a good move, but its launch was untimely. Punjab government imposed a "betterment levy" on the farmers. They were already suffering the fury of floods and the misery of droughts. How could they pay the betterment levy in February-March when it was not the time of any crop?

No one paid this tax. The government tried to recover it forcefully. Farmers were arrested and their properties attached. The farmers resorted to agitation, and in response, the government hardened its attitude. The agitators were beaten and fired at, at different places; the historic massacre at '*Jalianwala Bagh*[42]' paled into insignificance. The women also joined the men folk and courted arrest. The situation worsened.

As Karmi was the sarpanch, for her it was a new challenge. The Tehsildar came to her village to collect

---

42   The People assembled at 'Jallian Wala Bagh', Amritsar, against The Rowlette Act.General Dyer massacred more than fifteen hundred people there

tax. He called the entire village at the village gate and advised them, "Bhakra Dam is a temple for the farmers. On completion, your fortunes will change. Pay the betterment levy."

Karmi made her submission. "Sir, the year is coming to a close. No one has food grain left in the months of February and March. The stock of the past crop is exhausted, and the next crop is awaited. Even the government does not collect land revenue during this period. How can the farmers pay the betterment levy now?"

"You are the Sarpanch, dear sister. You should help us in collecting the levy. The farmers will pay if you advise them to do that."

"You can get it if anyone is in a position to pay. The meaning of betterment is prosperity. What has led to prosperity? The Bhakra Dam has not yet been constructed; the canals have not been taken out; the lands are lying barren. How have the conditions changed for the better? It is not proper for the government to impose the levy before the improvement in their economy."

The Tehsildar felt irritated over what the lady Sarpanch had said. He obtained orders from the sub-divisional magistrate for attachment and started the process.

The men in the village had already been taken out of their houses and assembled there. Only their families were left behind. They thought it to be the most opportune time to carry out attachments. The police inspector was handed the attachment warrants and sent to their houses.

.He went to the house of the member M. Kaur and showed her Attachment Warrant.

"What has this poor lady got to pay you? I have a child who is handicapped. Go to some affluent house where you can get something."

The S.I. was not one to care for prayers or to show leniency. He ordered his head constable, "Look at that bag of wheat. Have it carried to the truck. The buffalos and cows are also tethered close by. Untie a buffalo. The amount of levy will be recovered."

"Stop there. Don't touch the bag of wheat…. How dare you enter the house of a woman who is all alone in the house?" M. Kaur roared like a lioness. All of them withdrew in fear. No one touched the bag or the cattle.

The head constable got unnerved. He himself withdrew but pushed one or two addicts forward, who had been hired by the police. He said to them, "Why are you afraid of a woman? Go ahead and lift the bag."

As they tried to lift the bag, M. Kaur thundered, "*Do you see this sickle?* If anyone touches the bag, I will thrust it in his belly."

The hired addicts did not stop and lifted the bag as ordered. M. Kaur pierced the bag with the sickle. The wheat started pouring out. She warned the S.I.,

213

"I will have your belt removed if even an ounce of grain is reduced."

The SI got terribly afraid. He changed his stance. Withdrawing a step or two, he said to the others, "Are you blind, you bastards? Do not you see the grain pouring down? Why are you trying to put the dead serpent round your neck? Hold the bag properly!"

The addicts too got scared; one of them stepped forward and removed the buffalo's chain off the peg. The ladies in M. Kaur's neighborhood had already gathered at the top of the roof. They started shooting dung cakes at the police officer. The SI and his hired men ran away leaving behind as the women were chasing them.

M. Kaur snatched the staff of the fleeing SI and struck him twice. The police were driven out in disgrace.

When the police went to another house, the same thing happened there. The women were ready to do or die. They showered dung cakes from roof tops.

The farmers had risen against the government. The wealthy farmers, who could pay the levy, also refused to pay.

Their "bread in hand" was being snatched before the arrival of the new crop. The country was free, but the people were not being treated as the citizens of a free country.

Considering that the situation was getting out of control. Tehsildar informed the Sub Divisional Magistrate. He reached there and ordered, "Pay the tax within an hour—otherwise…"

Two hours passed, and then half the day, but no one paid the betterment levy. The S.D.M. issued the orders for arrest of all the members of panchayat.

They were arrested by the police but no tax could be recovered in spite of that. The SDM gave call to the D.C. "We have tried to convince the farmers, beaten them, arrested them, but all our efforts have failed. The police went to their homes to carry out the attachment orders, but the women reacted violently… The situation is quite critical…"

"If the attachment orders have little effect, try again to persuade them tactfully." said D.C.

The S.D.M. tried to explain. "After the completion of the Bhakra Dam the fields will turn lush green. Your condition is not so bad that you are unable to pay the levy. All of you are quite affluent. Punjab is the state of the prosperous people." They listened to the SDM but said nothing. Karmi saw that none of the men had the courage to say anything. She said, "Sir, your police have seen our prosperity after searching our houses. Their bins are empty, and the rats are starving. Electricity does not light the bulbs; how can the tube-wells work and irrigate the land. Let it be in working condition and it starts ushering in prosperity, we will pay the betterment levy also."

People started whispering to one another after Karmi had spoken. "The sarpanch has spoken the truth."

All the ammunition with the S.D.M. had been fired, but the Jats did not budge.

People got fed up sitting with empty stomachs since morning. Hungry cattle tethered to the pegs also bellowed.

The S.D.M. could neither leave the farmers nor arrest them. He requested the D.C. to send more reinforcement.

The D.C. reached there with additional force. The village was besieged as if it were some enemy territory. No one could go out or enter the village; it recalled the days of 1947. Earlier the goondas indulged in loot and harassment, and now the police force of free India was doing the same thing."

Karmi had been arrested. The police officer reached her house with his men. The house lay deserted. Whatever they could lay their hands on was taken away and dumped into the truck. They took away the cattle also. The same treatment was given to other farmers too. They had left nothing for the farmers' to cook for the dinner even. The village gave the deserted look as after enemy's raid.

The next orders of the D.C. were to "let the trucks, carrying the arrested farmers and their attached property move."

Bali, the daughter of the lady Sarpanch addressed the young girls, "Our parents have been arrested, our belongings taken away—how long we can sit as silent spectators? Let us seize the trucks."

She led them, and other women followed her. They lay down before the trucks. The women holding their children also joined them. The convoy of trucks came to a halt.

The D.C. got upset and rebuked the S.S.P. The S.S.P., in his turn, passed on his wrath to the D.S.P., "you are unable to control the situation."

The D.S.P. ordered the drivers, "Move ahead! Let anyone be run over."

The driver of the first truck started the engine and kept blowing the horn, but did not move. How could he? None else but his own sisters and daughters were lying ahead of his truck. S.S.P. rushed to the driver and said, "You son of a pig, why do not you move your truck ahead? You are simply blowing the horn."

The driver took out the key of the truck and threw it before the Police Officer. The other drivers followed suit.

The Deputy Commissioner ordered "Baton charge!" The police thrashed the drivers and then the womenfolk. They beat them mercilessly. Some suffered head injuries, others had their limbs broken; no one was spared. Those present on the scene were extremely pained to see the atrocities being committed on the women and children.

THIRTY-EIGHT

Karmi watched the ill-treatment meted out to the women daily. The news of kidnapping and rape were heard every day. Thrashings and inhumane beatings had become routine for the women.

Karmi noticed that a schoolteacher in her neighborhood beat his wife daily. She was also a teacher. She placed her salary on her husband's palm every month but did not have his permission to spend a dime out of that. The husband was such a miser as he even gave her daily fare for going and coming back from school. She carried two *chapattis* with sauce or pickle for lunch. She swallowed it with a cup of tea at midday. She attended to all the household chores. Nobody knew even then—why that foolish man beat her.

The wife was such a noble lady: though severely beaten, she never mentioned it to anyone for fear of her husband. He took undue advantage of her silence, and tortured her all the more, adopting new methods.

She kept enduring the cruel beatings like an Indian woman and did not leave him. An Indian woman crosses the threshold of her house twice in life—once, when she enters the house as a bride, and secondly when she dies and her dead-body is taken out for burial.

One evening, her husband returned home terribly annoyed. He started beating her on the excuse that she had not prepared the meals in time.

He put both her hands under the legs of the cot and sat on it. She kept on crying with pain; he kicked her all the more as she groaned. The children kept mum—they always feared their father.

She lived the life of a slave. One day she went to Karmi's house for a bowl of soup. Karmi noticed her injured fingers and asked her, "What has happened to you, *Sharni?* Your eyes are also swollen."

She started crying but said nothing. Karmi realized her agony. The entire neighborhood was aware of her painful life but "Why should we bother for other people?" was their attitude, and the days passed by.

Karmi consoled her and sat close to her and said sympathetically, "I am your elder sister. A sister is to share a sister's grief. If you tell me about your plight, I will try to find a solution."

Realizing that Karmi was quite sympathetic, *Sharni* related her tale of woes. She agreed even to lodge a report with the police. Her husband was called to the police station, but they did nothing. He was let off after he greased their palm. Not to speak of the end of her agony, his fury grew worse. The night set in. He started torturing her more cruelly.

"I will teach you such a lesson as you will never think of going to the police again." He took a three-foot-long electric cable and lashed her, leaving deep marks. Her shrieks were heard even quite at a distance. Karmi heard her crying. She called in the women in the neighborhood within no time. They had already been informed about it. They scaled the wall and went in. On seeing them, the husband lost his nerve. He tried to run away in fear. But they would not let him go. They caught him by his hair before he could jump across the wall. They lashed him with the same cable. The people in the neighborhood assembled, tarred his face with the soot of a hot plate, and took him to the police station in a procession. On seeing the crowd, the SI was upset. He registered the case and put him behind bars.

One night had hardly passed when he started imploring his wife in all humility, "I would not do so in future, madam. For God's sake, forgive me."

"Face the consequences of your misdeeds; I can't help you." Sharni retorted.

She left her husband's home, and taking the children with her, went to Karmi's house. Karmi rented a house for her. She felt happy living independently.

The case for a divorce continued, and Sharni felt frustrated. The case did not conclude for years. Had she not been in a job, she would have had to surrender again on the terms of her husband.

After a long fight she got divorce.

Karmi realized how important it was for a woman to be educated and economically independent.

She had already formed a cooperative society to make them stand on their feet. They could take a loan and start some business. But if they wanted to take up some course, a minimum qualification of tenth Grade was required. Their parents withdraw them from school after passing the fifth class as they were not in favor of co-education. Karmi raised the issue of starting a separate high school for girls in the panchayat. "Our future lies in women's education. With their getting educated, most of the problems are solved."

No one responded positively. They opposed her. "They are already studying in the boys' school. If you want to do something, do it for the boys. The whole village has gotten addicted to poppy husk. Build a stadium for them so that they can take interest in games."

One of the members cited an example, "Daroli, was known for drug addiction. The villagers had a stadium built with their own initiative. The drug addicts started playing. Every year tournaments are held there. People come from far off places to take part in games. The boys gave up taking poppy husk. They became fond of games. They kept machines for taking exercise. People in large numbers assemble for exercise in the evening. The village of addicts has been transformed into the village of players."

Most of the members were on one side, and Karmi was on the other.

Only one member, Kartar Singh, supported her resolution. "Girls' education is more important than the stadium. If they get educated, some would migrate on a marriage basis, and the entire family would benefit thereby. I would say that let us build colleges for women so that they might have an independent life of their own."

Kartar Singh's words had the desired effect. Hari Singh withdrew his counter-resolution.

THIRTY-NINE

Karmi opened the girl's school in the community building without any ceremony. Girls were admitted up to the eighth class. The girl students from the local school got their names transferred to Karmi's school. But no one came from outside. The retired teachers living nearby were recruited on nominal pay, and Karmi became their patron.

The staff worked hard and showed a hundred percent result. The following year, girls from distant schools also joined.

They needed a bigger building. A spacious house belonging to a non-resident Indian was lying vacant. He readily agreed to give it for the school. Some classes were accommodated there. Science teachers were also recruited for teaching physics, chemistry, and biology. The laboratory was fully equipped.

Keeping in view the need of the time, a library was set up. The girls spent their spare time in the library. It generated the interest in reading. There was one library period in a week for every class. Marks were given for reading extra books. Under Karmi's guidance the results were again excellent that year.

Establishing contact with the retired teachers helped in establishing relationships with the villagers, and this proved to be a boon for the success of the school. Due to their efforts, the entire village was cooperative. The people donated enthusiastically. The school made good progress all around.

The staff was well paid. They taught wholeheartedly. Because of good results, the number of students increased every year.

A school committee, consisting of enlightened persons of the area, was formed. The entire work was done under the guidance of the committee.

The annual function of the school was held. The people emphasized the need of opening a degree college.

With the increase in the number of students, the school's income also increased. A plot of land for the college building was bought near the highway. It became convenient for the students coming from outside.

Observing the resounding success of the school, the N.R.I.s started building rooms for the school in memory of their elders. Laboratories were set up, and the science department bifurcated. A hostel was also built. After everything was completed, approval for a degree college was also accorded.

When all the comforts and faculties were made available, even the NRIs admitted their wards to the college.

Karmi herself performed the role of a supervisor. She went to the college for one hour daily in the morning and looked to the minute details. If any shortcoming came to her notice, it was rectified immediately.

Special attention was paid to teaching technology. Because of its professional teaching, the college became famous far and wide.

Strict watch was kept on the performance of the teachers, and those not found up to the mark were fired and the able ones promoted. The spirit of doing better was inculcated among the staff.

A lady doctor visited the college every Saturday and treated the students for any problem. She also took a period in the senior class where she imparted knowledge about sex and the sex-related diseases.

Karmi herself took a period every week on character building.

Karmi's example was emulated by other people far and wide. They opened schools and colleges for girls in the villages and towns. The girls, by dint of their hard work, left the boys far behind in studies. They secured high marks in the examinations and got admission to medical, paramedical, and engineering colleges in large numbers. Because of their good qualifications, the girls were married to the boys settled abroad.

In view of the success of Karmi's college demand came up for. "Thanks to your sane advice and quick action the girls have benefited a lot."

College committee requested Karmi, "Now, sister, build the stadium in the college grounds. The girls can play, during college working hours and the boys can play in the evening. They will get health oriented."

"Let us all work together for the new project." Karmi agreed to their proposal.

When they started collection, only thirty five thousand rupees could be collected. They were disheartened. How could they build a stadium with such a meager amount?

Karmi consoled them. "Don't lose heart. When you want to do something great, it is the strong will that matters—it is more important than money."

Karmi went to meet the D.C. for financial help. He stipulated a condition that could not be fulfilled: "Transfer the ownership of land to the government." The villagers refused to do so.

Karmi suggested, "Do not pin your hopes on the government alone. Approach some NRIs of your villages. They will give you money." *Sardar Shavinder Singh* had come from America. Karmi, accompanied by the panchayat, went to his house. He was very happy at the visit of Karmi and the village panchayat. He agreed to help them in that project. The villagers appointed him the president of the stadium committee, and Karmi was made the secretary. He spent money from his own pocket as well as collecting from the relatives and friends settled abroad.

Next day the villagers started the filling work. Those people who had tractors used them, while others did the labor work. The whole village performed the job of filling in the stadium. It took three days to complete the job. It was all voluntary; if you calculate its value in terms of money (land inclusive); it runs into several hundred thousand.

The stadium was completed. This was the first village in the Punjab, where People built the stadium without any help from the government. Shavinder Singh and his family played the leading role.

FORTY

Karmi heard the sound of knocking twice at the outer door. There was no one close by to open, she herself went to attend. She saw a tall man, standing outside, who looked like a homeless fellow. His face seemed familiar but she could not recognize him. He kept gazing at Karmi without blinking.

Out of sympathy Karmi brought him in and made him sit. She was still unable to recognize him. Karmi looked at him very closely but failed to recollect. Watching Karmi's staring at him he laughed and his laughter made Karmi recognize and ask him, "Are you Paul?"

He nodded, "yes!" and tried to embrace Karmi like a lost lover. She stepped back abruptly and said, "Oh, no. Keep in mind I am a mother of three children...."

"It does not matter much; the mother of three children too has a heart."

"She has a heart but her heart is another man's trust."

"Where is the 'other man? ... I have heard that he has deserted you".

"If he deserted me, it does not matter, for a devoted wife. I consider him always present. It is the man who becomes unfaithful to his wife, a wife does not. She goes to the pyre with him and dies with the dead."

"No! Look at my wife! She gave birth to two daughters and then deserted me."

"Leave her aside. She may be one in millions. But what did you do with me? I returned the marriage party of a Feudal Lord for the sake of love; but you, instead of giving warm welcome, called me his 'left-over."

"Kammo, that was my mistake but it was not intentional… It had turned me mad. I am broken now. Please take pity on me…"

Karmi thought, "He is still off his head. He needs my sympathy." They sat down on the cane chairs and continued talking.

Karmi changed the subject and tried to amuse him, "Paul, you look like Ranjha, as if you have been grazing the buffaloes of some Heer.[43]"

"It would have been better, Kammo, if I had been grazing the buffaloes of my Heer. If there is anything left with me, it is the memory of your love."

Paul tried to explain his last time blunder; "Kammo, at that time I failed to fathom the depth of your love..."

---

43   Legendary love story of Heer and Ranjha: Ranjha served in Heer's house as cow-boy simply for the sake of her love.

Karmi started explaining her loyalty, "Paul! I had gone to you (my love) breaking the chains of Caste. You should have stepped forward to hold my hand. We should have shown the new way of life to the people. Charity begins at home. If we start to tread on new paths by setting our own example, we can bring in reform, show right path to 'the blind'. Our people do not set an example themselves. They go on giving sermons to others. No one cares for their formal sermons.

"You did not do the right thing, Paul. You broke my dreams. How nice would it have been if I could become the daughter-in-law of a potter! I would have felt proud that I had followed the right path of equality and fraternity shown by my great Guru[44]. I knocked at your door begging for your love. Alas! Had you understood! "

Listening to when Karmi explained her sincere approach toward him and his negative response, Paul repented. He started shedding tears.

Meanwhile Tara came in. Karmi introduced him to Paul. Tara met him very warmly and asked him, "Would you like to have a cup of tea or milk, uncle?"

"I will like very strong tea, my son." Paul felt as if he had met someone of his own.

Tara went to the kitchen. They continued talking. Paul said, "Karmi, I have undergone very severe

---

44   Refers to Guru Gobind Singh who baptized Sikhs and made them Singhs, who laid the foundation of classless and Secular Society

punishment for that blunder. I continue to suffer. If you do not forgive me, I will go mad."

Karmi said nothing. She was lost in thoughts. Paul looked at her with hope for some time, but she firmly stuck to her decision. Then he lowered his head.

After sometime he started the story of his marriage. "I made another mistake while getting married. I did not look at the girl but at her father's money—; his status as an officer. He was a 'Tehsildar' who had amassed ample wealth. But with experience I came to know that one does not become great by acquiring ill-gotten wealth, but becomes dwarf. 'Humanity' dies within him. I was caught in a web after getting married. The ill-gotten money turned me into an animal. I lost my moorings and turned into a slave of the woman, wine, and wealth. I got so much money that I thought it useless to practice medicine. I was drowned in pleasure-seeking.

"There is no comparison between you, and *Lachhi*. You are a goddess indeed. You have the blood of a great Social worker in your veins. He lived and died for the people. You know how to make sacrifices for others. Lachhi was the product of bad blood. The meanness of the corrupt father had made her mean. I failed to understand her.

"We thought of nothing, except the glare of money. What to talk of respecting my family…, she did not regard me as her husband. She made me a puppet to dance to her tunes, which I did.

"I have come out of jail recently after completing the life term. Lachhi had committed suicide by jumping into a canal after quarrelling with me. Her father filed a case of murder against me. His money turned the fabricated story into truth. Thank God, I was not hanged. There were two daughters, who were taken away by her parents.

"My parents died neglected and for want of proper care in their old age. The wretched woman disintegrated my family. I do not know where to go now!"

Karmi thought over for some time and said, "Go back to Ganganagar. Open a clinic there and serve the poor who need you."

"Who is my own there at Ganganagar now? I had four brothers and Lachhi did not develop relationship with any relative of mine. She spoiled her life and mine too.

"I have decided to live at Abohar, close to you, as a dejected lover, and have some cool breeze coming from your side."

FORTY-ONE

Assembly elections drew near. Posters of national leaders were pasted here and there. The rickshaw pullers, the cart pushers, and the cab owners started shouting through loud speakers, deafening the people. Public meetings were held and processions taken out in the towns.

The leaders repeatedly came to Karmi's door.

Tara too was afflicted by the election fever. On return from college he asked his mother, "To whom would you support, Mom?"

"I cannot say in advance as their manifestos are quite confusing and false. Party manifestos are always a show-piece, full of false promises.' There is no party in the real sense, they are business groups, and politics is their profession to make money. When one party earns bad name, they leave it and join another.

"'Last time, the blue party won in Punjab, They started behaving like kings. Nepotism became the cardinal point; all relatives were given berth in the cabinet. Their misdeeds resulted in the failure of agriculture; the industry went out of state and the people lost their jobs, nearly half the population is below the poverty line, pollution has made life hell. Food became unfit for eating, water unfit for drinking, and air unfit to breath—, everything seems to be cancer-causing. Any reporter, giving such news is kidnapped, if she is a female raped and ultimately eliminated to cover the crime.

"'This is not the case with Punjab only, go to Uttar Pardesh, Bihar or any other part of the country, the same situation prevails. The country is gripped by black money, which has taken deep roots. Out of one rupee, eighty-five paisa go to black money, only fifteen paisa are spent on public."

"We have nothing to do with these corrupt politicians, let us sit at home, Mom," said Tara.

Karmi reasoned with him, "This is bad; it is your regressive thinking. If everyone sits as unconcerned then who will save the country?"

They heard an announcement from the Gurdwara in the evening about the meeting of Blue Party. When they reached there, there was a huge crowd. Very hot speeches were delivered. One of the speakers talked of corruption under the white party rule, "To get rid of corruption make the Blue party victorious." Another speaker made a mention of the past sacrifices of gurus and said nothing about his own work done in the past.

Tara spoke as a leader of the United Front, "If you talk of voting for Shinder, he does not deserve it. He has been making money by fair or foul means all through the five years. If I am in the wrong, he should tell us how many starving people were fed by providing jobs? How many new schools were opened? How many patients were cured by building hospitals?

"About half the population in India is below poverty line; they remain under fed and do not afford enough food for two meals a day; without homes they go without shelter from scorching heat and freezing cold.

"There is an acute Power shortage: Agriculture gets power for two hours a day, and four hours for industry. Diesel is not available nor is enough gas at market rate but you can get it from black market. Agriculture and industry are bound to fail in such conditions. It will lead to more unemployment and semi-starvation.

Education is for sale, it became a dream for the poor. Children go to school but gain nothing, in papers the entire country is educated, but most of the people cannot write their names properly. Health services are almost non-existent. People are dying like flies and mosquitoes, either of malaria or dengue fever. Diseases like Aids and Cancer have come to stay permanently.

"Shinder is MLA and expected to serve the people of his constituency, he should visit them occasionally. The village had initiated the construction of the sewerage, and he did not help us in getting the grant. The Panchayat went to Chandigarh to meet him with this purpose. He took their application and did nothing to have the grant released. The sewerage work has been hanging fire. The dirty water of the village flowed into the fish pond and washed away fish seed. He doesn't deserve our votes."

'The villagers raised slogans against Blue party. When Shinder came to know of the fiasco, he was flabbergasted. He had no time during day, but in the evening he went to Tara's house, taking Ghuka with him.

Ghuka took him aside and reasoned with him, "We have had to approach the M.L.A. hundreds of times for help. Even when you do not want to support Shinder, say 'yes' for the sake of pleasing him."

Tara made his position clear in the presence of MLA. "No, Ghuka, this will not happen. Vote is a trust, and it is cast for the one in favor of whom our conscience permits. My conscious does not permit me to vote in his favor. Had he helped us in the village's sewerage project, of the village things would have been different." Tara made his position clear in Shinder's presence.

The M.L.A. felt offended at Tara's reply, "It means you will help the white party win the election and add to corruption."

"You can tell me: what have you done to root out corruption? I see no difference between both the parties. They are the two sides of the same coin."

"To whom else would you support, if you do not support the two parties?" The M.L.A asked him to make his position clear.

"We shall support the United Front."

"Your united Front is not going to win. You will only waste your votes," said Ghuka.

"If the votes go waste this time, they may be useful for the next time. If people follow us, Democracy would take roots," Tara said. Then he asked, "Any other service that I can do for you"

"Please, serve us Whisky; hurry up, lest your Mom comes in. She will condemn all of us."

Tara too wanted them to go away, "You take him to your home. I will come there. Ever since the M.L.A.'s name has been linked with the sex scandal, mom is very much angry with him. After seeing you here, she would turn me out with you. A meeting of the Cooperative Society is going on in the community hall. I don't know how long it continues. It would be better for you to leave before she comes back."

They were still arguing when Karmi came in. She got furious at the sight of Ghuka, but as the M.L.A. was present, she kept calm. "How fortunate we are, you visited us! Most welcome. Be seated please. Why have you stood up? Have you served tea to them, Tara?"

"We have already had," Shinder said.

"He is the people's representative and it is our duty to show him due respect. We would not let you go without taking tea."

The M.L.A. appealed to Karmi for her help in elections.

"Serve the people, my son, and we will help you. We need honest public servants for our Democracy."

He explained his position, "I have been doing public service, but you do not recognize it,"

"Helping a member of the mafia gang to be released from the police station is not public service. It is service to a handful of criminals. This service leads to increase in crime. How can I approve of this?"

"All right, you can think over once again." Saying this, he left.

Chain Brar got the White party ticket. He too was a big landlord, and the son-in-law of Ex-Chief-Minister.

He too went to Karmi's village seeking votes. He collected people on the platform opposite Gurdwara. He explained Indira Gandhi's Twenty Point Program which was for the uplift of the people. Then he started praising Ma'am Indira Gandhi. The same old things that the people had been hearing and had gotten fed up with.

Sarpanch Karmi spoke on behalf of the village, "These 'patriots' had transferred their surplus land to the names of their horses, dogs, and cats and did not let the law of Seventeen and half acres promulgated. The law was strangulated at birth. And the 'punishment' for breaking the law was, the award of

Chief-minister ship for one and a ministerial seat for another. 'M.L.As.' became their humble servants.

The joint families suffered badly. Those who did joint farming—, who had kept their lands in the name of their elders— already owned less than seventeen and a half acres. Their holding was declared surplus and distributed among the landless. They suffered the onslaught of the law. The smaller ones suffered, and the big landlords escaped through loop holes. They had become big by touting for the foreign rule. After independence, they captured state power and became bigger. The government being of these big landlords did not let the law (seventeen and half acres) take effect, the tillers of land continued to suffer. It led to food shortage.

"The black market is at its peak. After five years; the votes are sold and bought, making M.L.As. And M.Ps elected. Then M.L.A.s and M.Ps. are for sale, the state and central governments are formed.

"The sad part is that no party made efforts to save the democracy and improve the condition of the people. If any party did, it had no voice.

"In such undemocratic conditions, the starving masses lose faith in Democracy-: if they protest they are dubbed as *'Bhindran walas'or 'Bajrang-Dalia*, or *'Jehadis*[45]*as it suits them.*

"If the man of the street condemns them, he is kept under surveillance. If he asks for security he is

---

45   Jehadies are the Muslim Terrorists; Bhindran wala-Sikh terrorists; Bajrang Dalia-Hindu Terrorists.

denied; it is withdrawn if given already. The license for a weapon given earlier is canceled. He is eventually killed by a convict released on 'good conduct' from the jail; the people find it difficult to live a normal life. There is the fear of terrorists on one side, and that of the police on the other. There is fear psychosis everywhere and all the time.

"The government too does not believe in democracy. The ballot boxes are broken at the gun point and bogus votes are counted, making the loser elected. The loser becomes minister through muscle power...

"There is no justice from judiciary either. Election appeals are not decided till next elections. The 'defeated' candidate remains defeated all the five years. He is declared winner a few days/ or a few months before next election, and the democracy is 'saved'; it is a big blow to Democracy. People have lost faith in the elections and ultimately in the Government.

"The so-called People's representatives (MLA/MP) indulge in looting in one way or the other. They have stacked bundles of notes of black money to keep hold on seat; there is no punishment as they are above law."

Karmi's speech concluded. People started commenting, "She is saying the right thing. If she wins the election, she can bring change. We should request her to fight elections this time."

At the end, White party candidate stood up to give his closing speech. There was no one to listen to him. The villagers left him and gathered around Karmi.

FORTY-TWO

Karmi hoped that after completing his education Tara would get a good job and the hard days would be over... But luck did not favor her. He did his M.Sc. but remained unemployed. Some posts of Managers in the Punjab Sind Bank fell vacant, and Tara applied for that. There was no reply. After some time he came to know that he would not be called for an interview unless he had some approach.

One day a person, who could recommend him for the job, met with him. He went to his mother and said, "Yesterday I met Pritam in the bazaar. He told me, – getting service is not a problem; I will request the M.P and get you a job. We shall go to Delhi to see him. It is only the question of expenses for going and coming. "

"Do you think Pritam is a reliable man"?'

"He is your father's old friend. He used to come here and stay on for many days. No doubt, he is quite thick with the M.P. He got occupation of the disputed land of M.P. A man got killed by his henchmen. Both his sons and a brother were arrested, on the charge of murder. The M.P. assured them, 'I will see that no harm is done to the boys,' But he could do nothing. They were hanged."

"It means that he made a lot of sacrifice for M.P. who will surely listen to him. We should try our luck."

"You may try, but I don't think he is capable of doing it. If the work is not done, the expense of two would pinch and add to our problems. I do not have a penny with me at this moment. I will have to borrow from someone."

"Such an opportunity doesn't come at all times. We should not lose it."

Karmi could not refuse her son, "We have stored wheat for the whole year. You can sell it."

"That would be enough just to meet the expenses of fare for both ways. We may have to stay there for a week or so. We shall need money for that too"

"We have kept the seed for next crop; you can sell that too and try your luck. Who knows luck may favor you?"

The entire family felt encouraged at Pritam's assurance. Karmi got ready to even sell her house to help her son.

Tara loaded the wheat, including seed on a Tonga, and sold it in the market. He put the sale proceeds into his pocket and got prepared for going to Delhi. What would the other members of the family do now, losing their ration too? It was left for mother to think over.

Karmi went to the Gurudwara to pray for her son, "O my God help my son to get a job. I shall..."'

Pritam had come to them a day earlier. They looked after him to the best of their ability to please him. The entire family remained at his beck and call. Tara hovered around him most of the time.

In an undertone Pritam expressed his demand: "I am not feeling well; if I could get a little bit of opium I shall be in high spirits.'

Karmi was dumbfounded on hearing about opium. She did not want to listen to the names of drugs, and then they had to offer drugs to the honored guest, as he was going to make a recommendation for her son. Tara too held the same view as his mother. They were on horns of a dilemma.

"Tara, I told you before. Do not compel us to take beef (religiously forbidden for Sikhs)."

Tara was irritated too. After whispering something in the guest's ear, he lay down in bed. Early in the morning, without anybody knowing he brought some opium.

Next day Pritam and Tara reached Delhi. Seeing very wide roads and beautiful surroundings, Tara felt as if he had entered a new world. Finding him surprised so much, Pritam said, "'These people have done some good deeds in their past lives; they are reaping the reward in this life, my boy!'"

The sentry opened the gate after making some enquiries. They went in. There was velvety grass all around. Different types of roses bloomed on the edges. As they moved ahead, the sweet fragrance of jasmine enchanted them. Above all the moonlight was so heartwarming all the tiredness of the journey had gone. The bungalow seemed to be a royal palace.

Pritam took hesitant steps, and Tara followed him. They opened the door and entered a large hall where a wall-to to-wall red carpet had been spread. They removed their shoes outside the hall as if the volume of the Holy Book had been installed there. For them, the M.P. himself was the holy- man.

The M.P. was lying in a large bed, his body being as large as that of a bull. The supplicants had surrounded his bed, pressing his legs and arms. Pritam drew closer to him and wished him good evening; he too started rendering service to him, by pressing his feet. The M.P. moved his fat neck, like a pig, and whispered, "good evening!" in very low voice. Tara stood there awestruck, gazing around like a lost baby in the jungle. He even could not gather enough courage to say 'good evening'. Helplessly he too bowed his head and started massaging M.P. like the others. He thought, "It is nothing short of licking his shoes for getting job."

Beds for the visitors had been arranged in the servant's quarters on one side of the bungalow. Pritam led Tara to that side. There was a Punjabi restaurant close by. Arrangements for food had been made there... They had their meals and returned to their room. Tara heaved a sigh of relief as he had found the shelter; otherwise, serving the 'lobbyist' would have emptied his pocket instantly. Tara could not sleep. He spent the whole night building castles in the air.

They stayed there for three days. The M.P. did nothing so far nor did Pritam tell the purpose of his visit. Tara was getting short of money day by day, and this caused him immense worry. "All the money is gone. If nothing is done today, there will hardly be the return fare left with me." He pressed upon Pritam many a time during the day. On Tara's persistence, Pritam humbly said to the M.P., "Sir! This lad is Master in Chemistery. He is without a job. Kindly help him get a job for him. He is my distant cousin"

The MP made a feeble nasal sound— – 'Hhoon'— that seemed to have stuck in his nose. He turned his face to the other side. Tara waited for the utterance of a sentence after 'Hhoon...' for a couple of days "Hhoon" did not serve any purpose, as it was still half born.

And then he understood, "These 'big people' are good for nothing. They go on making lifeless laws, which decorate the files. That is why the peoples' problems, instead of getting solved, go on complicating. The common people have been unnecessarily considering them 'great people'. They are the puppets of the Prime Minister. The M.P., on whom you are pinning hope, is only an adornment; of the bed at home and the chair in the Parliament. Living in a palace, how can he have an idea of my pains and my mom's sacrifices for Me.?

"I have wasted half of my life in studying, and I cannot get a job now. If one has to remain a burden on one's parents even after getting such high education, how the country can make any progress I will ask the Prime Minister if he cannot give jobs to the youth of the country, why is he clinging to the seat of power. Leave this seat, and hand over the reins to someone else. If he gives no reply to me, I will squat there in protest.

"'It will be better for me to meet the Prime Minister through M.P. I have not come here to beg alms. Employment in the free country is my birth right. Go to the Prime Minister as a respectable citizen rightfully and ask him where his socialism is?!'"

Tara requested, "Sir! My mother has very high hopes in me. She has spent all her assets on my education and now I am unemployed. I had applied to the Punjab Sind Bank for the post of a manager. What to speak of the post of a manager—, I even cannot get a clerical job. Where should I go now? Kindly help me meet the Prime Minister just for once'"

The M.P. was surprised to hear him. He said, "Oh, my boy! I have never dared meeting such a great leader so far… and you….?" Truth escaped his lips.

Next day Tara got into a bus and reached Prime Minister's residence. There was a long queue of visitors. Tara also joined the queue. They could see everything through the gate bars. The persons clad in white, were adorning the chairs spread in the green lawn. A supplicant from Himachal Pradesh stood ahead of him. He lost his nerve at the sight of M. Ram, the Congress leader, sitting inside. He started abusing him. "Who will listen to my woes? M. Ram has come here also ahead of me. It is his son who has raped my daughter. My First Information Report was not allowed to be registered at the police station. Rather, he called my daughter, a prostitute."

As he stood there, he heard the stories of other leaders.

After some time, an officer came out, holding in his hand a red diary. People guessed that he was P.A (Personal Assistant to P.M.). He had come out to write down the people's complaints. A stirring was noticed on his arrival. The sentries at the gate also saluted him.

The supplicants had come from far-off places. When they started relating their tales of woes, their heart rending stories caused a chill in the spine of those who listened. They had come to the Prime Minister's house a number of times but it was all in vain.

Tara's turn came. The P.A. looked at him as if he suspected him to be a terrorist, and asked Tara, "What brings you here?"

Tara felt annoyed at his arrogant behavior. He said in his mind, "To condole at the demise of your government." But he controlled his anger and said, "To see our Prime minister."

"What is your problem?"

"I have passed M.Sc. in Chemistry. I have been without a job for a year."

"Go to Employment Exchange," he said arrogantly.

"I have been going there again and again but without getting any job. That is why I have come here. Millions of youths are rotting on the roads. What is the use of independence to us?

"I wish to ask the Prime Minister— on one hand you are rearing the crocodiles, and on the other hand, people are starving. Unemployment is as acute as the people are denied the Basic Right to live."

"Get lost, do not bother me," said the enraged P.A., pushing him behind.

"I will go back only after exposing your socialism." He had not yet completed his sentence when two policemen appeared, held him by both the arms, and pushed him back so badly that he fell flat. The striped constable said, "Leave him, the bastard is mad...wants to see the Prime Minister!"

Another one said, "Thank God he is not saying - *'I am* the Prime Minister.'"

He kept abusing: "Bastards talking of freedom. Such a bad situation did not prevail even during British rule… Even the Mughal Emperors heard the supplicants in the open court." He was boiling with rage. Ultimately he made up his mind to stay on in Delhi and show them what he could do to expose their 'Socialism'.

"Freedom is hiding itself here in air-conditioned bungalows. It unfurls itself at the Red Fort on 15th of August...I will show them the Pearls of Mother India rotting on the rubbish heaps."

Looking for the Red Flag of The Great Martyr, Bhagat Singh, he reached a place where three flags of the same color were flying. He went to their offices one after the other. They talked of 'revolution' and dubbed others as 'traitors.' He got into the labyrinth. Whom should he regard as a revolutionary to bring change in the rotten system- so called Democracy- and whom, a counter-revolutionary?

But one thing he understood was that those who fight among themselves could not bring any change for the good of people.

Tara failed to understand, "The White party has gone mad after enjoying state power, but what ails the followers of Bhagat Singh? The Chair sans Power had turned their heads. In such a condition Real Democracy-Power with the People- will remain a dream."

Tired after going from pillar to post in desperation, Tara returned home. He felt terribly ashamed and lay indoor. His mother thought, "My son is tired of the journey. Let him relax. Why to disturb him?"

On the third day, he heard his mother's affection-soaked voice, "Are you O.K., my son? You are lying like this—."

Tara said nothing. He cursed himself lying there condemning him day and night, "Why did I go for high education in the country of fatalists who always live in the past and never think of present. In the country of sages and the orthodox, I just wasted my time over collecting Degrees. I should have recited God's name, read some religious book, become a Saint with matted hair, meditated in the fire, or ice cold water. Here in this country ignorance is bliss. I should have become 'Saint' like *Dharindra Brahmchari* or *Chandra Swami*, applied the royal mark on forehead. The President, Prime Minister, Ministers would have come for my blessings. What to talk of a job, big 'ashrams[46]'spreading in miles would have been mine; these so called leaders would have walked to me for being blessed. They would have offered me planes to fly, and limousines to ride in. I could then order the demolition of Babri Masjid or order the building of Ram Mandir. What was the use of getting so much education?"

"Tara! See the sun has risen so high. There is no cooking material; all pots and pans are empty. I have been borrowing for so many days."

He could not face her Mom; much less give a reply to her. "Whatever little she had, I had sold to pay for my visit to Delhi."

---

46 .Head-quarters of saints

He was cursing himself, "Even the rickshaw pullers are better than I. They place at their mother's
palm a crisp hundred-rupee note in the evening. My
degrees have made me unable even to do the manual
labor and earn the livelihood."

Without removing the quilt from his face, Tara
replied to his mother, "I am not feeling well, Mom.
You can borrow Ration for a few more days."

Lying there, it came to his mind, "You shameless
brat! How long would you keep lying in this way?
Get up and do something."

Tara got up, had a wash, and went out to the village square. Ghuka met him there. He took him to
his house and told him on the way, "If you had supported Shinder in the elections, you would have
got a job. How long would you go on carrying the
corpses of the old patriots and singing national
songs? Shinder is within my approach. Just tell me
what sort of job do you want to have? You went to
the Prime Minister and returned after losing whatever you had. You should have told me. I would
have got you the Manager's post. But if you ask my
opinion, leave aside the manager's post. I can make
you Deputy Superintendent of Police- D.S.P. If you
had done Law, I would have managed to appoint you
a judge. Why are you mad after a manager's post?
The Chairman of the Punjab Service Commission
was appointed on the recommendation of Shinder's
mother-in-law. He is on contract basis. He sells jobs

on commission basis. Everything is done under her directions.

"Now tell me what do you want to become? ... Of course there is one thing….some time is required for procedural formalities. You cannot be appointed D.S.P. directly. You will be appointed an Inspector for some time, and then promoted to D.S.P., golden chance to mint money in police Department.

"Some fee is required to be paid for every post. If you do not have ready cash, sell some land. Such an opportunity does not come one's way again and again. You have got the genuine Degree; I will manage your selection with less money. People are becoming officers by obtaining fake Degrees.

"There is no need to go to Chandigarh. The Chairman himself has no power of his own. For any job required, Madam would give the chit. Hand over the chit to Chairman. He will send orders at home."

"Ghukka, perhaps you are inebriated and talking tall. There is no logic in whatever you are talking. Your mind always works in the reverse gear. You became a sycophant for your greed to become a drug peddler, and you are marring the future of the coming generation too. You know quite well that my father went away to fight the Nazis in the Second World War. He has not returned so far. My mother has grown old, fighting 'the enemy' within the country. Do you think I would taint their fair name?"

Tara said to his mother, "We have a misconception that a job will be given to us on the basis of Degrees. We have been groping in the dark. Jobs are sold. Degrees have no value. There are touts hawking about. These days Ghukka is also doing the business of a middle man."

Karmi got irked at the mention of Ghuka's name. She said, "Do not mention his name.... Just get a bag of wheat from the neighbors. I have talked to them. Be strong, my son. These hard days will also pass off."

FORTY-THREE

Clashes had been going on with Pakistan, but when the war broke out with China, India had an assessment of its military power. The army had to be strengthened. For recruitment of officers, age relaxation was given. It suited Tara. He could not get a job anywhere, and he started thinking of joining the army. He sought his mother's permission. She was not willing to send him in to the Army. She said, "Leave the idea of going to the Armed Forces. What had your father gained? What a ruin he had brought to the family, and it has not been undone till now. You are the hope of my life. And if you go away, what would I have to look forward to?"

Tara pleaded with her, "If I do not get employed anywhere, should I not go to the Army? I should be able to earn my living."

"Start some business."

"I have tried many times and failed. Only money makes the mare go."

"If you are so much determined of going to go, you may go. I will manage myself. My blessings are with you.' " As she said this, tears stood in her eyes. She took Tara in her clasp and said, "Go! Go happily!

I am mad and I get emotional. Do the mothers ever cry sending off their sons to Front? They send them with garlands around their necks."

Tara was confident of his ability. He could pass any type of test. He was fully prepared.

Tara was called to Meerut-cantonment for the test.

Written test was given on the first day. Only blanks had to be filled in. There were objective questions, to be answered in Yes or no. Such questions helped to understand the trend of a person's mind. His aptitude to become an officer could be judged.

Next day, groups of five or six boys were formed. Every group was given a project. The needed equipment for completing the project— – ropes, planks, supports, et cetera— – was given. The group had a mutual discussion. Everybody gave his technique for completing the project. There was unanimity over Tara's scheme, and he was accepted by others as the leader of the group. He completed the project. If he had not succeeded, others would have been given the chance to do that job.

Next day was the competition in rope-climbing, wall-scaling, et cetera. Tara won those hurdles too.

The following day was for the debates. Tara had a treasure of knowledge with him. He impressed others in all the subjects.

At last the boys were called for interview. They were put questions to test their general Knowledge.

Tara was asked, "Which was the power behind P.M. Indira Gandhi's murder?"

"There was no power behind her murder. She was murdered by religious fanatics because of the Blue Star Operation at The Golden Temple."

"China has attacked India. Should we take revenge" was the next question.

"No, sir," Tara replied confidently.

"Why?" The Chairman questioned his view.

"We can take revenge if we are capable of doing so. Only the army does not fight the war alone; the entire country has to fight. People start taking advantage of emergency. They hoard the necessities of life in vaults and create famine. Our economic condition is not good comparable to that of China. Therefore it would be wrong to think of taking revenge."

The Chairman felt very pleased.

A Conference was held the next day. Tara appeared before the Service Selection Board. The Chairman again put very intricate questions.

"What are your hobbies?"

"Reading newspapers and magazines, and gardening."

The Korean War was going on in those days. America was causing great losses to North Korea. The Chairman asked Tara, "Will China jump into the war directly to help North Korea?"

"China will not join the war directly. Its guerillas are already fighting there. Joining directly would make it a world war."

The board members clapped and cheered him for this reply.

When the result was declared, Tara had topped the list. He passed the medical examination also.

His desire was fulfilled. He got a decent job, an opening to move ahead. He was quite confident of his abilities.

He was weaving the dreams, when he received a letter from the President, informing him, "You have not been found fit for grant of Commission in the Army."

Tara said to his mother, "Mom, I had decided to risk my life to join the army service, but the government has not found me fit even to die for the motherland."

"The Government of India did not like your Independent thinking. They want yes-man."

"Why did they not like my independent thinking? There is nothing wrong in it."

"Then fault lies with me: Two policemen came; they said, 'Congratulations, your son has become a Lieutenant. Give us a bottle of whisky, Mom. "

"We do not drink. I can bring sweets from the shop.

They said, "What would we do with sweets? Give us a bottle of whisky. He would become Lieutenant on the basis of our report. If you do not want him to become an Army Officer, it is up to you."

"They were annoyed and returned spilling venom. A doubt had arisen in my mind even at that time that they would write something adverse. During the British rule, they dubbed the freedom fighters as 'perverted minded.' Your father was an I.N.A. Veteran. So they wrote against you too. The police have not changed. They are more corrupt than ever before. Their behavior is not like the police of an Independent nation. But the Government does not need patriotic officers. Such type of police would not fill their coffers. They have the pro slavery attitude. They are corrupt to the core. There is nothing bad in you, my son. You are my Lieutenant at home. We shall fight against the enemy within."

FORTY-FOUR

Karmi had become a heroine of the people. But the political leaders living there began to consider her as their political enemy. They tried to make her path thorny as to dishearten her in local politics.

Pauli a congress leader was her Farm neighbor. His land on the high way was adjoining to that of Karmi's. He had got the city bypass sanctioned through her land. He thought, "If she is dispossessed of that land, she would be in a tight position, with no source of income, and compelled to leave the village." More over Pauli's land had become gold by the city's bypass. Blue party leader Shinder also joined with Pauli as Karmi was their common enemy. Shinder also gained by the city's By-pass-Pauli's Project.

Karmi came to know when the time given for filing the objection had elapsed, it was all kept secret.

One day Dad brought in a paper from outside and said to his daughter-in-law, "This paper was given to me by the Tehsildar's messenger, saying that the city bypasses would pass through this land."

Karmi lost her wits on hearing the news. She said to Tara, "Go to the Tehsil office right now and find out the true facts."

Tara met with the Revenue *Officer and* said, "Sir, before acquiring land, the owner has to be given some notice. You did not do that."

"The notice calling for objections was duly given in advance. This is the second notice to vacate the land.

The period of filing objection has elapsed. You will be paid compensation for this land."

"Any proof of serving the first notice? Show me," insisted Tara.

"It was our job to serve the notice under section two, and it was given. You can check the mail-register"

The Qanungo showed Tara the dispatch register. The notice had been entered in the register.

"We have not received it. All right, show me the map of the bypass," Tara requested.

Tara looked at the map and understood how it had happened. Paul's land was adjacent to theirs, and next to that of Shinder's. In order to increase the value of their land, they had managed that the bypass should be on their land, touching Pauli's land.

Tara returned home and said to Karmi, "The bypass has been approved. The last date for filing objections is also over."

Karmi said, "The last date might have passed, but the date to go to the people's court has not expired. Go and meet the other affected farmers. Let us get together and fight together against the high-handedness of the local leaders."

The news spread like wild fire: Poor Karmi is ruined. Her land has been acquired for bypass…it is a gross high-handedness of the Land lord Lobby." Many people came to sympathize with her.

The stock reply that Karmi gave them was, "I do not know why these people are bent upon driving me out of the village. But I would not go away in this way. I shall fight back."

Lacchhman Singh's government was supported by Congress party that was ruling the state at that time. Congress Leaders like Pauli were taking advantage of his weakness.

One day two young men came to meet Karmi. They said, "Aunt, our land has also come in the bypass. Your land is adjacent to Pauli's, and ours is next to Shinder's. We have also received the notice. We have come to tell you that we are with you. There is no one educated enough in our family to take further steps to resist this. We know how to fight with muscle power. If no one listens to us, we will kill him or get killed."

"There is no need to lose your wit, my son." replied Karmi. "We need to keep cool. We should not think of violent means. Will you get your land back if you get killed? No. You will not. We will fight the legal battle. We will succeed. People are with us."

After a few days an old man clad in ochre robes, came there., touched Karmi's feet and said to Karmi enthusiastically, "I have come to know that your land has come in bypass.'

"Yes, my son, you have rightly heard."

"The bypass cannot be allowed to be built here. Here lie the '*samadhis*[47] of our ancestors"

"Everyone knows about the 'samadhis', my son. Pauli also knows this. But he has been blinded by power."

After he had gone, Karmi asked Tara, "'Who was this man?"

"Do not you know? He is Piara *'Cheena.'*[48]

'Yes, he had suffered a lot. His parents died in China. His uncle himself married the Chinese woman. He sent him back to India to live with her grandmother.

"When his grandmother died, He took to bad ways of making money. How could the rivals tolerate his misdeeds? They thrashed him and made him run away. His devotees believed in his spiritual powers. They came to see him from far and wide at full moon. When he came to know about the bypass, he came to sympathize with us. He seems to be a useful guy. Have a small hut built for him and make it clear to him, 'Do not drink or indulge in any other evil' while he is here."

Karmi obtained a copy of the land under 'Samadhi'. She had a case made out and submitted it to the Governor.

The officers from various departments came to visit the spot. They were impressed finding that a spiritual

47 symbol of so-called graves
48 Chinese citizen by birth

old man was staying there and looking after the sama-dhis in ruins. Half the battle was won by Cheena.

The Governor instituted an inquiry through the Judicial Magistrate. All the officers were unhappy with Pauli due to his undue interference in their work. So they reported as per record, taking this opportunity to set him right.

An ex-MLA, Roop Lal, gave his statement before the Magistrate, "We come here every year to pay obeisance to our elders."

The Magistrate recorded his finding: "The sama-dhis stand at the land in question, worship is done and people come here to take mud, which is consid-ered holy by them."

Pauli had sidelined the report, and it was not taken into consideration.

People came to know that action was not being taken on the report at his instance. During the Chief Minister's visit, they went to his village. As he saw the villagers coming from a distance, he directed the police officers, "Let them come, do not stop."

Pauli was already sitting with the Chief Minister. On seeing him, Baldev said, "Do you expect jus-tice from him? He is already sitting in the lap of the Congressmen. We can gain nothing. We should not waste our time here."

Tara reasoned with him, "We have come now. Let us talk to him. He would not swallow us like a crocodile."

Both the sides were on the point of grappling with each other before initiating a dialogue. Noting the atmosphere was charged, the Chief Minister said, "Do not worry. I will visit the disputed site and take the right decision." He decided to hold the next meeting at Abohar, and the disputed site lay on the way.

On the day of Chief Minister's visit, the police had come there early morning. The Chief Minister did not come till five o'clock, but the people stayed put. His convoy reached at about six.

He called both the sides. The entire public was with Karmi. Only Pauli and Shinder were present on the other side.

Observing the huge gathering of the people, the M.L.A. went to stand at a distance from both the parties.

"Tell us, Madam, what wrong has been done to you?'" The Chief Minister asked Karmi.

Pointing towards the line drawn for the bypass, Karmi said, "'There goes the bypass crossing my field. The adjacent urban land belongs to Pauli. This has been left out. The next tract of land is that of Shinder. That too has been saved. Another fifteen to twenty small farmers have been wronged—.-deprived of the land.'"

After listening to Karmi, the Chief Minister looked at the bypass line minutely, and kept examining it. Then he said to Pauli and Shinder, white Party leaders, "Now you can tell me what you want?"

Pauli spoke, "The by-pass should be at the site where it has been approved. This is in the interest of the city."

"If it passes through your land, the city benefits all the more. It would be nearer and less expensive." replied the chief minister.

"No sir, we will be ruined." they argued.

"On the-spot study shows that government will have to incur double expenses and the farmers of the other villages are being uprooted."

The M.L.A. supported Pauli and Shinder, "They are the political pillars of our area and should not go disappointed."

The Chief Minister addressed the M.L.A., "You are the common factor. Talk of justice. By building the bypass in the land of these villagers, they are making their own land valuable. You must think of the other families, Look here, my friends: I cannot ignore the glaring facts. The present scheme is rejected. I hereby direct that the bypass for the city should be in the city land."

FORTY-FIVE

Karmi was saved from the onslaught of the bypass. She went to pay thanks to the people who had supported her. First of all she went to the ex-MLA Roop Lal Sathi.

He stood up to welcome her and said, "Dear sister. You have done wonders. The self-styled kings of this area have been defeated. They are exposed before the public, their political career is ruined."

"Credit goes to the people who fought to save me. In fact, I had lost all hopes of taking land back. It is the people's support and your statement in the court of magistrate that clinched the issue and made me win."

"This was my duty, dear sister. I have told the truth. I have not obliged you in any way."

"Dear brother, how many leaders have the courage to speak the truth?"

"In fact it is Dr. Paul who really deserves to be thanked. He held the flag of the United Front High and went round the villages and visited every house." Sathi said and gave a call to Paul.

.Karmi thought, "What a wonderful thing is love! Without my appeal, Paul started mobilizing people in my favor."

Then she told Sathi, "Dear brother, Paul has something common with me from childhood. We studied together and played together."

Sathi said, "The way the government is sustaining on the support of Congress, nothing could have helped you. As a matter of fact, the United Front has helped you win. People had come in your support in such a big way that the Chief Minister had to side with the truth. In my opinion, the people should form United Fronts in all the villages and towns. I am with you in organizing people on these lines."

Karmi took Paul with her and went to the other houses too.

When Karmi returned home, her mother-in-law was waiting for her. She advised her, "Mere expression of thanks won't do. Donate some money to some Gurdwara or school." Dad endorsed her views.

Karmi said, "Dad, I know the donation given to the Gurudwara is good, if it is spent for the welfare of all.

Only a handful of people misuse it to capture state power and make it a family estate. I would prefer spending money on the spread of education. I will give it to my college.

FORTY-SIX

The next meeting of the United Front was held in Karmi's village. She congratulated the United Front on its victory and added, "The credit goes to our young brigade. As a matter of fact they are our Red Guards. I wish that their representative should be taken in the executive. The post of the Vice President and the Deputy Secretary should be given to them" It was unanimously passed.

The stage Secretary welcomed Mr. Sathi, the new member of the United Front, and requested him to express his views.

Mr. Sathi said, "I am pained to see the downslide in the condition of Punjab. It is worsening day by day. Punjab was a basket of food for the whole country. It is now on the verge of starvation and living on drugs. There was a time when India was regarded as a golden sparrow. Today it is passing through the curse of unemployment, starvation, and diseases of different kinds. If we hope that the government will do everything for the welfare of the country, provide education, employment, and save the people from drugs, it is all a fallacy. People should form United Fronts everywhere,"

The stage secretary supported the views and requested the Veteran Mehar Singh to give his views.

"Ladies and Gentlemen, I support the views of Sathi that the cause for the bad state of affairs in the Punjab is the government itself. It has gone into wrong hands. The vested interests has wrested power in the name of religion. The good of the country lies only in separating religion from the state. India is a secular country. The United Front will not permit anybody to misuse religion."

The members present clapped to welcome the suggestion. He advised them to unite and fight under the flag of the United Front.

Kartar suggested, "Let us redress the economic problems first. The farmers are under debt and compelled to commit suicide as their lands are attached by the moneylender by cheating them. The most important task before the United Front is to save the land from attachment."

Gulzar, present in the meeting, brought another problem in to the notice of the committee, "The inputs used in farming are mostly adulterated by the dealer as well as by the retailers. The yield is reduced because of adulteration. It doesn't cover the cost of the crop. The farmer has to borrow money to meet the expenses from the commission agent, the money lenders and wealthy landlords. When he fails to return the money they grab his land. The adulterators bribe the government machinery and adulterate the seed, fertilizers, and insecticides. Our dedicated workers should locate the wrong doers, blacken their faces, and take them out in processions."

Karmi returned to the stage and said, "We should not indulge in violence. The police will arrest and put you behind bars. Our work will suffer."

The young leader got excited. He said, "We have seen enough of the path of non-violence. We have been starving for a very long time. Government has done nothing all these years to stop adulteration. When the United Front blackens the faces of one or two guilty ones, others will learn the lesson."

Pandemonium prevailed. The doves opposed violence. The President appealed for maintaining order and keeping quiet.

"When you come out openly to resort to violence, the United Front would be faced with a new problem. The matter would go to the police and you will be entangled therein. Reforming the black marketers, you will yourself get entangled in a problem. Don't go beyond sit-in strikes and protests."

Still, all the hawks did not agree to this point. Ultimately, they all agreed on blackening the faces of wrong doers. A copy of the resolution was forwarded to the government and another to the media. News appeared in the papers and over the radio and television.

This had a very good effect. The businessmen, ministers, and the government servants, got scared. Adulteration of seeds, fertilizers, and insecticides stopped to a great extent.

PART IV

The cattle got afflicted with mouth and foot disease. Every other day two to four cattle heads were lost. Those that survived were worse than the dead. They could not plough the field, nor could they pull the cart. The milk cattle got dried.

It was a good chance for Nikka to pull Karmi's leg. He called for the village people and addressed them, "I tried to make you understand that a woman sarpanch would not be able to do anything good for the village. Don't elect her as Sarpanch. You did not listen to me. Now the cattle have been dying and she is doing nothing. If there were a man in her place, he would have tried to take some preventive steps."

His mere mention of a lady sarpanch made the people furious. A man was sent to call Karmi. He said to her, "Do something for the cattle, dear sister. The disease is spreading fast day by day. Nikka is misleading the people and instigating the people against you."

Karmi stood up and followed him without any delay. The entire village had assembled by the time she reached there. Nikka was delivering his lecture. After he had finished, Karmi said, "I call the doctor every year to give injections for the mouth and foot disease, but nobody listens to me. Even now it is not too late. I can call the vet."

Illiterate villagers paid deaf ears to Karmi. Nikka again stood up and said, "We have been getting exorcism done every year, free of cost. Why should we pay money to the doctor?" What the Hindus do, the Muslims would not. The village may suffer a loss, but he had to oppose Karmi on one pretext or the other.

Bhago's Bachan said, "We won't go in for the western treatment. That treatment aggravates the disease. The holy thread given by *a Muslim of Kotla* is quite efficacious. He has Guru's blessings."

"Last year, you had got the exorcism done but the cattle are still dying. Why is it so?" Karmi left them speechless.

Bachan replied, "All the cattle in the village were not brought under the spell. *Jamuna* had made fire in her hearth. Milk was churned in some houses. How could then the spell be effective? This time, Panchayat would impose a fine of Rupees five hundred on any one obstructing the spell." The addict himself made the decision on behalf of Panchayat...'

The villagers had agreed to go in for exorcism. Bachan was sent to Kotla. , Karmi felt a great humiliation as illiteracy and ignorance prevailed upon over wisdom and .knowledge.

Bhago's Bachan used to swallow a ball of opium of a berry size. His mother also had the same quantity of opium.

Her husband had died at an early stage. She settled for remarriage with his elder brother and gave birth to Bachan.

Her second husband considered the boy a bastard and drove her out. Who was there to listen to her woes? The poor woman faced the problem of square meals. She also had the responsibility of bringing up the child. She could not do without opium. An acre or so of land that came to her share was very small... Its income was insufficient to meet her expenses. So it was disposed of. After that there was no source of income left. She had to resort to some underhand means.

All sorts of rumors were floated about her. The women assembled at Taro's house for spinning, talked of her: Dialo said, "Have you heard, Bhago is having an affair with Sucha, who is old and handicapped?"

Taro objected to her statement, "What does it matter to you? It is her life, let her live as she likes."

Dialo, in support of her story, said, "Has she then found a young man? He is an old man, unfit to do 'justice' to her."

Taro questioned, "What can the poor Bhago do otherwise? Her own man betrayed her. She sought another one who was available in those circumstances. Do you think she should jump into a well? How could 'she bring up her child? She had to pass the hard time. Bhago's pain can be felt by Bhago only. Her new husband produced the child and deserted her. Nobody was there to question his high-handedness. Had he been a man of some morale, he should have brought up his son, educated him, and put him to some job. Nobody could make him realize his responsibilities towards Bhago and her son. It so happens because she is a woman and easy to put blame on her. People flog the dead. No one blames the man who ditched her. You are a woman; you should condemn her husband instead of condemning the poor lady. This tragedy can happen to you also."

Bhago felt very much perturbed, listening to what the people were saying about her. There were some tablets in her house for killing the mice. She swallowed some and gave one to the boy. She got rid of her wretched life, but the boy started vomiting and survived. He grew up rotting here and there. He did charms and made both ends meet. At the time of performing '*yag*' (free lunch of sweet rice to please the Goddess of rain *or* curing the mouth and foot disease) and Bachan was the leader. That day was a day of festivities for him.

He went to Kotla every year, and brought charm for the cattle. One, who disturbed the charm, was summoned to the village square and made to dust off the shoes of the congregation. Everyone in the village obeyed Bahcan's dictate. Nobody could dare to question him.

It was Sarpanch Karmi who irked him. The time had not yet come to deal with her. He was on the lookout for an opportune time.

Before the spell function, Bachan instructed the villagers on the loudspeaker, "The amulet will be hung tomorrow early morning in the village square. The people in the village would take their cattle through the street of Pundits and pass under the amulet and go home. The 'passing under amulet' would end at eight A.m. No fire shall be ignited in the hearths before the function is performed. The villagers will bring the milk to the langar (Kitchen for free food). No churning of milk on that day. Tea would be ready at eight in the morning. Everybody will relish breakfast in the langar. Anybody creating a hindrance in the spell will be fined."

The devotees cleaned the lanes with brooms, sprinkled water, and spruced up the path one day before the spell.

The amulet was hung in the lane early, at 4 AM. They placed two large pans full of charmed water on both sides of the lane. Volunteers stood there. They dipped the twigs of 'the neem' tree and sprinkled water on the cattle passing under the amulet.

The volunteers started with their own cattle. Others followed them. This continued uninterrupted. There was a big crowd in an hour or so, as if it was a fair. The villagers were happy at the hustle and bustle of the occasion. The devotees sat down in rows, ate 'langar' and went home.

Bachan passed remarks, "May God save us, someone has violated the rules of spell this time too. Animals may not be cured." He shot the arrow at Karmi.

As he uttered these words there was a great hue and cry.

"Who is the one who disobeyed the dictates?" The President of the Gurdwara committee expressed his surprise and raised the issue...

"It is not for me to say anything. You can yourself look around and see. One, who has not joined us, would have done this," Bachan said.

"Of course, the lady Sarpanch is not to be seen here. Her cattle have not come for the spell," said Baba Dhanna.

"Summon her to the Panchayat. Is it good to violate the spell?" Nikka added fuel to fire.

On receiving the orders of the self-styled 'punches' (members of the village council), Karmi understood, "Nikka has played this mischief to humiliate me'. Who is he to summon me? Some devil's hand is there behind him. I should act very carefully. I don't understand the people, who change so much. I had called the doctor for their good. He was stopped by them, and they went after the spells and amulets. They will come to their senses when the cattle start dying in large numbers. In fact, people are not to blame. It is illiteracy which that impels them to do such things. Bhago's brat indulges in all this to make his both ends meet. Nikka makes him dance to his tune. And moreover, I do not let their opium be sold in the village, and they have turned inimical to me"

Karmi went to them and said to Bhago's Bachan, "You are misleading the people and finding fault with me. It is just to make money. I started the treatment of mouth and foot disease. I called for the doctor for giving injections to the cattle. Finding fault with the scientific treatment, you started making spells. If the cure could be had by threads and amulets, the cattle would not have died. The cattle are dying even now, you will be held responsible for their deaths."

Bachan said, "You need not talk to me, The Panchayat has summoned you. Talk to them...."

Then Karmi turned towards other people, "you have made me a Sarpanch and now appointed Nikka as my boss?"

The leaders of the amulet gang got tongue-tied.

Continuing, Karmi said, "On the one hand you have faith in *'Sri Guru Granth Sahib,* and on the other, you practice the hoax of spells and amulets. What kind of Sikhs are you? Following the addicts and idlers, you are insulting the Guru. A true Sikh does not believe in amulets and or any other spell. His thinking is scientific. Now tell me if you still recognize me as your Sarpanch or someone else? If you find a better Sarpanch, You are free to do so... I have no objection."

The ex-Sarpanch said, "Dear sister, sometimes we lose our balance of mind and do the wrong. Now kindly call the doctor and start treating the cattle. We are with you."

Udhe was getting education at Amritsar. He lived with his aunt. He was not taking keen interest in his studies. He often went to see movies or wandered about aimlessly like other teenagers.

One day Tara went there to give him money. Udhe was not at home. He waited for him sitting in his room. Tara started searching for some books to read. He noticed the photographs of foreign girls kept in the notebook.

Seeing the photos, he got lost in thoughts, "He is not serious in studies. He is busy in keeping correspondence with the girls. He gets crossed with one, starts correspondence with another."

Udhe came at midnight

When asked about photographs, he said, "They are my pen friends."

What could Tara say to his grown-up brother? Tara mentioned this to his mother on reaching home

When Udhe came to see his mother, she asked him, "You were not in your room till midnight. Where did you go? "

He kept quiet. There was nothing worth mentioning that he could tell her.

His silence pinched his mother all the more. She said, "Udhe, have you ever thought of us, of how do we meet the expenses of your education? We sell milk and spend on you. Is this good at my age, to carry big bundles of fodder on my head for cattle? Tara, Bali, and I go to fields and bring three bundles of fodder before the people wake up. Then we chop it before they go to college. The entire family remains at tenterhooks to feed them then, get milk and meet your expenses. You should have realized our position before you waste money and precious time on romance. You are living in a dreamland. What comparison do you have with the foreign girls? They correspond with you to know about India. They have so many other pen friends all over the world. Simpletons like you think that they are in love with you.

"They have so many other boyfriends to die for. They live with them and make merry but do not marry. They get married after completing their education. The boys also do likewise. They study and work side by side. If still they are unable to meet their expenses, they draw loan from the banks. They can spend money on their girlfriends, and they tour the other countries also with their money. You are studying at the expenses of your family. It does not look proper for you to run after girlfriends."

"On getting some girlfriend's photo you take it as if she has become your own. Neglecting your studies, you have become a Majnu[49]"

---

49   a legendary lover

Udhe did not like what his mother said to him. He thought, "She has gone mad as she talks like this."

He said arrogantly, "after some time you will come to know when I reach England. My girlfriend has invited me there."

His mother reasoned with him, "She has not called you for marriage, but only as a friend. You have not understood what is in her mind. Earn money and go, I will not stop you. Here, the boys have no money to go abroad; they can't afford to pay their college fees even. Look at Tara. He takes tuition work to earn money and pay for his education. You have not been able to do F.Sc (12th Grade). You have been trying in vain for two years. We were hoping that you would become a doctor.

"Just listen to me. This is the last chance. If you get through, well and good— otherwise come home and do some job. We cannot afford wastage of money in the name of education."

Udhe felt very bad at the way his mother talked to him.

He showed reaction, expressing anger in one way or the other and did not talk to his mother. How could Karmi bear the annoyance of her son? She herself talked to him and cajoled him.

Next day she went with him to leave him at his aunt's place. Udhe went to college. The sisters-in-laws talked freely.

Karmi said, "Dear sister, Udhe is not taking interest in his studies. Just keep him under check. You understand our economic condition very well. I could not educate my girls. They got their education privately, at home.

"But we did everything to educate the boys. Satti and Bali were put to work. I discriminated against the daughters, and they did not resent."

Karmi praised her daughters, "The girls bear all the discrimination with fortitude. Satti has been married and gone to her house. Still she worries about us. She sends the tractor, to help us in sowing and plowing. I had given Bali a little hint about ourselves, being hard-hit for money and suggested her to open a shop for sale of carpets *and cotton blankets.* She agreed and sat at the shop. At the same time she continued to study at night. Her schooling was disrupted. She was the eldest one and completed her education last of all. The girls have been working, and we earned a few chips, which helped in educating the boys. Now it comes to my mind sometimes that I had done so with high-handedness."

Aunt said, "You acted wrongly. Not a little but very much, especially with regard to Bali. You have taken revenge of some past era from the girl. Will the boys put you in the cradle to swing? What your aunt did to you, now you have done the same thing to your daughter. Will your daughter stop this practice in future? She would discriminate against her daughter. The boys would create hell but never bear discrimination. Possibly they might strangle the one who discriminates against them. We have seen this happening at many places. The fault lies with the parents. They pamper them in the first instance. Whatever is good in the house, they give it to the boy. Right from the boy's birth they shower all the affection on him, regarding him as the successor to their throne. And if they come to know that the infant in the womb is a female, they go in for abortion.

"The girl, who survives, to her good fortune, is not treated well. There may be thousands of laws favoring girls, but the parents still do not give them the share of property. They write their will in favor of their sons. Not only do they disinherit them, they append their consent to the will. As soon as the father writes his will, the sons change their attitude. They kick their parents out in a short time. Surprisingly enough, the daughters look after them till their death. Then they repent over the discrimination against their daughters. And they die heaving deep sighs. I can't say anything about Tara, but Udhe will surely ditch you. Then you will weep bitterly. Ultimately, Bali and Satti will come to your help."

"I have come only to say this. Udhe has gone astray. Keep an eye on him. He keeps girls' photos in his pocket. And have you looked at his fashion? He wears pants of free style and poses himself as a filmy hero. Tara is of different views. He talks wisely. People praise him like anything. I pray to God that rest of my life may go to him."

Karmi had not yet returned to the village, when Udhe had already reached there and stood before her to say, "You have returned, Mom, without giving me money. I have to pay for the tuition."

"I handed over the money to your aunt. Go and take it from her."

Udhe passed his F.Sc. barely getting through. The marks obtained were not sufficient for joining any course. As a last resort, Karmi got him admitted to B.Sc. "What will he do? What job could he be put to? The elder one is still idle. Every year a chunk of land goes away."

Tara asked for money to do B.T, but she ignored. Tara again said, "You have not replied me, Mom. Did not you hear me?" "I did hear you, my son." Karmi explained the position to him. "You know how hard hit we are? The question is not that of your fee alone. We will have to give donation too for admission. Bali has grown up and is of marriageable age."

Tara did not lose heart. He said to himself, "how long would you look to your mother Do something yourself. If mother has not got anything to give, how can she give you? I am a Master in Science. There will be so many tuitions. Get admitted, and there will be no dearth of money. Neighbor's daughter is not even matriculate, but she gives tuition in Math's to the primary class children and earns money. Even the poorest go in for tuition. You will have no need to ask your mother."

FORTY-NINE

Tara's college started B.T.[50]classes from that year, and it became easier for him to do the teaching course. He managed to get admission and did not have to offer a donation too. He rented a room near the college. He gave tuitions and managed his own expenses. In odd times he helped his sister also. After a few days in the college, Tara understood that, there was nothing new to learn or teach in the B.T. course. It was the same old syllabus, and the same routine method of teaching.

Some of the boys just went there and positioned themselves at the college gate. Their eyes chased the girls and awarded them marks. Some one was adjudged as World Beauty, another as Indian beauty queen.

A girl named Bindery studied with him. They had given her the title of World Beauty. She was really a dashing beauty, and the boys waited at the gate to welcome her. Some passed remarks and teased her. Tara used to watch them. One day he could not restrain himself and jumped into the fray. Wordy

---

50   Bachelor of Teaching

duals led to physical assault. His courageous act saved the world beauty.

The next day another Romeo sprung up. He clashed with Tara and said, "why are you feeling so irked, you bastard? Is she your sister?"

Tara was not to be cowed down. He retorted, "Come here, and I will make her your sister too."

Tara gave him two heavy blows. Having been beaten, he grumbled and went away. Tara knew that the so called modern lovers were capable of doing that much, and they can do nothing more. He forgot all about the incident.

After an hour or so he returned along with two or three ruffians, holding bats and hockey sticks. Tara was empty-handed. What could he do? They gave him a sound beating with hockey sticks, hurting his arm badly. The situation was saved because it was the market place. People intervened and disengaged them— otherwise they might have killed him.

When he went to college the next day with bandages, everyone sympathized with him. Bindery especially felt for him a great deal. She said, "I have no words to thank you, Tara. You risked your life for my sake. I would not be able to repay the debt of gratitude throughout my life." After that incident, their closeness increased with every passing day. Whenever there was a free period, he went to the library and she followed him. Sometimes they went to the canteen to have a chit chat.

Bindery was aware of Tara's haunts. She hurriedly got out of the bevy of girls and reached wherever he could be found.

Reading in the library was just a pretext. They kept a newspaper or magazine before them and talked endlessly. The Annual Day of the college was celebrated. The function began with Bindery's dance. She was quite well versed in singing and dancing. She surpassed even Hema Malini in dancing. The audience was simply captivated.

When Tara was called upon to speak, he was lustily cheered. He spoke on the subject of Indian Woman. He said, "You talk of Human Rights for Woman. In this land of sages and savants, a woman has no existence of her own. She is regarded as a machine for producing children and a maid for her husband. Even a maid does have some place of her own; she gets some money also and has some reckoning, but a housewife even does not have that much of reckoning or remuneration. She is considered a commodity, which can be bought or sold. Passing through hell of services and selling body in piecemeal, she turns into a skeleton after some time. People worship a lifeless image of Goddess, offer it sacrifices, but the goddess in flesh and blood is treated no better than a pair of shoes. Her place is not even equal to a mud image of goddess."

There was loud clapping. After hearing his views about women, Bindery felt greater attraction for Tara.

She said to him, "Tara, your views impress me. I can say your mom and dad must be worthy of worship. Your house would be like a temple. I would like to go on a pilgrimage to that holy place."

Tara was reluctant to take Bindery home.

"I can take you there with me, but I am afraid that a nymph descending from heavens to a rustic's house may not go back to the high skies."

"I am not the one who would run away, Tara. I can walk on the hot deserts for you. Just try me."

Tara talked to his mother about Bindery, "a girl from Ganganagar is my class mate, mom. She wants to meet with you. If you allow me I can invite her?"

Karmi was pleased very much to hear of Ganganagar. She got more eager than Tara to invite Bindery to her house. She said, "For me even a sparrow coming from Ganganar is very important. I will feel highly elated to meet that girl."

Bindery, accompanied by her friend *Neelam,* went to Tara's village. It was a part of the city. There were metaled roads, brick-lanes, electricity and water supply system.

Karmi had cleaned and tidied up the house before Bindery's arrival. The old furniture and other things had been properly arranged. There were two cane chairs in the verandah and a divan in the sitting room with two chairs on the sides, and a table in the center. There was a big bookshelf full of books. Everything was in place and looked well.

As his mother saw Bindery from a distance her joy knew no bounds; his son's beloved had come. She said, "The full moon has appeared to my good luck."

"I have been asking him almost every day to come here but Tara was reluctant. When I came to know that you were also brought up in Ganganagar, I have been very keen to see you," said Bindery.

"Where do you live in Ganganagar?" Karmi tried to know more about the place because of Paul.

"We live in Model Town, near the courts and where have you been living?"

"We lived two miles away from Ganganagar in the village. When my aunt died, we returned to our village. But the girls do not have any place of their own. Their home becomes the place where they go after marriage. This is my village now. I might have known your parents. What are their names?"

Bindery was afraid of disclosing the names of her parents. She said, "My mother has left for her heavenly abode long ago. My maternal grandmother and grandfather brought me up. I have a younger sister."

Karmi said, "A boy, Paul, who was my class fellow lived there. He had become a doctor. You might know him."

"OH! He was my father," she interrupted Karmi.

"Then you happen to be my own daughter. Come here let me caress you." Bindery drew close to Karmi reluctantly. She was afraid of her father being exposed. Karmi moved towards her, and took her in her clasp, and tightened the grip. Karmi had heard the whole story from Paul. She just kept everything within herself. Bindery too did not want to move ahead with her family's story. She got sad. Karmi got lost in thoughts, "what a strange way of nature! The love which could not blossom in the first generation seems to be coming to fruition in the next."

Bindery diverted Karmi's attention, "you seem to have lost in thoughts, Mom."

"Bindery, it seems to me as if you have been related to me in some past life."

Then she made a mention of her father, "How is your Papa, now?"

"I know nothing about him. But my grandfather tells me that my mother had drowned in the canal and my father left home in grief. There has been no news about him since then. For us he does not exist. He would have come had he been alive."

"It is very important for the children to have both the parents. The life of children remains incomplete without them. They float in the air like a kite whose thread is cut. I would suggest you to search your father. He should think of marrying you, after finding a decent match. How can the old grandparents guess about your aspirations?"

"The grandparents may not understand, but God has given me a mother who can understand my aspirations."

Karmi fully understood what Bindery had said. She asked, "Why should I not give an advertisement about your Papa. He should come back and give a befitting send-off to his daughter."

Bindery laughed. Karmi understood the meaning of her laughter. Bali brought in tea. Tara and Neelam also drew closer. Neelam said to Tara, "You have not replied to my question. I do not see Uncle here."

"Mom, please answer *Neelam*'s question."

"Neelam, even God has not been able to fully understand man. How can I? Only he knows why he has gone away?"

Bindery laughed, "Tara, our horoscopes have tallied."

Neelam said to Bindery when they came out, "you are lucky, dear. Mother is even nicer than the son. Do not miss the great opportunity."

FIFTY

When Bindery returned home, her grandmother asked her, "Why are you so late today, girl? Where had you gone? We got terribly worried."

"There was a function in our college, dear Mom," Bindery made an excuse.

"One should speak the truth, my child. We know where you had gone. You should have told us."

Bindery felt it bad. She said to herself, "Grandma is always keeping an eye on my movements. Only God knows what she had been doing in her youth?" She went out of the room in a sullen mood. Her grandfather looked at her quietly.

Grandmother told her husband, "Neelam's mother had told me that both of them had gone to the house of a boy, who is their class fellow. It is not proper for the girl to take so much liberty. Let us find a match for her and marry her off."

The grandfather said, "Yes, it is not proper. That is why we fear that she would marry a teacher of hers. A teacher has no extra income. She would starve. I have a high officer in view."

"If so, try to make a decision. It would be better to do this before it is too late."

"The boy is an A.D.C.; he will be D.C. in course of time.'

'"Why is he still a bachelor?"

"He was married but divorced. The high status of an officer covers up all the faults. He has been promoted from the post of a Naib Tehsildar and reached this level. He has minted lot of money. He had been charging a hundred thousand for each case. He has so much money that it is not easy to count it."

Bindery was overhearing this in the adjoining room. When she saw that they were planning to hitch her to a *divorcee* she got furious and said to them, "I would not marry a divorcee."

Her grandfather tried to convince her, "you mad girl, understand! The boy is an officer. He will be promoted as a D.C. very soon, the master of the entire District. It is not a small thing."

"For me suitability of the match is more important. How can an old man be a match to me? He has spent his life, and I am a young girl. Most of the officers are corrupt, womanizers, and money seekers, and also devoid of human values. Their wives are seen bemoaning their lot. I do not want to lead life like them."

Grandma sent her husband to his room tactfully, "mind your business, please. We should not argue with a grown-up child."

She said to Bindery, "your grandfather is your well-wisher. If you are not willing, forget it."

"Grandma, you have seen that money cannot give you happiness; rather, ill-gotten money turns the house into hell. Were my parents happy? They had lots of money and did no work. They sat idle and quarreled. They ended their lives, leaving us to live as orphans. Only parents can give parental love to the children. There may be anyone trying to shower affection, but no one can equal one's own parents.

"I will choose my life partner myself; I am not a child now. I will marry a man but not an officer. A wife needs her husband who loves her and, shares her joys and sorrows. Another thing, please note, I have already chosen a boy. I have invited him here next Sunday. I will not do anything behind your back."

"All right, I will talk to your grandfather."

Tara said to his mother, "Bindery has invited us next Sunday. You will come with me, right?"

"All right, I will."

"Let us take along Uncle Paul too," suggested Tara.

"Please do not raise this issue at this stage. In fact, Bindery is Paul's daughter. Her mother committed suicide. Her grandfather had registered a case of murder against him. He would never like to face his father-in-law. Before making them meet, we will have to plan a new strategy. Otherwise everything can go wrong."

Tara reached Bindery's house with his mother on Sunday. He was well dressed; he had borrowed a suit from one friend and a tie from another.

Who was there to look at his suit and boots? For the old grandparents, their visit was hardly welcome. They had agreed to it very reluctantly, feeling utterly helpless.

Bindery introduced the guests, "Grandpa, he is Tara…"

"…who saved you from the goons?" Grandpa completed her sentence.

Grandma blessed him. "Bravo, my son. Live long!"

Karmi got seated close to the grandparents, and Tara moved closer to Bindery. Her younger sister, Nandi, went to the kitchen to prepare tea.

"Do you keep good health, Dad?" said Karmi to break the silence.

"It is so-so in this age. We are just pulling on. Keeping indoors all the time is not a life worth living!"

"I also belong to Ganganagar. Bindery is my own daughter as such. She is a very sweet child."

"We are living for them. What else is there for us to survive?"

Their Grandpa and Karmi continued talking. Nandi brought in tea and placed the tray on the table. She got seated next to Tara.

Bindery knew that her grandfather would try to go very deeply into their background. She took Tara to the adjacent room. Tara, considering the time opportune, broke to her some fresh news, "Bindery, your Papa is alive. He was sentenced to life imprisonment on the charge of murdering your mother. But the truth is that your mom committed suicide."

Bindery was annoyed with her grandfather. "This is the doing of the old man. He made out a false case against our father, but he had been telling us a made up story."

The grandparents were busy talking to Karmi. Grandfather said, "Bindery had told us that you belong to Azim-Garh, near Abohar. How much land do you own there?" "We hold about six acres. Tara has done M.Sc. He is doing B.T. now. He will become a teacher and make a good living.

Learning from Karmi that the boy would become a teacher, grandfather acted as if he had no interest in knowing anything further. In fact, he had already made the necessary enquiries. He initiated another topic just to disturb Karmi's peace of mind, "you could have brought the subahdar with you, and we could meet him."

Karmi explained the factual position. "I don't know where he has gone? A woman cannot go anywhere."

"We too are very unhappy in this regard. Their father has also gone somewhere, leaving behind two daughters to be looked after by us."

Bindery got enraged at hearing the false statement about her father, and her attention got fully diverted towards him.

"All right, God willing, we will continue to meet. Let me see Grandpa." Tara too understood what she meant to say, and stood up.

As soon as they had left, Bindery flared up and asked her grandpa, "where is my father? Don't hide the truth from me. Otherwise I...." He understood that the girl had got enlightened about the truth.

"Charged with the murder of your mother, he was sentenced to life imprisonment. It is not known what happened to him later on." The girl did not believe him.

"I will try to know the real position. I will locate him." The grandfather was totally upset at what her granddaughter said. He felt as if the ground was slipping under his feet.

FIFTY-TWO

After completing his training, Tara was appointed as a teacher in a semi-government school. His salary was one hundred and twenty five rupees only He was thinking, "I have spent seventeen years of my life in studies, and my salary is equal to that of an illiterate and untrained worker. A teacher is treated like a rickshaw puller or a cart pusher. A waiter earns by way of tips more than a teacher is paid after a month—. His teacher's Treaining is rewarded, the least. This is an insult to a teacher... What kind of scholar or scientist will he produce and regard himself a Guru? It is but natural that he would suffer from an inferiority complex.

"A teacher, who himself suffers from an inferiority complex, cannot produce *Mannu (Philosopher) or Chanakya (Statesman)*. He would certainly produce parasites on society.

"What is the fault of a student if he/she does not get good education and does not succeed in life? What is the fault of their parents who, keeping themselves half-starved half clad, send their wards to school?

"Here is the Government to blame, who failed to change the educational system in line with the changing time.

"A student is just like a raw material that can be used to make a tractor for the production of food or a tank for destruction. A child is like the potter's clay; which can be used to make a beautiful Statue of Liberty or an ordinary bowl. The greatness is not that of the iron ore or the clay—, it is the greatness of the artist, who makes a master piece of art. A Teacher is an artist who works on a child's brain to make him a great man, a doer of things and a builder of nation.

"In the ancient times, a teacher enjoyed the status of a Guru. Very prestigious Universities like Texila and Ujain were imparting education to thousands of students from India and abroad. Research was conducted in Mathematics and Science.

"With the passage of time, the *Brahmin* who was considered a Guru started misusing his position. He became a broker between man and God and lost the status of guru, his teaching and learning stopped. The respect for the guru too was lost. Whatever little respect for the teacher was left was reduced to zero during the British rule. Their policy was to produce clerks.

"After independence, the new government failed to bring in any change in Education, and continued to follow the beaten track.

"The schools are functioning in the eyes of the world, the children go to schools, but they learn nothing there. They can attain something if the teachers have the proper qualifications of a Guru.

"The spirit of a Guru can be instilled in a teacher if dedicated people, highly capable and having due aptitude for teaching, are appointed as teachers and paid high salaries. Why should his qualification, capability, training, and salary be less than that of an Indian Administrative Services Officer? He has to produce the future citizens, the valuable gems who can take the country forward."

Tara saw that in his school, the S.V[51]. Teacher was hardly middle or 10th Grade qualified. "How can he be a capable teacher to give good education to make a student 'Einstein'? His salary is insufficient to make both ends meet. He is impelled to collect Food Grains at the time of harvesting season... In doing so he loses self-respect... The primary school teacher is in the worst position; his salary is less than that of an S.V. Teacher. His meals are brought by students from home.

"The teacher is a human being. He too has his needs, without the fulfillment of which, there is no other go.

"The innocent children suffer because of the wrong policies of the government.

"The parents also suffer when their wards fail to get proper education and enter into the army of unemployed and become burden instead of relief.

---

51   senior vernacular

Ultimately entire society suffers. The uneducated citizens turn terrorists or criminals. They are easily misled by religious fanatics. It is the main cause of poverty in the third world. A student becomes a graduate but still is unable to write his application for a job. Who is mainly responsible for this sad state of affairs? Undoubtedly, it is the Authority who runs the 'show'.

"The teacher should be able to understand the psyche of the child and teach him accordingly. The child should feel that he has gained something, learned something. An ordinary person cannot teach in accordance with the psyche of the taught. Only an able teacher can do so.

"A child's morality should be the central point of our educational system, but the teacher's morality comes to an end when he bribes the minister to get a teacher's post. He is always worried about repaying loans. He goes to the class room in name only and returns without teaching. If he teaches properly in the class, they would not go in for tuition. He will be unable to repay debts.

"Some of the teachers start coaching academies. They help the students in copying to pass the examination. The students play truant and join the 'academy.' The 'academies for copying' are flourishing, and the schools are failing. They are bound to fail, in the absence of Gurus, as robots have replaced them.

"In league with the officers of Universities and Education Boards, they have set up corporation. Copying, leaking out papers and sale of Degrees/ certificates has become their roaring business. The corporations have the paper setters and printers in their pockets. A night before the examination, the paper reaches every branch. If any student fails, he can get through in re-evaluationn, paying fees to the corporation".

""They are caught once or twice. But no one comes to harm for obvious reasons. Ministers Scandals come to lime light. If Corporation's Scandals are leaked it matters little. Inquiries are made, the case lingers on…ultimately, and the case is closed.

"Only poor students stay in the schools as they are paid Stipends. They have nothing to gain except the monetary benefit. Ultimately they too 'go to any corporation for help to get a certificate'. Education is for sale due to the weak policies of government. Most of the students do not get the opportunity to get admission in professional schools/colleges as they cannot afford big amount of Donations. But they can buy 'certificate' or 'Degree' of any quali- fication from the market. It is a very sad state of affairs that after spending a golden period of life and hard-earned money on education, the young people are not able to pass any competitive test for job. They make an addition to the Army of the Unemployed. "

FIFTY-THREE

Tara realized that the political parties were using the teachers as their party cadres. They no longer did teaching in the schools. The education of the schools suffered. Moreover, it was a setback to the Government Teachers Union too. There were as many teachers' unions as the number of political parties. The teacher did not remain a teacher but became the puppet in the hands of the politicians.

The White party was defeated because of its bad deeds and poor performance but it ascribed the defeat to the teachers. The leaders were transferred to far-off places. Tara was transferred to Kanga, the remotest end of the state.

The Blue Party came in power. It too lost some seats in by-elections; the wrath for such loss fell on the teachers. The Masters and lecturers were transferred out of the district, and the Junior Teachers out of the *tehsil*. The teachers became homeless en masse. For them the year of partition of the country repeated. They became refugees again. Tara had just returned after undergoing the first punishment of transfer. He was transferred again."

Karmi said, "Tara, the government has transferred all the teachers; all of them could not be bad. Everyone has been punished. Is the government teachers' union unable to stop the revengeful transfers?"

Tara gave her the factual position. "No, it is not able, as they are divided and there are so many teachers' unions... The internal disunity has made the unions lifeless."

"The teachers should realize this that without unity nothing can be achieved."

Tara got lost in thoughts when Karmi said this.

The Blue Party, after making the teachers homeless, compelled them to think of unity. They started feeling as if there had been a tremor. Yes it was a tremor for the teaching class; family life was disrupted. The husband was at one place and the wife at another and their children somewhere else.

The revengeful approach of the Blue party upset the very educational system. It was big blow to the economic condition of the teachers. They were not able to bear that blow. The shake-up brought teachers to their senses. Though holding different political views, they got prepared to forge unity. They only needed leadership. The teachers started thinking, "Such whirlwinds would continue to come, and the way to safety lies only in unity."

The question of unity dominated the teachers' thinking. Tara initiated the move for unity in his school. He said to his colleagues, "Dear brethren, we had become hand tools of the political leaders as the unity of the G.T.U[52] is broken. We are suffering the consequences. Our families have been uprooted, one member of the family at one place, and the other at another. How would we bring up our children? How would we educate them? Now is the time to get united and start the battle against government tyranny."

The teachers agreed with Tara's reasoning. The unity movement started at Dhudi-ke (in Moga District). Four teachers used to take leave in turns and went on two motor cycles. Every day they covered five to seven schools. Gradually the unity movement gathered momentum. When it was seen that the teachers favored unity very strongly, a team of four teachers was constituted in every district. They went round all the schools in Punjab like a whirlwind, and this became a strong movement for unity. A convention was decided to be held at Philaur. This was also given good coverage by the media.

There was a very hectic activity for unity, even more than the Assembly/Parliament elections. The question of maintaining their own identity for the teachers of leftist/Rightest groups cropped up. They explained their election manifestoes— the left declared, "If leadership comes into our hands, we will have the transfers stopped and the norms for transfers made."

---

52   government teachers union

The teachers of the rightist views talked of increase in salaries. The Teachers of both the camps struggled hard to get the leadership of the Government teachers' union.

The day of the unity convention arrived. By eleven o'clock there was a huge gathering. It was bound to be, as there was the confrontation between the right and left. The hall was full to capacity, and it became difficult to accommodate all the teachers. Therefore, the stage was set in the school compound.

Tara had initiated the move for unity, and he took the stage and appealed to the teachers to take their seats. Their leaders occupied their seats at the stage.

Tara proposed the name of a colleague for stage secretary. Voices were raised from the audience, "Tara will preside over the convention and do the job of Stage Secretary as well—, no other person on the stage is allowed."

Tara placed the proposal before the house. It was unanimously approved. He started the proceedings. Another proposal came: –"the leaders should tender resignation as presidents of their groups and come down from the stage."

It was passed as well.

The Presidents of different factions tendered their resignations, left the stage, and sat down among the teachers. It was a very peaceful atmosphere. There was a wave of joy all around. The teachers raised slogans very loudly. If anyone wanted to say something else, he was not permitted.

Tara placed before the house the basic principles for unity:

A teacher on the payroll of the government on Election Day will be entitled to vote and become a member of the Government Teachers Union by paying one rupee.

It was passed with one voice.

2) A presidium will be formed by all the elected district presidents and decisions be taken by a majority vote.

"The resolution is passed unanimously."

3) The elections for the district and block presidents will be held on the same day and at the same time— – a voter will be given two votes, one for the district president and the other for the block president.

The resolution is passed

4) Annual elections of the Government Teachers Union will be held every year. Electoral disputes will be decided by the presidium.

"Passed….passed…..passed."

Tara was unanimously made the convener till the elections were held and it was also decided that he would conduct the elections. Nomination papers for the district and block presidents would be received next Sunday at Doaba College, Jalandhar.

The organization of two hundreds thousands, Government Teachers Union came into existence. A sum of two hundreds thousands rupees was collected by the union to meet its expenses. Twelve presidents were elected in the twelve districts of Punjab— – nine were of the leftist views and three were rightists.

The newspapers gave the news of the Unity of Government Teachers Union in headlines. B.B.C. praised the development with comments-: "G.T.U. has come up as an organization in the world where the voter, while casting his/her vote, gives Rupee-one with it."

Elections of the G.T.U. were held in a peaceful atmosphere, and no objection was raised anywhere. The teachers gave a proof of their high moral character.

On the other hand, the elections of the government are conducted by the Election Commissioner, ; when all the arrangements are made, the police is present in a big way, still fair elections are not held; there is firing, murders, and kidnapping of candidates. Foul means are resorted to at every step and money flows like water. Bogus voters cast their votes, and the real are denied. The trucks load of bogus voters are caught and handed over to the police but no one is punished, and those going to file a report are murdered.

The Government Teachers Union became a role model for the entire country, and, even during the emergency days of 1975, annual elections were held without any problem.

The unity of teachers triumphed. Government bowed before their unity and the transfers were cancelled. Tara returned home. He was able to tell his mother, "The teacher has woken up. He does the teaching work and he will be, no longer, a tool in the hands of political parties."

FIFTY-FOUR

Bindery's grandmother said to her husband, "we have already lived our life. How long would we go on saying – 'do this, don't do this'? Let the girl live her own life and do what she wants. She wants to meet her father, let her. If she marries a teacher, let her. Why should we annoy anybody?"

"Laccho's Mom, having experienced the onslaughts of time, I too have come to senses. Children should not be coerced. Let them do as they wish. We tried to impose our will on Laccho. What did we gain? Had she been well educated, she would have understood the meaning of family life and would not have died an untimely death. We had no time for her! We kept busy in making money. Did the money earned by us served any purpose? My conscious now curses me.

"Now we should move with the time. We harm ourselves with false prestige and harm others too, call Bindery."

Bindery came in... Her forehead was furrowed with rage.

Her grandfather said in an undertone, "I have realized now, my child, that we should not impose our will on you. Marry the boy of your choice and live your life."

Hearing the happy words from her grandfather she clung to him and said, "Tara is an ideal boy, grandpa. He loves me from the core of his heart. A.D.C. is an officer. Most of the officers go off their head inebriated with power. They cease to be good husbands"

"You can try to search your father also so that I can return to him his trust. Let him take care of his family, his house. I will devote some time to help the old people. " He expressed his desire to go to the Senior Citizens Home.

Bindery accompanied by Tara and Karmi went to Abohar to seek her father's blessings. Paul had least expected that his daughter would ever meet him. As she reached there, she bowed and touched his feet he took her as Tara's wife. He turned towards Tara and said in surprise, "O Loafer boy! You have married keeping it secret from me."

The three of them laughed heartily. Karmi said, "What an irony of fate! The father had forgotten his own daughter."

Noting that he had got bewildered, Karmi said to him, "Paul, your prayers have been heard by Almighty. She has been sent to light the lamp of joy in your barren life!"

Paul tried hard to think and then Bindery's recognition dawned on him, "oh, Bindery, you have grown up so much!" He embraced her tightly, and forgot all the misery of the past.

Paul was not in robust health. The miserable life as a dejected lover had reduced him to skeleton.

"Papa, you have suffered a great deal. I would not let you rot... Come with me to Ganganagar and live in your own house. Grandpa and grandma are going to the Old people's Home."

"This is also our house cum clinic. Where would my patients go? What would happen to them? "

Paul was a noted child specialist. He treated children taking keen interest. He derived pleasure in serving them and he was always in demand.

"I have understood life now, Bindery. The joy of living with your own earnings is boundless. Living in Ganganagar, I did not understand life being inebriated with money. Ill-gotten money was the cause of all my ills... I lost my job and lost my family. I will return to the same position if I go back there. I would like you to live here. It is your place to live, made for you by your father with honest earnings. There is a fragrance of life in every particle of this house as I have mingled myself with it."

Karmi said to Paul, "Bindery does not belong either to this house or to that. She will go to her own home now. It is not good for daughters to remain too much attached to their parental home. It is harmful and does not let them live peacefully in their in-law's house. Look for a suitable house for her, so that she can live there happily."

"Why should I find one when she has already found? Am I right, Bindery?" Paul took her in his fold and gave a kiss on her fore head.

She laughed and said, "You are absolutely right, Papa."

Tara held Bindery's arm and said, "You have met with your father now let us go home."

"Not in this way. You must come here as a bride groom, and I will go with my Dad's blessing in palanquin as a bride.'"

"Yes, you are right, my child,'" said Paul, feeling very happy.

"'Yes…how is Nandi, my child? What is she doing?"

"She is studying in college at Ganganagar."

"Oh, I have just forgotten. Paul, your father-in-law has invited you. You should go. He has forgotten the past. You should also forget. Let Bindery's marriage be performed there, in your old home," suggested Karmi.

"Let me make some arrangement for my patients. Bindery will stay with me till then."

Tara and Karmi left Bindery with her father and returned. Paul's deserted house bloomed up.

After a few days, Bindery returned to Ganganagar with her father. She rang the bell. The maid opened the gate. Her grandparents stood before them, their heads lowered. The mother-in-law held a small bowl of oil to be poured on both sides of the gate. She poured oil and welcomed her son-in-law.

Nandi came from behind and embraced her father. He got so emotional that he could not utter a word. Caressing his daughter, he took her in his arms.

The father-in-law said to his son-in-law most humbly, "forgive me, my son, for what has happened in the past. Now you should stay here, we are leaving for the senior citizens home. We will serve the needy there."

Sipping tea, they talked about Bindery's marriage.

Her grandfather said, "We have made all the preparations for the marriage. I have deposited half a million in their names and each has been given a house too... Now look after your family and allow us to go. "

Paul said respectfully, "Why should you go? Convert this home into Nursing Home. People would bless you. Let the girls build their homes with their own earnings. The joy that one feels by one's own earnings cannot be had from a gift."

"We have to marry off Bindery but not with much fanfare. In the olden days, dowry was exhibited, but now along with dowry, the people and their money are also exhibited.

"Marriage is the meeting of two minds, a tie of love. But now people have made money the main thing and the girl as part of property. Marriage is a secondary thing. They may be happy or unhappy; they cannot get out of the stranglehold. That is why it is common that brides are burnt and the Police justify it as 'a stove explosion.' We will not ape the people. We have to tie the husband and wife in bond of love."

To give the final touches to Tara and Bindery's love story, they performed the ideal marriage. No dowry was given; no gift was taken. After the marriage ceremony, they had their meals at their residence.

Bindery and Tara visited their grandparents again, they entrusted the money deposited in her name to them, and said, "Here is your money. Spend this on the Old People's Home."

Bindery went to her in-laws, and her sister went to live with her father at Abohar.

"Tara, where do you propose to go for Honeymoon?"

"We will celebrate the honeymoon at our tube-well. You will see there God prevailing all-around."

FIFTY-FIVE

"We are married now, Tara, and I wonder, how have we been living without each other so long? Now the life without each other seems to be a drag. Have you ever thought of about Mom and Dad, who live without their spouse? They have no life of their own." Bindery gave Tara a new idea to think over.

"I never thought of this problem, Bindery. You are right. They are not living their lives; they are just waiting for their deaths. Life is incomplete without the life partner. Life is meaningful with husband and wife living together. Man is a social animal; he cannot live alone. In the West, people don't go by the age—, old or young, they always seek company.

"Take the case of dad. If he has a heart attack at night, there is no one to take care of him. If the life partner is at hand, life can be saved. You know what happened to Angola, our neighbor? He lived alone. He had strained relations with his wife. He had a stroke at night. He fainted and passed urine and stool in bed. After a day the neighbors suspected something wrong, and they broke open the door. Now he is in the Nursing Home at the mercy of others. His wife too is not happy. She is confined to bed in her daughter's house. Had they been living together, they could have shared each other's agony, and things would not have come to such a pass."

"Tara, loneliness gives birth to worry, and then there is a brain hemorrhage or heart failure.

"Instead of getting paralyzed it is better if they marry and live a happy life."

As they were talking, Paul came in. He said, "I thought, being off day, I should meet with you. I had spent my life in vain, and if God has been kind to bring us together, I can't do without seeing you. Nandi is missing you more badly than me. I have come to take you with me so that you could get her admitted to the next class."

Bali went in for preparing tea.

She brought in tea with a plate of sweets and also called Udhe. The family got together. They made chit-chat as they sipped tea. "Give me a rupee, Udhe, for seeing my face,"[53] Bindery teased her *'devar'* (husband's younger brother).

Udhe handed her a two-rupee note, saying, "One Rupee for unveiling your face and another Rupee is for sitting in your lap. Let me sit now."

Bindery shied and said, "No, this is not acceptable." But Udhe advanced towards her to sit in her lap. There was a peal of laughter. They talked merrily for an hour or so. After taking tea, Bali and Udhe moved out of the room, leaving behind the newly-weds and their mother and father.

---

53   It is a custom that after marriage the brother-in-law gives one Rupee for seeing face, and one Rupee to sit in her lap

In order to break the silence, Tara said, "Dad, Bindery worries quite a lot about you. She says, – 'my Dad has been passing through an agony all alone for a very long time….' "

"'I have lived my life, good or bad, and this is a second phase of life, I have to face loneliness for the sake of you people.

"Children have their own lives and you have your own. So many people are sitting like you, awaiting death. What a punishment it is! Is it life, Dad? Just think over it. Expressing their opinion Tara and Bindery stood up, "Tomorrow is our working day and we have to get up early."

Karmi, sitting with him said, "Paul, you have not understood them. The children wish you to marry and settle down."

He laughed and then said, "Kammo! They said to both of us. You are also sailing in the same boat. You too are passing through the same agony. The where about of your husband is not known? Nobody knows whether he is alive or dead. It is just possible he may have brought another woman. You have been wasting your life waiting for him."

"It is quite different, Paul, in the case of a woman. If a woman crosses the threshold, man considers it an act of unfaithfulness. Society does not let her live; even if she just talks to another man, they make a mountain of a mole hill. This is the punishment our society inflicts on woman.

"These are all the old notions. If a man becomes unfaithful to his wife and brings in another wife, why should she not remarry? He says *'divorce'* thrice, and divorce is complete. He relishes woman like mango fruit and throws her like its seed in the dust-bin. *He ruins her life without giving any reason.* He himself does not feel satisfied with one marriage, and goes on marrying again and again.

"Let us change the rotten society, Karmi, and bring in a revolution in woman's life." Paul was still hopeful that Karmi would give her consent.

"My husband is alive, Paul. Worshiping him till his last breath is my foremost duty as an Indian woman."

"Karmi, how long will you bear the injustice meted out to you by your husband, deserting for no fault of yours? You are setting a bad example for other women. You should have divorced him and started a new life."

"Paul, the woman is an embodiment of sacrifice for the sake of her husband, for her family, and for the society at large. These institutions exist due to her contribution."

"Karmi, you talk of 'husbands', you know some husbands are cruel and bring misery to their wives: some expect her to sell her body.

You talk of sacrifice for family it is the institution of family where daughters-in-law are burnt alive for the demand of dowry.

"You fear 'society'; it is the society where a virgin girl is married to lifeless statue of God. Her life is lost in entertaining the priests. Society drives her to lead the life of a prostitute in the service of God.

Karmi, please visit Pakistan or Afghanistan and see what the Society and the Highest Court give in justice to the raped woman. If she fails to prove herself innocent by giving the four witnesses of men, she is stoned to death.

"In the African Sub-continent, women's condition is still worse. They are bought and sold like property. The Parents raise their daughters not as human beings but as commercial crops."

Karmi had no answer.

FIFTY-SIX

One day Bali was lying in bed, covering herself with a sheet. She had cooked food but did not eat. She told Karmi, "I have no appetite."

A suspicion arose in Karmi's mind, and she asked, "Why are you retching?"

"Do not torment me unnecessarily. Let me sleep," Bali replied curtly, and again covered her face.

Karmi called Bali's friend, next door, over the wall, "Tari! Your friend is lying in bed but tells nothing about what ails her... What should I do? She is unwell and I am worried to the bone."

"You should not worry, aunt, unnecessarily. It may be a problem of indigestion. Give her tea boiled with aniseed. She would get well."

Tari reassured Karmi in this way, and herself went to Bali and said, "Get up and do some work. Why are you pretending illness? Aunt has gotten worried, to see you lying down."

Instead of laughing at what her friend was saying, Bali started crying. She said nothing and stepped towards the bath room, as retching had begun. Tari also got suspicious. She followed her into the bathroom and said, "You are vomiting. Have you done something wrong?"

Bali started crying bitterly and said nothing.

"You must tell me instead of crying like this," Tari insisted.

"On the night of Lohri festival[54]…," Bali related the entire incident, related with her rape. In order to keep secret from Karmi Tari went out looking the other way. She did not want to let Bali's Mom know about her rape. That would cause storm in their home.

Tari's going back quietly, added to Karmi's suspicion.

She got terribly upset. Next day, she took Bali to the lady doctor, despite her initially refusing to go. The doctor diagnosed that she had been pregnant for two months. Bali said nothing but started crying again. Karmi felt like spitting venom but did not rebuke her. Bali told her everything when they returned home. How long could she hide it?

"It was during the Lohri night, when I and Tari went to attend the celebration. There was a huge crowd around the bonfire. People from the whole village had assembled. We sat there for about an hour and sang songs. The boys continued with their *bhangra* dance. Some drunkards also came there and started shouting. Tari continued to sing and did not leave. I, judging the atmosphere turning tense,

---

54   Lohri is a winter festival. The whole village gathers around the fire; they dance and sing together.

walked toward home. I had hardly come half the distance when a car stopped close to me. Someone put a piece of cloth on my face, and made me unconscious. I don't know what happened after that. When I regained consciousness, I was lying naked below the waist on the road side. I got terribly upset. Then I took courage to cover myself and walked home. The outer door was still open, as I had left before going. I came in and lay in bed. I was so much scared that I did not have the courage to tell anyone."

"Did you recognize any of those boys?"

"They had covered their faces. I have some doubt about Minister's Kuku."

Karmi was a wise lady. She owned her mistake and said to herself, "You have erred. You did not consider her a grown-up girl. She should have been married at the proper age. Being a mother, you never cautioned her about guarding herself against any pitfalls, nor do they do so in the schools or college."

She fell on the bed, and got lost in thoughts, "Open nudity is shown in the cinema houses and on T.V. Obscene songs can be heard on the cassettes played everywhere.

"Has anyone ever thought of the bad effects of all this and that? If we do not understand the sexual problems faced by the grown-up boys and girls, and do not help them, is it their fault? Actually, we ourselves create the atmosphere of promiscuity.

"We feel shy of telling a daughter about her sexuality. The result is before us, and then we go to the extent of killing her.

"If a boy tries to violate anyone's modesty, we do not bother and keep quite. And in case of a girl, she has to suffer with no fault of hers.

"Had Bali been married at the proper time, she would have gone to her house and lived her own life...— but I had absolutely no money to marry her off?! It is her father's fault. He kept producing children. He should have brought them up, educated them, and married them, and then could have gone anywhere he liked. I did whatever I could do as a single parent. What more can I do?

"And more than this, the blame lies with society where dowry is a symbol of social prestige. If there was no question of dowry, she would have been married timely. The 'leprosy of dowry' is spreading day by day. It is not known how many 'Balis'' pyres instead of their palanquins go out of their houses.

The political leaders have been singing songs of democracy for over sixty years. If our daughters' and sisters' blooming youth is sacrificed at the altar of dowry, our government too is to blame. Why does it enact toothless laws? The laws are not framed to be implemented, but only to hoodwink the public. We used to hear that on the attainment of freedom, a goat and a tiger would drink water at the same place.

Drinking water at the same place is a far cry: the tiger is tearing apart her kids too. Nobody is ashamed of it.

"The consequence of rape is suffered by women, and the rapists move about freely and arrogantly."

Karmi had been lamenting till Saturday, when Tara was expected back. Tara did not come, but Udhe came in. There was a hushed atmosphere in the house. He saw the eyes of his mother and sister swollen. He could not keep silent. He asked her, "Mom, What is this mourning in the house? Both of you have been crying."

His mother remained silent. He looked towards Bali. She too lowered her head. Karmi conducted herself in a formal way and gave him tea. After taking tea he went out to meet his pals.

He returned home drunk at dusk. How had he come to know? He got after Bali as soon as he returned. He said furiously, "Whose sins are you carrying? Just let me know, who is he? ...You have tarnished our image. We can't show our face to anyone."

Bali kept quiet. She kept shedding tears. She did not have the courage to tell him, afraid she was of the cruel ones. Udhe was insistent on knowing the name of the rapist. He drew closer to her and thundered, *"Why do you want me to kill you?"*

Bali shrieked with fear. As she heard the noise, Karmi rushed in. She held Udhe by the arm and dragged him in. She said in panic, "Why are you making a noise for the world to hear about the tragic happening? Cannot you talk in an undertone?"

"Mom, I am dying of shame, and you are asking me to speak in an undertone! It is already known to the world….This girl has cut off our nose. And she tells nothing. What should I do? Where should I go? … O my God! Where is the well into which I should jump?

"I should know from her who has dared play with our honor! She should name him. I will suck his blood…. Now she is sobbing."

"Ask her if she tells you; otherwise I will…."

"What do you mean by "otherwise"? What will you do? Will you kill her? I tell you who was he. Go and suck his blood.…" Bali placed her hand on Karmi's mouth, "No, Mom, no. Why do you want the entire family to get exterminated? We will not tell him."

Not only Bali, but everyone was afraid of Kuku. This type of high-handedness and cruelty was a routine with the Kukus. No one gave an inkling of the wrong done to him or her and just pocketed it.

Karmi could not restrain speaking the truth to Udhe, "Why do you think of killing her? She is not to blame in any way. Only we are blameworthy. We did not marry her in time. We just put her to work. What do you know where the money came from that had to be paid to the creditors every month? She worked for us, and you studied. Tara had been studying earlier than you."

After Karmi did the plain speaking, Udhe mellowed. He said calmly, "If we keep quiet, Mom, the world would not let us live. They will point their fingers at us... We will have to live in shame. It is better for me to die rather than to live a shameful life….. I am looking at her face and if she does not tell me I will—….."

Noting his fury, Karmi said, "Just listen to me! If you raise your finger at her, you too will face the result. If I have been bearing your misconduct, I will have to bear her bad experience also. You could have said all this rightfully, if you yourself were clean. No one is thinking about Bali, the victim, but only about society.

"Let the people say, whatever they want to. I and not the society have to make a decision to punish her. The people would say she has tarnished our image, and we should kill her….' I would not do that. If the girl cannot retaliate, it does not mean that we should kill her. Scores of people, considering themselves as saviors of society, are wandering about. People like *Kuku and Kaka* go about victimizing our daughters and sisters. It is not known how many girls do they rape every day? We come to know only those cases that are reported in the press—. – A German girl in Chandigarh, a Russian girl in Goa, a Japanese girl in Kashmir, the entire world knows about them. Where are those saviors then? These 'saviors' are real rapists. Today Bali has also become their victim. Because she is your sister, your eyes have opened.

"With whom will you grapple with all yourself? It is for the entire society to deal with these *Kukus/ Kakas*"

Udhe went in and sat down helplessly, waiting for Tara.

Tara reached home at about eight in the afternoon. He was dead tired. No one thought it proper to talk to him. He took his bath, had his meal, and went to sleep. As he got up next morning, mother and son started whispering. Udhe woke up late, had a cup of tea, and sat down near Tara.

"Have you heard, Tara, what Bali has done?"

"I have heard. We are educated people, and let us solve the problem as the educated ones do. It does not behoove us making noise. Mom settles the disputes of the entire village. Let us also leave this to mom, and do as she tells us to do. Bali is not a stranger; she is our own sister. We have to think about her future also. We would not do anything in haste that might cost her future and make people laugh at our foolishness." Tara tactfully handled Udhe, and the atmosphere in the house calmed down.

As Bali was sitting alone, Karmi said to her, "You have been such a wise girl, my child. How did this senseless thing happen, making us lose our face?"

Bali felt hurt at what her mother said, and started crying bitterly. She said, "I will not let you lose your face…do not worry!"

Karmi got unnerved. , thinking, "it will be terrible if she jumps into a well or does something else. She got up and brought a glass of cold water from inside and asked Bali to take. She sipped it and put down the glass.

Karmi kissed her forehead, Bali calmed down. Udhe came in and said to his mother, "I have found out...Sitting quietly would not do. I am going...." With these words, he rushed out. A boy on a motor bike was waiting for him outside. Tara ran after him, followed by Karmi, but in vain; they could not reach him.

FIFTY-SEVEN

Udhe kept on thinking, '"Mom is in the wrong. You would not be doing any good by forgiving the culprits. It will encourage them to do it again. It will be more harmful to file complaint with the police. It will be another mistake. If any victim ever reported she had repented. The police added to her woes. They themselves resorted to raping her. She had been compelled to commit suicide.

"People are never in the wrong. It is 'Kukus' doing. Nikka settled an old score with the help of Kuku. If I keep quiet now, they will not let us live in peace. What will Bali think? 'My brothers are calling themselves valiant fighters.' What have we done for her in taking revenge?

"Keeping quiet won't help. I will take revenge. It will be a tit for tat."

Thinking of all this and that, he reached the den of the Maoists.

The Maoists embraced him. It was a godsend opportunity for them. They told him that it was a case of rape; it is Kuku who did it. Acting against Kuku would mean confrontation with the government. But the fight against the government is not an easy job. You have to join our Militant cadre and set your own example to mobilize the people.

"When government fails to do justice, people resort to other ways to take revenge, ultimately they join us."

They told Udhe plainly, "If you want to take revenge be ready to make all sorts of sacrifice."

Tara kept quiet for some time and started thinking of all the consequences. One Maoist said, "It is very difficult to give up all hope to live. But revenge is not possible if you hide in your mother's lap, and we get killed for your sake. It is not a small thing, taking revenge against Kuku. Everyone hides his face when the time to make a sacrifice comes, because life is so dear, my friend."

"Alright, I shall join your cadre and you do your job."

The Maoists were not so powerful, at that time, as to be able to punish Kuku. For action they deputed two boys to go with Udhe.

The daredevils had not yet done anything except just preparing the plan, when the intelligence got the hint. Because of the danger of terrorism in Punjab, the intelligence was at work in right earnest. The police nabbed three of them in daylight. They were kept in the torture cell in Amritsar for a week. On the first day, they tied their hands and legs, powdered fine sugar on their bodies, and made them sit near an ants' colony... The prisoners cried the whole day but admitted nothing. The Next day they were suspended in the well, heads down. They fainted, but revealed nothing. A day after that, they were held by the hair and dipped in water turn by turn. They confessed, "We were going to kill Kuku"

Still the police could not recover the weapons. In fact, they did not have any. The weapons would have been delivered to them at the time of 'action'. That was a different party charged with the responsibility of delivering arms. Both the parties, the one to take action and the other to deliver the arms, did not know each other.

A few days later, one of them, Bawa Bant, was killed in a 'police encounter'. His eyes had been taken out, the finger nails been pulled and the starved face looked like that of a kitten. He was in such a terrible shape, that one shuddered to look at him. The whole matter was in the air.

The police had planned to make up another 'encounter' to kill all three of them

The news spread like wild fire. People besieged the police station. The Government got nervous lest the infuriated mob should set the police station on fire. Udhe and one of his pals were let off.

After being thrashed mercilessly, Udhe returned home.

Karmi reasoned with him, "Rape cannot be revenged by force of arms. It is not easy, for avenging, single-handedly. *The Revenge is* taken by the people only. Our job is to awaken the people. The battle for justice would not end at Bali. It has begun with Bali."

Karmi was still not sure of Udhe's change of mind— – she knew about his anger. He could still harm the girl.

Karmi broached the subject of Bali's future in the family meeting, "Some people know about what happened to Bali, and many still do not know. Find some needy match and let us marry her off."

Bali felt humiliated and had no interest in their talk. She had not slept for many days. She stood up and, wanted to have some sleep upstairs. As she was ascending the stairs, her foot slipped. She collapsed, and fainted. She was rushed to the hospital. Her life was saved, but the baby in her womb died.

After a couple of months, Bali's family again discussed about her future. Tara suggested, "Everybody knows about the rape. No one seems to be agreeable, *Neela* may agree. We should ask him" Then he said to his sister, "Bali, you have to live your life. If you are willing, we can ask Neela."

Bali kept quiet.

Udhe protested, "As he is a weaver's son people would talk about us in many ways."

"Let them talk. Is there anything bad in it? I will regard him a great man if he accepts Bali. If we find another boy, where is the guarantee that he would keep her? The incidence of rape does not remain a secret," said Tara.

"I like your suggestion, my son. Neela is the right person. He would be able to keep her. His handloom work is not bad. The sons of Jats do not earn as much as he does. What do we have to gain from a Jat, if he behaves badly later on?"

All the members of family agreed. When the question of approaching the boy arose, Bali protested, "what wrong have I done to be hitched to an uneducated man? Like other people, you too have regarded me as rubbish to be thrown at the heap. I have not done the rape. I have been raped. You failed to punish the rapist, and now you are going to punish me. You will get rid of your responsibility by hitching me to a weaver's son, and I will have to undergo punishment for life."

"What do you want," asked her mother.

"I want you not to push me out of the house. The money that you want to spend on my marriage should be used on a training course. I will do B.Sc. in Nursing and stand on my own legs."

That day the meeting of the United Front was held in Kartar's village. The proceedings of the last meeting were read out and passed unanimously. The meeting started with the speech of the Secretary, Paul: -

"...India has been grappling with the problem of corruption already. Now adulteration has become the order of the day. No food article is fit for human consumption, milk is artificially made with urea, fruit and vegetables are injected with toxic drug to supply early to the market. Even the water is not pure, it contains urea; the life of the people has become hell. But the more important thing is to save the farmers, the backbone of country, from the moneylenders. Now Kartar will give us the report how that problem is more harmful than the adulteration."

Kartar said, "Benarsi does the money lending business in our village. He has no license or other concomitants. He shows correct rate of interest in papers, but in practice he charges a very high rate of interest. He has maintained two separate ledgers. He charges a reasonable rate from well-to to-do borrowers to show his fare business; for others his rate of interest is exceptionally high, and breaks the law. He does not depend on his Ledger alone. He keeps the thumb impressions on blank papers, gets attachment order on these basis. Money makes the mare go in the court too. He greases the palms and obtains attachment orders. The poor farmer cannot afford to hire the lawyer even. Most of the farmers under debt are committing suicide and the government is not checking the high-handedness of money lenders. I have verified it.

"There are a few well-to-do families in every village and the overwhelming majority is of the poor. The problem is very serious. It calls for our immediate attention. We must do something. We should teach a lesson to some crooked money lenders. Let us first catch Benarsi red-handed, take his ledger and blank papers with the thumb impression of borrowers in our possession, and then a garland of shoes be put around his neck and a procession be taken out. If he is taught a good lesson, others will come on in line."

Some conservative members suggested that it was a good case of fraud. Do not resort to direct action that will involve police in money lenders' favour.

Kartar, who himself was a lawyer, contradicted them, "What would you gain by making out a case of fraud? The case will be deferred again and again, and no decision will be given. We will get entangled into litigation. A better solution would be at the village level. Teach him a good lesson and set an example for others. It will tarnish his image, and his business will be adversely affected. He will be set right."

The president intervened in their discussion, "If the United Front also limits itself only to checking papers, we will be no better than government servants. Here is the question of the United Front's prestige. We should inquire about the real position from other sources in the vicinity and take action quickly against the defaulter."

Gulzar said, "Besides professional money lenders the corrupt businessmen also aggravate the problem of Agricultural debt. They mix poor quality of seed with high yielding seed. They also adulterate Fertilizer and Crop Medicines. It increases cost and lowers income of the farmer and thereby pushes him into indebtedness.

"The sowing time has not yet come. Of course, I have cautioned the small and big businessmen that anyone found selling adulterating seed, fertilizers and insecticides, will not be forgiven. If any farmer commits suicide on the ground of a poor yield due to above causes a case of murder will be registered against the men responsible for increasing his debt." ,

President delivered her presidential address, "The practice of adulteration is done at the instance of ministers at the top level and government officials at the local level. The dealers are selling adulterated seed, fertilizers, insecticides and fungicide, bribing the officials locally.

We should lay siege to the corrupt ministers too and expose their malpractices with the Business Houses. Official machinery will automatically fall in line.

The Farmers should raise their high quality seed themselves.

"The farmers should become self-sufficient with the help of the Cooperative banks. They should meet their basic needs themselves and depend on the government only when there is no other way out. They should make use of the natural resources. They should prepare gas by using cattle dung. Those who can afford may use solar energy. With a little effort, they can produce gas and power themselves. This will also help in decreasing pollution."

All the members agreed with the president's views, and the responsibility of producing 'Gobar Gas' (Cow dung gas) was given to Hari Singh. He inspected the gobar gas plant at a village in Bathinda District. He raised loan from the Cooperative Bank on behalf of Panchayat and installed a community Gobar Gas Plant. Two laborers were employed to collect cow dung from the village houses. They brought the push carts full of dung to the gas plant and put it into the well. The people who could afford they got the plant fixed up individually in their own houses. In six months' the electricity needs of all the households were met. Moreover, they got natural manure and so were able to produce fruit and vegetables for themselves.

Encouraged by this experiment, the United Front had the gas plants installed in many other villages.

FIFTY NINE

Bali completed her B.Sc. Nursing and got a job in the hospital, close to her house. It helped Karmi to enjoy her company. But how long could she keep the daughter with her? She started thinking of her marriage. Karmi advertised in the newspaper for a suitable match. Many letters were received. When she sent her reply with her photograph, making it clear - "dowry seekers may please excuse," she got no further response... Some dropped after knowing about her rape and others because of no dowry. When Karmi saw that her daughter, though beautiful and well versed in all virtues, was unable to get a suitable match, she widened the circle for Bali's marriage. She dropped the condition of caste and class.

She received so many letters from tailors, goldsmiths, and others, and Karmi was surprised, "There are more educated people in other castes. All the castes had advanced ahead of the Jats. The Jats had with them nothing but their arrogance of caste."

She started negotiation with a Ramgarhia doctor. The boy-Bant Singh was ten years older than the girl, but he was an American citizen. While Jats demanded not less than a million rupees in cash besides dowry, the Ramgarhia was ready to accept her, only in the dress she was wearing. He saw many virtues in the girl. Karmi informed him about her rape, because later on, such things might get complicated. He laughed and said, "She is a wise girl who did not commit suicide and started studying further."

The date of marriage was fixed. A week before the marriage, Bant came to their house. He took a letter out of his pocket and placed it before Karmi, saying, "What sort of revenge are you out to take?" The letter did not bear anyone's address; it was typed –:

Innocent bird,

You have been entrapped. Bali is already married. She has had an abortion also. Her husband is living in America. As he had gone there illegally, he could not take her with him. This marriage is being performed only to go there. As soon as she lands in America, she will go to her house and you will be left behind, holding the bouquet.

Yours Sincerely,

Karmi was flabbergasted on reading the letter. "Someone has done this out of enmity. They are after me like anything. Now they have not spared even my daughter. You need not believe me. You can inquire from anyone in the village. You will know the truth."

Bant thought that if she had been married the Registrar's record would show this. He went to the office straightaway, to obtain a copy of Bali's marriage registration. He said to the clerk, "I need it just now."

"Apply for it today; you will get it after a week."

Bant put a hundred rupee note in the clerk's pocket and made his application 'Express.'. He started rummaging the records, leaving aside everything. Bali's marriage had not been entered anywhere. He wrote down, "There is nothing on record to show that Bali, daughter of Bhag Singh son of Didar Singh, is married." Bant was satisfied, and the date of marriage was confirmed.

Karmi performed a simple marriage. Only five persons came with the marriage party, and they took away the bride after the marriage ceremony. It was a time-saving and a money-saving way with the appreciation of all the sane people.

Ordinarily, the cases for migrating to America were cleared in three months, but in Bali's case, even after a year, there was no sign of her going. Bali remained quite upset. Doubts cropped up in their minds. : Karmi, too, worried a lot and wondered whether Bali's case had been processed at all or not. On inquiry, it was revealed that Dr. Bant's previous marriage had not yet been annulled. Divorce papers had not yet been issued. They had to wait impatiently for another six months.

It was a lucky day for Bali when she received visa. Ticket was purchased, and she left for America within fifteen days. After giving a send-off to her daughter, Karmi thought, "I was going to hitch my daughter to an uneducated and poor boy, and now with her courageous and firm stand, she has reached America. She has been married to a doctor. Her virtues and education washed off the stigma of rape."

The doctor earned lot of money, but he had to work day and night. Although Bali had done her Nursing in India yet she had to pass the American test too. She passed the test in the first attempt and got a job in the hospital, sometimes she had to work for two shifts. She attended to household chores also.

Bant's mother had died, and his father lived with them. In addition to her husband, she had to serve his father too. Doctor's first wife had left him for this reason only. In a way she had been called upon to cater to the needs of two husbands. This problem was faced by Bali also. Her-father-in-law was a drunkard, and, when dead drunk, he did not care for anything except his lust. Bali proved to be wiser. When Dad sat to drink, she slipped out on one excuse or the other.

Bali complained to the doctor about this problem, and he kept quiet. Some days passed, but how long before the evil day could be warded off. ? The same complaining and lamenting started. The doctor had returned home, dead tired, blamed Bali, "you are telling a lie and raising an accusing finger at my father…"

Bali kept quiet. Her father-in-law wanted to take the benefit of her silence and started acting foolishly;

she gave a call to 911, "my father-in-law…." The police reached there. They found Bant's Dad dead drunk and her complaint was found to be genuine. He was ordered to go out of house for two hours.

The doctor was not at home. It was snowing outside. Wherever he stepped outside, he got stuck knee-deep. The doctor returned home in the afternoon; he did not find his father there. He was undergoing punishment outside. Bant tried to slap Bali angrily. Bali warned him, "Listen to me. There is no need to fight. If you want to live with me, you are welcome; otherwise file a divorce. Do not suffer yourself and make me suffer. Father-in-law is like my father, but when he trespasses the limits I have to keep him away"

When Bali said all this firmly, he mellowed down.

He went out, looked around. His father was laying half-conscious against the back wall of the house. He brought him in. He was set right with this punishment but his son did not. He harassed Bali every day on one pretext or the other.

Bali got pregnant in the course of time, and after that they lived happily, caring for each other. All the past grievances were forgotten.

One day Bant said to Bali, "If you bring your mother here, it would be very helpful. We can bring up our child easily.

Elections to the State Assembly were announced. The United Front members insisted on Karmi to be their candidate. Karmi had the past experience of confronting the mafia in the elections. She thought, "defeating them is an uphill task, it calls for a long drawn-out battle. It is to be fought not by Karmi coming to the fore by herself: There is the need to prepare a team to fight.

"The selection of a candidate should be done by the United Front. We will not commit this mistake like other parties. The political parties leave all decisions to be made by the leaders, who get sold. The mafia obtains tickets from them. We have to leave the decision on the members of United Front. We have to establish the convention of conducting elections for the selection of candidates within the party."

Kartar understood her point and said, "'What Ma'am is saying is correct. It is not an easy task to challenge the mafia and suffer its wrath. After the first elections, the mafia tried to grab her property. They were out to kill her younger son in a fake police encounter. Only the people of the area saved him.

Had the people not besieged the police station, the police would have killed him on the following night.

"The decision about the candidate should be taken through elections within the party. It will help in making a team. We should fight election as a team under her command.

"Not only our state— should the entire country follow this system to elect the proper candidates." *Kanwal,* an N.R.I., gave his opinion.

The primary elections of the United Front for selection of a candidate were contested by many. Karmi was also got convinced to participate. It was a neck-to to-neck fight between Karmi and Hari. Hari was supported by conservative people. As Karmi was an established leader, she won the primary election and became the common candidate of the United Front for the ensuing elections.

The Blue party had fielded its old candidate Shinder. Talking about him in her speech, Karmi said, "This is the man who broke Longowal-Rajiv Agreement and made Longowal the target of terrorists. Longowal signed a peace treaty to stem terrorism and save Punjab from burning.

"Shinder gave a misleading statement: Longowal sold Punjab to the Centre. The Terrorist shot him dead to make the agreement null and void. Shinder exploited the sentiments and got elected. He has the support of that Communal party who demolished the 'Babri' mosque and created conditions for riots.

The die-hard Hindus roasted the Muslims alive in the ovens.

"White party is supported by those communal forces that burnt the *Sikhs alive* in Delhi riots of 1984. Chain Brar is their candidate.

"If either of these two candidates wins the elections whatever is left of democracy will be decimated."

At the end, Karmi expressed her views, "we have seen how our country is being looted in the name of democracy. If you are pinning hope on them for doing any good to the country, it is like groping in the dark.

"To protect you against their machinations, the united fronts should be formed in all villages and towns all over the country.

"Now a single member of the mafia is leading the entire village by the nose. At the time of elections, wine is being distilled everywhere. Anyone can go there to drink. Police does not stop anyone. Their quota is fixed. Anyone can have hashish; opium eaters can have opium. Do you want to live like pigeons and keep your eyes shut, or to live like valiant fighters? Work for the success of the Front."

Gulzar reported, "The canvassing for the election has stopped, but the trading in votes has begun. There are hectic activities. The buyers and touts are doing their worst. The price of the vote has been rising high— one hundred, two hundred.

It was ten o'clock at night. The price rose to five hundred. Wads of notes were un-laden. The time for the throw of a hammer had arrived. ... The price of the vote rose to one thousand. Only one quarter of votes had yet to be sold. The candidates themselves reached the scene. The deal was struck by Shinder at two thousand, and even three thousand in certain localities.

We are gone, Madam. Our votes too have been bought. Our people have been enticed by paying those three thousand each. Do something."

Karmi called Udhe, "You were made the head of the Red Guards. Where have your guards gone? Our votes too have been sold."

"Our voters would not go anywhere, Mom. They will receive money from them and vote for you. You should relax." Udhe had worked out everything, as he said this to his mother very confidently.

But Karmi was not convinced. "Go and take care of our votes now. Do not get lax. It is your responsibility. Do something," Karmi **counseled Udhe.**

It was mid-night, still Udhe stepped out. Someone fired in the air. He had a hunting gun he fired twice in return. People went indoors. Neither the Blue Party supporters nor that of the White Party were seen anywhere.

The field was left to them, and the Red Guards only remained there. They had the spirit of sacrifice; they had an ideal before them. They had to seek a remedy to solve all the problems. Udhe had deputed Red Guards to protect their votes in all the villages.

They were able to bring back their solid votes or who had wavered.

Shinder came to know about the change in his vote bank. He could not sip water. He came out in a jeep full of his henchmen. The White party was also terribly shaken. Atmosphere got tense. The question was no longer that of winning or losing election, but of life and death.

Police was on duty all around. It was 8:00 A.M. Two long queues of the voters were formed, women in one queue, and men in the other. Polling started.

There was a huge crowd by mid-day. Fake voters came on trucks and buses to cast their votes. Red Guards apprehended them. Instead of stopping them, the Presiding Officer permitted them to cast votes. Red Guards complained to the Returning Officer, and they were caught red-handed. After some time, they were let off under political pressure.

Knowing that he was losing, Shinder fired in the air. People started to run in all directions. There was utter confusion. The ballot boxes were being grabbed. Police was trying their best but still the situation was getting out of control. A bullet struck Udhe. He was injured.

Karmi and her supporters took him to the hospital. He was admitted in the I.C.U. . . . .

The voting came to an end at 5:00 p.m. The boxes were sealed and deposited. The election parties of other booths continued depositing their boxes till mid-night. The room was sealed in the presence of S.D.M and guards took positions. Red Guards stayed with them even at the risk of their lives

Udhe's condition was worsening. Karmi remained by Udhe's side till the counting began. Blood transfusion was on, and treatment was being given, but the boy lay unconscious. Leaving Tara and others with him, she went to the Town Hall.

Karmi and Shinder were having equal votes as the counting was on. One went ahead by a few votes and then the other did likewise. At 5:00p.m., Karmi was ahead of Shinder by eight votes and then continued the lead. The counting concluded at half past eight. Karmi was winning, but under political pressure, Shinder was declared elected by one hundred and twelve votes.

After the counting, Karmi went back to the hospital. Udhe was taking his last breath when Karmi reached. The doctors tried their best to save his life but in vain. Fighting for democracy, Karmi sacrificed her son.

There were huge crowds all over. Heated slogans were being raised, "We will avenge the death of Udhe-Fight for Democracy will continue..." Karmi mellowed them, "You will kill one or two. The mafia will not be eliminated by your killing. Killing is not your job. Your job is to awaken the people. The people will take revenge; we have to just lead them... have some patience. You should be reasonable.

Nothing will be gained by getting violent; we would lose much. Organize the people under the flag of the United Front. Getting them organized is the only way to avenge Udhe's killing. Only then true democracy would be established."

Karmi was left alone in the whole world. The near and dear ones came and returned, after offering condolences and counseling her to bear the irreparable loss with fortitude. Tara and Bindery also went back to their places of work. With Udhe's support, she could have accepted even the greatest challenge. Udhe's death broke Karmi's back; she was a mother after all.

She tried to forget him and think of other things, like reading or taking up some other work, but left everything untouched. She did not like to do anything at all.

If someone came to see her she talked to him. But still her mind remained with her son, and she started crying. There was no life without her son. She was just pulling on.

Tara sent Bindery to stay with his mother for a month or so. Much less gauging the intensity of her pain, she remained glued to the T.V. Karmi did not like T.V. Her wound was tender, and she wanted seclusion.

Every daughter-in-law cannot develop good relationship with her mother-in-law. A week hardly passed, when Bindery held her purse and went back to her husband. She told him, "Mom does not talk to me properly. Her brow is always furrowed. I feel suffocated there."

Tara gazed at her face. What was she saying? He said to her calmly, "Bindery, you had gone there to help mother tide over the grief. She could feel easy if you got up early morning, served her tea in bed, took her to meet some relations and friends, talked to her sympathetically to blunt the edge of her grief, got her some book to read…, and she could have got re-engaged in day-to-day life.

"In fact, it is not your fault. You have been brought up without parents. You can't fathom the depth of a mother's agony. Your grandparents were of the old model, and you did not mix up with them much. You spent your time with your girlfriends. You learned from them how to enjoy life but not how to share grief."

Bindery felt offended on being told like that. She went in and lay down, covering her face. Tara could not bear her lying so much annoyed. He went to her to reconcile. He tried to pull the sheet off her face, but she flared up, "I am married to you, not to your mom, right"

Tara was wonder struck. He got lost into thoughts as he stood there, "Bindery has not regarded herself the daughter-in-law of this house. A pampered girl as she was, how could she have an idea of our pain?

How can she like her mother-in-law, who is smoldering like a damp dung cake?"

Bindery had gone. Karmi remembered her husband, "The news of Udhe's murder has appeared in the newspapers. Enemies have killed our son, a promising young leader of the United Front. He should have come back by now."

Howsoever hard she tried, she could not forget her son? That agony would go with her to death. "He was a hero of the time, who sacrificed his life for others. Even stones had cried at his demise. Why did his father's heart not melt? He should have come back to his senses on learning about the tragedy."

She heard a knock at the outer door. She felt as if the Subahdar had come. But how could she be so fortunate? Paul had come. He said to her, "Nandi has done her B.A., Kammo. His result was declared yesterday; Udhe had great attachment with me as if he were my own son. I have been thinking of marrying Nandi to Udhe. They would have made a very good match. But God willed otherwise. Nandi was never tired of talking about him. Now she goes on crying. What can be done? One cannot die with the dead, even though the intensity of pain is great. Has Bindery not come?"

"All of them came to me turn by turn and Bindery too. They have gone back to their respective places. Tara is trying to get himself transferred to the village school. Then it will be easy for me to pass the time."

"Well take care of your health. I am going. Nandi will be waiting for me."

"Tara was transferred but Bindery could not get a job. She had to do the household chores. She had never done this earlier, and whatever she did lacked wisdom. She put the lentils to boil, filled the cooker and made it tasteless, which did not go down the throat nor could it be thrown away. The chapattis baked by her too were over burned or half-baked, which swelled in the mouth. One day she tried to boil rice; she put so much water that it was not drying up; she tried to dry it with a hair dryer.

It came to Tara's mind oftentimes, "Bowled over by her beauty, I am caught in an odd web. Distant hills look green."

"We had come here to serve mom, but mom has to serve us. Bindery cannot work, and mom has to do everything for us."

He said to his mother, "Mom this is the time for you, to relax. You should not work so hard. Let her do most of the work, she will learn."

"She has not been used to doing work, my son. Now she finds it hard to do so. She would learn gradually."

"I am just managing to understand the reality of life, Mom. When would you get any comfort? What is the family for? It is for serving the elders but not to yoke the elders to work."

"Don't worry about me, my child. A long life is ahead for being served. I would not lose anything in helping you. Mothers feel happy doing something for their children. What kind of mother is she who does not take pleasure in helping their kids? Do not worry about me. Take care of your family life." Karmi advised him to be broad minded.

"I will make her find some sort of a job. When she start doing some work, she would understand how hard it is to earn money and stop wasting it.She had asked me to engage a servant, as she could not do the cooking. I told her that we could barely manage the house with my salary. How can we have a servant? Then she told me that she was not demanding money from me but from her grandfather."

Karmi said, "No, my son, we should not get anything from her grandfather. You may starve, but do not come under their obligation."

"Now she is insisting that if she does not get a job, she would start tuition work, and with her earnings she would hire a girl for help."

"Bali has called me to America many a time. I think I should go to her for some time. Meanwhile your Bindery will adjust with you in this house."

In order to get diverted from her pain, Karmi made up her mind to go to Bali and stay there for some time.

Karmi was just talking of going to America when she got a call from Bali, "I am going to be a mother, Mom. I have mailed your sponsorship papers, Please, get your visa and come here."

Karmi was pleased very much to know that her daughter was in the family way, but she did not feel like leaving her country. She always thought of doing this or that.

She wanted to know the where about of her husband but she had failed to get any hopeful information from his colleagues. With the death of her son she felt lonely and had a great urge to live with him.

She handed over the charge of the United Front to Kartar and the responsibility for the college to the Committee. She got free to visit America. She applied to the Embassy for a visa. On receipt of the interview call, she went to Delhi.

While traveling by bus, she was just thinking of her contribution to the family and her reward by her husband, "I married this old man and raised his family, giving birth to two sons and a daughter. He did not give any weightage to it He took me as a child bearing machine. He had no sentimental attachment with me."

She reached the American Embassy. She was called from window No. 3, and she went into the Visa Officer's booth. As he saw her alone, he asked her, "Where is your husband?

"I do not know. Long ago he left the house without telling any body and never returned…."

He sympathized with Karmi and said, "Show me your certificate of marriage. Without that you cannot prove yourself to be Bali's mother."

She did not have the marriage certificate. She was thinking as she stood there, "I gave birth to the girl, brought her up, educated her, married her off, and still I have not become a Mom; Father did a little action, that too for pleasure seeking he became creator, the father of the girl; it is strange. It is man's highhandedness. The Woman is discriminated in this male-dominated society at every step."

Disappointed, she returned home.

She took the village headman and two witnesses with her and went to the Tehsil office. She filled the form to get her marriage registered. As the registration was to be done from back date and her husband was not with her, Tehsildar kept raising objections. She gave all the answers he required. She was the leader of the area, and he did not dare to demand illegal gratification. He continued harassing her till five o'clock and, while leaving the office, he signed the paper. She obtained the marriage certificate and returned home. The following week she went to Delhi and got her visa. Within a fortnight she boarded the plane.

SIXTY-THREE

Karmi arrived in a new world. She observed that American people work very hard; they are busy, day and night. Even pregnant women do the job till the on-set of birth pangs. Bali too attended her duty up to the time of delivery. She went to the hospital at the last moment. After giving birth to a male child, she was discharged. She came home the second day. The baby boy was put in a different room.

Karmi was surprised, "in this respect, even birds are better than these people. They remain with the baby in the nest till their young ones are able to fly and feed themselves".

Her baby cried a lot for mom's nipple, but it did not matter for them. They gave milk bottle according to time schedule. They do not want any interference in their personal life."

After living there for some time, she realized their real problem, they cannot pull on if both husband and wife do not work, and otherwise it becomes difficult to pay the bills. It is the necessity; under their set up.

The children are looked after by the baby sitters, and mothers go to work. The mother's attachment with the child is only till its birth. The new born baby neither gets mother's nipple to suck nor the warmth of her body. An artificial nipple takes the place of Mom's nipple, and baby-sitter replaces the real mother. The bond of love that develops between mother and baby by natural inter action does not develop. Without mother's love, the baby remains irritant and unhappy. Remote control of baby costs her much that she realizes later on. Some other short comings creep into baby's Psych. When the parents get sick of the babysitter's behavior, they call their mothers / mothers-in-law. But they too cannot serve the purpose of real mothers in baby's growth. Mother is a Guru of the baby; grandmother cannot be the Guru of Mom's Standard as natural love is a tool with Mom for baby's teaching.

A child can be brought up by 'Dollar'- mothers, no doubt, but the human values can be inculcated by natural mothers only. Without human values they turn into robots and problematic personalities.

Without their natural growth they grow abnormal. A large number of such girls become mothers before school graduation. Man should learn from nature. A fruit plant yields good fruit when it attains maturity to yield. If it yields fruit before maturity it affects its health and the health of fruit also. Similar is the case of human being. Woman's life is ruined, and she realizes it later on. Moreover she has to depend on social security or some other aid. She becomes a burden on the nation.

Karmi thought, "I am a grandmother; I have love for the baby and the baby too has attachment with me. But those kids who do not have their mothers/grandmothers and grow up with 'Dollar'- mothers… their behavior is not normal.

"The mother too is a loser in the long run. Her earnings are taken away by the baby sitter; and her baby, when grows up, leaves her like that of an animal's. She becomes bankrupt in the real sense and lives all alone in the company of pets. This is the time of old age when she/he wants to be loved and supported by someone of her/his own. "

SIXTY-FOUR

Her daughter's father-in-law was a pleasure seeker. He danced like a pea-cock at Karmi's sight. With the setting of sun, he started drinking. He used to drink so much that he lost his senses. He passed urine or vomited almost every day. While cleaning the baby was her duty, she had to do this job for the old man also. It was the question of her daughter's future life.

Bearing a child and cooking food for the family is considered as woman's duty, but looking after her daughter's father-in-law, was a new phenomenon.

Bali did not return home, sometimes two to three days at a stretch, as she had too much of work at the hospital. There was a shortage of nurses, and she had to do others' duty also. Dr. Bant used to come home in the evening, but the phone remained glued to his ear. Both of them had no time for their new born baby. It was the grandmother's concern only.

Karmi got fed up with life in USA in about a month, but the purpose for which she had come, could not be lost sight of. She did not leave the child to the maid's care. One Sunday, a lady in the neighborhood took her to the gurdwara. Reaching there she felt as if she had reached her own village. She met the Punjabi community there, and talking to them she felt very happy. The monotony was broken. She drew close to the lady who took her to the gurdwara every Sunday.

She could not sit idle. She started teaching Punjabi to young children in gurdwara and this helped her in feeling at home. The children could neither speak nor read Punjabi. English was their mother tongue. The Punjabi parents got enthused to send their children to learn the language of their roots. Following her, so many Punjabis came to the fore to help her in teaching. The number of students also increased.

Karmi felt that Punjabi books of good quality were not available in gurdwara. Only handbooks of hymns *and s*tories of the Guru's life were available. No one took interest in them. One day Karmi appealed to the congregation, "Gurdwara has lot of income, please, start a library on one side. Books to suit the taste of everyone should be kept there. It will help them to develop interest in reading Punjabi books. The religious books are read only by the old people; the new generation has no interest in them."

The people agreed with her proposal. A room was given for the library; funds were sanctioned for buying books. Stories, novels, and poetry books were purchased. The people spent some time on reading new books on Sunday.

Karmi was very particular that the literature should be of constructive nature. Newspapers and magazines published in Punjabi were subscribed to. The constructive work done by Karmi prompted all the Punjabis in America to start libraries in temples/gurdwaras. The libraries started functioning. The books to learn Punjabi were also got printed in Roman script and made it easy to keep new generation in touch with the culture of their roots.

When the Punjabi community came to know that Karmi had set up a girls' school in her village and it became a college later on, they started giving donations to the college.

Karmi did babysitting for her grandson at home. He too enjoyed her company. One day after playing with the children, grandson got into his grandma's lap and said, "Become a monkey grandma!" Whatever he saw in his books he asked his grandma to do that.

She could not say 'no' but started making excuses, "I am old now; my knees and ankles do not work. How can I become a monkey and jump like him? You wanted me to become an elephant, my child, I became one. You wanted me to become a horse, I did so. But I cannot become monkey and leap like him. "Then you can become an owl." He made her task easier.

"No, I am dead tired now. Go and make your grandpa an owl." Grandmother passed the buck to the grandfather. He went to him and asked him to become an owl. The grandfather was already annoyed with Karmi and said to him curtly, "first of all make your grandma an owl, then your mom, and come to me thereafter." He turned his back on his grandson.

The child felt very bad at his grandpa's refusal. He started crying.

Grandfather did not care for his crying. He thought he would keep quiet after crying a little. He started to read a book.

His grandson got furious and flung the crane in his hand at grandpa's temple. The temple bulged, and his spectacles were broken. The grandfather frowned and wished that he could give him a severe blow. But he was also afraid that someone might ring up the police and he would be put behind bars. He could do nothing but said only this much–: "How spoilt he is!"

In this way Bali's mother and her husband's father staged a one-act play with the child daily.

One day Karmi got too much tired, playing with the grandson. She said to his grandfather, "Please take care of him for some time so that I can do cooking."

"I cannot do it. The bulge at my temple hurts too much."

'Carrying the child on her flank, Karmi came out grumbling, "My life is hell over here. I have not even had a time to wash my face…they are taking revenge of some past lives."

Dr. Bant came in. He stood quietly and listened to her woes. When he went ahead, he found his father was fomenting his temple with a piece of ice. He asked, "What has happened, Dad?"

He was already enraged greatly and kept mum for some time, and then said, "This brat hit my temple with the crane and caused a bulge. He also broke my glasses."

Bant asked him to forget such a petty incident and advised the baby, "A good child does not do like this, sonny. He is your grandpa."

The child felt hurt on making him realize and started crying.

"Don't cry, my son," saying this, he took the child in his lap, caressed it, and he got silent. Then he turned to his father and said, "He wants someone to play with. If there was another child, he could have company. And now he asks you to play with him. When you do not listen to him, he gets annoyed."

A child loves to be loved. He did not feel happy playing with his grandfather but felt happy with his grandmother. She had to attend to all the household chores and in addition, looked after the child. She was on tenterhooks the whole day.

The same exercise began the next day again. Her grandson said, "Grandma, I want to have a cookie." The cookies were downstairs in the pantry. Karmi carried him on her flank to the pantry. The child was very heavy. The old grandmother carried him with difficulty. She felt very uneasy, and, descending the stairs, she could not restrain her tears. She was stepping down and crying. As she was still in the stairs, Bali turned up. Looking at her mother shedding tears, she said, "Is everything all right, Mom, you are crying?"

"Yes everything is all right but—..." saying this, she started sobbing, "When I was at my own place, I did not have to do all this, ; working the hand-mill, so to say, I was free to go to sleep and wake up when I liked."

"The child must have harassed you?"

"Harassed? My goodness! The whole day he keeps me in a tense position. When I try to sit down, he says, 'Up, grandma up. I want to bathe in Mom's tub.' I carry him upstairs and give him a bath. After having his bath, he says, 'I want to do potty in potty-chair, hurry up.' When I wipe him, he orders me to go upstairs, 'Up, grandma, up, I want to play in the toy room.' Upstairs and downstairs, is the whole day practice. My legs have gone stiff and heavy and I have a back-ache too. When so hard-pressed, I feel I should not have come here. I was all right by myself."

"Mom, we have not come here on our sweat-will; we have been compelled by our odd circumstances to leave our mother land. I was raped, what worse had not happened with me? Did you experience any happiness there? Your dearest son, with all the quali-ties of a rising star, was killed there. Your own life was not safe. You do not face those problems over here."

Next day the grandchild saw, through the window pane, birds moving about on the lawn outside. He looked at them with keen interest as Karmi lay in bed. He insisted on going out to play with the birds.

In order to divert his attention, Karmi tried to make him read a book, "This is the police car blowing a siren." He liked the police-car sirens, and, taking the book from grandma's hand, he started reading. He leafed through for a while. Seeing that he was busy going through the book, Karmi tried to relax. As he saw his grandmother lying down, Noor lost his temper. He flung the telephone receiver at the window pane and broke it. He started crying, looking at the broken pane, and felt afraid lest anybody should rebuke him. Grandma got up to assuage him but he feared her. As she drew closer, his cries got louder. Grandmother was afraid that her son-in-law would feel bad at the loss. She gave the child a chocolate to silence him.

He got silent on getting chocolate and got busy with eating.

His grandfather felt annoyed, "Bant has told you so many times not to give him chocolate. It is bad for his teeth. But you do not listen to anybody. You should at least act upon the advice of your doctor son-in-law."

Karmi was already sick of him. He never took care of the boy and had given her no relief. She retaliated, "If you do not want to lend a helping hand in work, please do not torment me unnecessarily. I am not made of steel, I too get tired. If I have given him a chocolate to stop his crying, heavens have not fallen down. You could take him, rather than condemning me. You could say so if you ever took care of him."

He felt insulted. As soon as Dr. Bant entered the house, his father started poisoning his mind, "Your mother-in-law lies down the whole day. She does not care for the boy. He has broken the window pane. And when I tell her to take care of the child, she retorts vehemently."

Bant also got furious, looking at the broken glass. He said to his mother-in-law, "What a big loss have we undergone, Mom? As soon as I enter the house, you make me face a new problem daily. You cannot look after even one child. It is so cold we shall freeze with the broken window glass. We will have to spend money."

Karmi was not the one to take it lying down. She said, "Your dad was also sitting here. He could have taken care of the boy. How can I do everything all by myself? Should I attend to the kitchen or look after the boy?"

"You insult my dad at every step. Had you requested him properly, he would have taken care of the boy." "Taking care of the boy? Forget it, he sits to drink whenever it comes into his mind and orders me, 'Fry eggs for me. ...' "

As they were arguing, Bali too came in. Karmi got emotional on seeing her. She started crying.

"What has happened, Mom?"

"I cannot become a wife of every man in my old age."

"Who is asking you to become a wife? You are sulking unnecessarily."

Karmi got silent, fearing more conflict. She suppressed her anger. When calm prevailed, she told her daughter everything, "One day, when he was dead drunk, he held my arm, but I pushed him back. The child thought that we were fighting. It started crying. Seeing that the child was crying, he stepped back. Now he always spits venom at me and instigates his son against me. Today his son also had flared up unnecessarily."

Bali had not forgotten the old man's doings. But except for showing sympathy, she couldn't do anything for her.

"God is unkind to you, Mom, putting you in a new trouble every day. I thought you would become happy after coming to America, but your position got miserable here. "

"It is not God, who is after me, it is His men. Firstly your father betrayed me. Had he not gone out, all this would not have happened. A husband is a lifelong companion who protects her wife. In his absence everyone starts looking at her lasciviously.

"Your father-in-law thought that he had gotten an easy prey. He has made my life a hell. He used to take the boy out in the park—, he did vacuuming and all types of cleaning—, but now in order to torment me, he does nothing."

Bali was on the horns of a dilemma; she could not say anything to her husband, she was not in a position to share her mother's agony in any other way.

Next day they were invited to a party by one of their friends. They took Karmi and their son along.

Karmi looked like a maid among the well-dressed guests. No one took her for Bali's mother. Thus, feeling small, she occupied a back seat.

The party began. They had their pegs, drank a little and danced. The old man too was busy drinking. Everyone called him 'Dad'. The child started playing with children. Bali too got busy. So many snacks were lying on the table, and people came and helped themselves. She thought in Indian way, "I will have something if anyone asks me, to take it." No one asked her, and she did not take anything.

The party ended. Everybody stood up. Bant told Bali on the way, "You should ask Mom to dress properly while going to parties. She looked like a maid in this dress." Karmi felt humiliated. She was not asked if she was hungry or had taken something, rather they started criticizing her unnecessarily.

Bali talked harshly to her, "In this suit you got us humiliated, you look like a baby-sitter and not our mom."

"I put on my Indian dress and the shawl over my shoulders. I could not have become a *'ma'am'*[55] like you overnight. I sat there in the room without taking anything in the party. Lest the people misunderstand me as a maid."

Next day she did not prepare breakfast. She even avoided taking care of her grandson. Instead she went to the kitchen garden just to while away the time. As she eyed the blooming flowers, she felt as if the entire world was blooming joyfully. Tending to the plants and flowers she felt relieved. She plucked the dried up twigs and killed the black bees clinging to the roses.

Bali had to go for a two o'clock shift that day. She saw her mother sitting in the kitchen garden. Bali went to her and said, "You have come out so early, Mom. You have not taken your breakfast. What is wrong with you?"

"Nothing is wrong with me. I have 'lost my senses'. "

Mother's reply infuriated Bali all the more.

When her daughter talked so rudely Karmi felt like flying back to India.

Karmi remained lost in worry throughout the night, "There is no son or daughter relationship in this world. All is based on self-interest."

"What a husband is to wife, and wife is to husband, no other relation can be. I should live with my

---

55 fashionable lady

husband. My honor, my dignity, is with my husband. It is just possible, that good sense may prevail upon him, and he may return home."

Next Day she told her daughter, "I have had enough of your America, buy me a ticket for India. I want to go back."

SIXTY-FIVE

Karmi reached Delhi. The entire family was there to receive her. As she put her foot on the motherland, she felt as if she had gotten all the best that life could give. Tara presented to her a bouquet and clasped her in his arms. Her daughter-in-law touched her feet. Paul folded his hands from a distance and greeted her. Karmi embraced Nandi and clasped her to her breast.

Next day they reached home at dawn, the whole night passed in travelling by car up to Abohar.

Karmi saw that everything had undergone a change— – there was velvet grass in the courtyard, flowers of different kinds were blooming and made the air fragrant. There were different types of vegetables grown on the one side of the house. Karmi was overjoyed at the hard work done by her daughter-in-law and son.

Bindery brought tea in bone china cups with saucers, and Tara placed before her a plate full of *barfi (sweet)*. Nandi brought in hot '*samosa*[56] looking at the barfi in the plate, Karmi said, "Tara, everybody knows that Indian sweets are adulterated. Earlier air

---

56 Snack-wheat cake stuffed with boiled pea nuts and Potatoes.

and water were polluted, and now even the food-stuffs have become toxic. You have brought barfi. Milk contains lot of Urea."

Tara had no reply. He removed the plate.

Looking at the bone china set, Karmi said to Bindery, "It appears you have got a job."

"No Mom, jobs are for sale by ministers. We cannot afford millions to get a job. She remains busy with tuition work," said Tara.

Karmi felt very happy at the changes made in the house. She said, "East or West, Home is the best. You cannot get this type of sincere love anywhere in the world. If you want to know the truth, it is your love that brought me here."

"Really...?" asked Paul in a romantic way.

Karmi smiled on his comments. He understood the meaning of her.

Paul said again, "No one comes back from there, and anyone who goes there sticks to that land. That you have come back is really the expression of your love."

Karmi diverted the topic. "Now tell me, how is your medical practice?"

"Very fine, it is child care that pays. The children get sick frequently, and the work goes on uninterrupted. I have bought this car out of my practice."

"This Honda car shows that you have a roaring practice. You should now think of bringing a life partner to sit with you in the car."

"The one I love has come." Paul was still trying to win her back.

Karmi said, "Talk sense, please."

Paul felt it and said, "Kammo, you seem to have changed." Paul stood up to leave.

"No, Paul you are not to go!"

"No I should go now, you should relax now. You have come after a long journey."

Karmi was tired, she went to sleep. Bindery awakened her in the evening, "Dinner is ready, Mom, get up. You can sleep afterwards." Karmi went to the dining table.

"You have prepared such a heavy dinner, Bindery! How have you learned cooking all these delicacies?"

"Practice makes a man perfect. One has just to make a beginning."

Tara got a chance to praise Bindery after a very long time, "She does lot of work now, Mom. We have rented a room in the city. She gives tuition work there. In the evening she does the cooking. She devotes her spare time to gardening. She thus remains extremely busy all the day."

Karmi felt very happy. She said, "You have done wonders, Bindery. Your efforts have brought in a sea change in the house, which sparkles now in every way. This is called life," Karmi again kissed Bindery's forehead.

"I have learnt quite a lot from Tara, Mom. One gets transformed in accordance with the situation.

Tara has helped me. Now I derive lot of pleasure in doing work.

"To my good luck I have come out of the old situation. Had I remained dependent on my grandfather's money, I would have met the same fate like my mother."

As they were talking, Gulzar and the President of the United Front, Kartar, came. They had learned about her return. They broke to her the good news: – "The United Front is on the great ascendancy all around. Small organizations are united under the banner of the United Front. The number of Red Guards has tremendously increased. Wherever they notice any injustice, they fight against it. The people also join the sit-ins and demonstrations in a big way. We are sure to win the next elections.

"Earlier the moneylenders could get farmers' lands attached, but the things have changed now. The United Front does not let any attachment go through and fights by tooth and nail.

"Formerly the farmer's produce was priced at the sweet will of the buyers, and they did not even cover the cost of inputs. A Price Commission of Agriculture Experts has been appointed this time. They fix the prices of yield, keeping in view the expenditure on inputs. Because of the pressure, one member of the Farmers' body has been nominated to the Commission. He is from the United Front.

"The bonded labor has been freed. Earlier, the big landlords gave some money in advance and kept exploiting them against interest payments. Now it is not so. The labor at the kilns has also been freed."

Karmi laughed and said, "That means you have established real democracy. But you must bear in mind that these serpents cannot be killed easily. They have yet to build the *'Ram Mandir' 'fight Jihad,'*, and the *'sanctity of Gurdwaras* has to be upheld.' They mislead the people in the name of religion or giving misleading slogans such as above, to create communal tension."

Next day Karmi went to college. She felt very happy at the progress made by her institution. The money sent to the college from America had been well spent. Post-graduate classes were being run.

A humble attempt for the education of the girls had succeeded admirably. Karmi's institution looked like *Shanti-Nike tan*[57].

---

57   This is an institute Founded by and known after the name of Rabindera Nath Tagore, Noble Laureate.

SIXTY-SIX

It was Sunday. Every-body was relaxing at home. Karmi asked Tara, "any progress made about locating your father, Tara?"

"The one, who went away from the house like a thief, has not gone to come back. He might have jumped into some well or canal. Otherwise he would have come back."

Karmi did not like Tara's curt reply. She had returned from America with the hope of finding her husband. Her son's reply disappointed her. He had driven his father out of his mind, taking him for dead.

She said to him angrily, "All right, call a taxi for me. I will go alone. He is dead for you but for me he is alive; I am living in the hope of finding him."

"Why should you go by taxi? You can go with Uncle Paul in his car"

"When my own son refuses to go with me, why would Paul like to go? Is he related to me in any way?"

Bindery felt bad at Tara's non-cooperation, and she said, "You need not ask anybody. If he does not go, I will go with you. I will feel obliged to accompany you, Mom." For the sake of Bindery, Tara also got ready to go. He said, "Our vacations begin next week, all of us will go together. We will take this opportunity to pay obeisance at the Golden Temple."

They booked two rooms in *Guru Ram Dass* Inn *Amritsar* and went there. After taking some rest in the rooms they started searching for the Subahdar. They looked into the special rest houses, called bungas, and a ward for the old and infirm people. All men there looked alike— – long flowing beards, pressed-in cheeks, wrinkled skin all over their body, and sunken eyes. They had started looking for him after about twenty-five years! Recognition was very difficult. There were so many old people like him.

Next day they checked the rooms along the corridor, community kitchen, and everywhere in the golden temple. Tara got disappointed and said to his mother, "We have not found him here, where should we go, now?"

"My inner voice says that he is here somewhere. We will certainly find him!"

"But your inner voice should also tell his whereabouts."

"He must be doing service here. We have not yet seen him in the *'pingalwara'*[58]; Let us go there."

Tara turned the taxi towards 'Pingalwara.

The volunteer rummaged through his register, but there was no entry in the name of the Subahdar Bhag Singh. Karmi was not satisfied with that much... She

---

58 An institution founded by Bhagat Puran singh for homeleas people suffering from various chronic diseases

went in herself and checked the destitute, invalid, lepers, and those suffering from incurable diseases lying in their beds and awaiting death.

When they were about to return disappointed, the volunteer on duty said, "There is another room on the back side of the institution. You can see there also. T.B. patients have been isolated there. Their entries are in a separate register with the supervisor."

The mere mention of T.B. scared Bindery, who feared going inside. She said, "let us go back, mom. We will not find him but might contract some disease."

Tara also refused to go in. He said, "Bindery is right. We might get infected." Karmi agreed.

They were going to get into the car, when Karmi stopped. "My conscience says he is here."

The volunteer on duty said to them, "There is an army veteran ever since Bhagat ji's times among the TB patients. You can see him. He may be your man. Even if he is not the one you are looking for, he would be able to tell you about your man. He knows everyone. He is a very good person. He is now hard of hearing, and his eyesight is nearly gone. Earlier he could read the newspaper and watched T.V. also. He just lies down counting the beads of his rosary. He is a benevolent person. He received hundreds thousands as arrears, which he donated to the Pingalwara."

The mention of arrears reminded Karmi of the subahdar. She said, "He must be our man."

"What is his name?"

"'I do not know his name. We call him Veteran / Fauji."

"Let me satisfy myself, my son. It should not remain in my mind that I had not tried there." Karmi left them there and went in.

As soon as she entered the T.B. room, on the right side, a tall man with a long white flowing beard lay in bed, counting rosary beads. Karmi called, "Sardar ji." He raised his ears as if he had recognized the voice. He peeped through the aperture of his closed fist carefully and said after a few moments, "Who are you?"

Karmi also recognized his voice. The love had sparkled. She replied, *"Karmi!"*

"Yes, repeat it, please, what have you said?"

She said, "Karmi!" loud enough to make him understand.

He sat up slowly and asked again, "Are you Karmi?"

"Yes I am."

"God bless you, Karmi….may you live long," He folded hands for prayer and said haltingly, "O God! Accept thanks in million times of a sinner who has been heard."

Tears of joy flowed down his cheeks. Karmi wiped his tears with a corner of her head cover...

Hearing them, Tara and Bindery also came in and touched his feet.

Karmi introduced him to his son, "he is your Tara."

"My Tara!" saying this, he tried to stand up but could not. Karmi and Tara helped him to stand. After a couple of minutes standing, energy was restored into his legs. The subahdar embraced Tara with all force. Then Karmi introduced Bindery, "she is your daughter-in-law."

He caressed Bindery's head. He started moving in front of them with the help of his stick and reached the volunteer on duty and occupied a chair there. Others followed him. They all took seats close to him. Then he inquired about his parents.

"They expired long time ago. They were very keen to see you till the end."

"Oh ho!" he sighed. "Satti must have been married"

"Long back, she has children, with God's Grace. Bali has also been married. She is in America."

"I do not see our Udhe with you...?"

Karmi could not reply, her throat got choked and she started crying.

"What is the matter? Is everything all right?"

She kept on crying but couldn't utter a word. After some time she said, "He has been put to death by your own near and dear ones."

"Who is he to do the heinous act? I have never harmed anyone."

"He is your nephew, Nikka!"

He said after a long pause, "It happened because of my absence. Had I not left my home, this would not have happened. I am responsible for his loss, Karmi." Tears flowed down as he said this.

All of them got sad. Karmi kept on crying by the side of her husband.

"Let us go home, Sardar ji."

"No! Karmi, I have no right to go there. I always put you in trouble. Had I done anything good to you, I could go,"

"Forget the past. It was my fate!" Karmi blamed her fate and forgave her husband.

"It is not your fate. I am your culprit."

"When the government sent me home empty handed, I had gone off my head...it was bound to be....I had spent the whole of my life fighting for my country but got starvation and poverty in return. I had lost my rank and returned home utterly disappointed. Thank God I did not commit suicide.

"I felt relieved a bit on reaching home and meeting you people, but all of a sudden, finding Udhe in our house, I suspected your illicit relations . . . The suspicion upset my mind all the more. I left home in desperation....

"I should be punished for what I did, Karmi. Let me die here."

His son also insisted on his going with them, "Dad. You have performed a marvelous job in the liberation of the country. Now give us the chance to serve you."

Volunteer sitting nearby could not restrain himself, "Your services to the people have borne fruit, Dad. God has heard your prayers now. You have struggled with death for a long time. You are lucky to have chance to live among your family members for the rest of the days,"

"No!" Dad declined curtly and sat tight in the chair.

"You should listen to someone, Sardarji," saying this, Karmi held him by the arm and made him stand. Tara, his wife, they all, helped karmi to pull him up. Dad stood up and stepped ahead.

The Pingalwara volunteer made entry in his register and said; "Now you can meet with the President and go home."

SIXTY-SEVEN

Karmi, reaching home gave a bath to her husband and dressed him in new clothes. His cot was put in a separate room. Dr. Paul came in. He examined him; checked his blood pressure etcetera, and told them, "Take him to the Civil Hospital for a thorough check up."

Blood tests and X-rays confirmed T.B. disease. Doctors prescribed the medicines and sent him home.

He was accommodated in a separate room and was served food there. Karmi herself looked after him. She gave him medicines, massaged him, bathed him, and changed his clothes daily.

She gave him milk and boiled eggs in the morning for breakfast. During the day he was given fruit and chicken soup. At night he was given 'chapattis' with lentils or rice curd and meat.

Karmi took him out for a walk with the help of his stick, morning and evening. After a few days' care, the subahdar became much better and, impressed by Karmi's valuable services; he expressed his gratitude, "Karmi! You are my Ganges.[59] You have given

---

59   The Ganges is a sacred river. People call it 'mother Ganga.' It is true as Indian Economy mainly depends on the Ganges

me life. You have purified the impure one. I am a sinner. I continued to commit sin, and you kept on forgiving me, purifying me like the Ganges. How would I repay your debt of gratitude in this life?"

"Rendering service to her husband is the duty of a wife, *sardar ji*," saying this, she went to the neighbor's house.

The subahdar was singing Karmi's praises, lying in his bed. Someone called from outside, "Uncle, are you in?"

"Who are you? Come in, I am here."

He came close to him and touched his feet and said, "I am Nikka."

"What is in common between us now? You killed my son and broke my backbone. There is nothing left for me to survive."

"I have come only to clarify the position, uncle. Aunt, on the instigation of other people, gave my name in the list of murderers. Kukku is openly declaring that he attempted to murder Udhe and Karmi many times before but failed; He succeeded at the time of elections to kill Udhe.' Aunt feared Kukku and did not mention his name. I can go to Gurdwara to say the truth on oath," and he swore by the sacred book-Guru Granth Sahib.

As Nikka swore, all the subahdar's doubts were cleared, "Possibly, Karmi did so erroneously." He said to himself.

Uncle's anger was mellowed, and they started talking about ordinary matters. Uncle asked him, "What is going on in the gurdwara? ..."

"The priest is a good person, well learned, well at devotional singing. His *prayer is worth listening to*. He makes you ecstatic. You should also come." Nikka knew that his uncle was of a religious bent of mind. He won him over by talking of religion.

"God willing, I will come on Sunday."

"I will meet with Aunt later. I am in a hurry to go elsewhere."

Nikka avoided his aunt as he was a liar, he did not have the courage to face her.

When Karmi returned home, the subahdar expressed his desire to go to gurdwara, "Tomorrow is Sunday. We shall go to gurdwara to pay obeisance."

"You can go. I don't have so much time."

SIXTY-EIGHT

In order to please his uncle, Nikka made arrangements to honor him. When the subahdar reached Gurdwara, there was a good gathering. The congregation stood up with garlands to welcome him. He was laden with garlands as he went in. Nikka made his speech praising the Subedar like anything, "He has played a great role in our freedom struggle. He fought at the I.N.A. Front for many years. He was made a prisoner and when released came to Pingalwara and started serving there the sick and the invalids. He did not remain attached to his family. Whatever arrears he got, he donated to Pingalwara.

The president put a yellow scarf around his neck. They were photographed. Slogans of 'God is great' were raised. The subahdar was overjoyed. He forgot the murder of his son.

By enacting the drama of honoring him, Nikka won his heart. He went to the gurdwara daily. Nikka met him there. Day by day his influence on the Subedar got cemented. It posed a problem for Karmi. She could not say anything to her husband nor could she stop him from going to gurdwara.

One day Nikka spread a rumor; "Someone has burned the *Granth Sahib*[60] at *Sehlina*. This is the handiwork of the Hindus. We will avenge this mean action."

The Subahdar interrupted him, "Talk sense. You should think before speaking. It could be a Pakistani spy, an ISI agent. Pakistan wants to create a wedge between the Hindus and the Sikhs. Pakistan is bent upon destroying India's Economy. Mohammadan schools are everywhere in Pakistan and injections of religious fanaticism are given there. The pupils are taught to kill the infidels. You are wrongly blaming the Hindus for burning the Holy Book. They have more faith in Guru Granth Sahib than that of ours. They keep it at home and read the hymns. In same family, some members are Sikhs and others Hindus."

Ghuka contradicted him, "Someone must have been born as Gangu.[61] Others supported him, "Yes, yes, it is possible."

They silenced the subahdar. A procession was taken out the following Sunday and they made the subahdar lead it. They made provocative speeches at every crossing and talked of the burning of the holy book. They also raised the slogans of a Separate Sikh State. A procession with naked swords was provocative to the Hindus.

60

61 Gangu was a cook of Guru Gobind Singh JI. He was a Brahmin by caste. He betrayed and got two minor sons with their grandma arrested by the Muslim Governor, WazirKhan.

In retaliation to the procession of Sikh Fanatics, Puri got a chance to lead a procession of the Hindu Fundamentalists. He was a Drug lord of International fame. He had a very high income. The officers were very close to him. He had become the defender of the Hindu faith against the Sikh Fanatics.

He called the meeting of all the Hindu Fundamentalists such as *Shiv-Sena'*, *Bajrang Dal*, and addressed them, "What has happened in the procession of the Sikhs, you have seen; and what they have been saying, you have heard. Will your eyes open only when a Sikh State is established like Pakistan and you become refugees again? Shutting your eyes like a pigeon would not do. If you want to live in Punjab you will have to give them a befitting reply.

"We will take out a huge procession on coming Sunday. The volunteers would hold Tridents[62] in their hands, at the sight of which the Sikhs would themselves leave Punjab."

After Puri, other speakers also supported the move to take out the procession and passed the resolution to this effect unanimously in their meeting.

Karmi heard the call with the beating of drums for taking out the procession by the Shiv Sainiks and other Hindu Fanatics. She got worried, "The wretched Nikka has created riotous conditions by taking out the procession. The Hindus will retaliate

---

62   Three pronged Spears

by taking out processions in other cities and raising provocative slogans, and there would be looting and arson. The situation will get out of hand,"

As Karmi was cleaning the pans and pots striking one against the other loudly, subahdar said, "Why are you so angry today, dear?"

"Why should I not be angry? I am not made of clay. Those who tormented me throughout my life and those who took my son's life, have become so dear to you. You lead their procession. And I, who sacrificed my life for your sake, have become your enemy now.

"The question of Hindu-Sikh, which the mafia had failed to raise for years, has been raised by you, leading their procession. You have created conditions for Hindu-Sikh strife.

"What would the people think? The husband is leading the Fundamentalists and the wife is leading the Democrats, they are playing with our sentiments. You have wasted my labor of years. I struggled throughout life for establishing democracy, and when success was at hand; you have pushed it back by a hundred years. You are the chief culprit for these misdeeds." Karmi thundered angrily.

He said, "I am sorry, Karmi, I have made a mistake. I relied on Nikka's swearing by the Great Guru. Please forgive me. I cannot repay the debt of gratitude even in seven lives."

Karmi called the emergent meeting of the United Front at night. Roop Lal Sathi, Kartar, Gulzar, and other leaders came to participate. Kartar said, "There is no time to think now. There is an urgent need to calm the situation. We should do something."

Sathi expressed his views, "The United Front should take out a Peace and Amity Procession before the Hindu Fanatics does it on Sunday. We should do it one day in advance on Saturday. A public announcement should be made tomorrow. Our Red Guards will go from door to door requesting the people to join us to save the country from another partition."

At the conclusion of the meeting, Karmi said, "The Peace and Amity procession will be taken out at 11:00 a.m., and Dr. Paul will make all the arrangements for the procession."

The Procession was taken out through the city. People came out in large numbers. The public responded overwhelmingly. Kartar and Sathi appealed to the people at the crossings to maintain peace. Passing through the lanes and bazaars, the procession reached the old grain market. Karmi made the presidential speech, "My dear countrymen, awake! The enemies of the country are going to partition your motherland for the second time. The first wound of the unwanted division has not healed yet. Half the population cannot afford a square meal twice a day, do not afford clothes to cover their nakedness, and have no shelter to hide their head from freezing cold and scorching heat. If the division takes place again, the country will be totally ruined and a barbaric stage will come.

"The last procession was taken out with naked swords and fiery speeches, the procession with '*Trishuls*[63] will be taken out on Sunday. There would be violence, arson, and bombs would explode. If the atmosphere continues to be vitiated like this, and processions with swords and tridents continue to be taken out, there would be riots too. The arsonists lose nothing. Only you and I will suffer.

"The mafia will rule supreme; the leaders like Nikka and Puri will take rein of the country. Democracy will remain a dream forever.'"

A young man standing behind the stage was feeling uneasy when Karmi mentioned the name of Nikka. He twisted his right moustache and then left. He was heard mumbling by those standing close by –:

"...Your death is looming large, Karmi!"

Karmi roared like a lioness as she exposed the Mafia. "It is the Mafia who gives birth to Fundamentalism. Nikka and Puri are its bye-product." When she mentioned 'Nikka' again, the young man, tearing through the crowd, got on the stage and fired at Karmi— but, saving Karmi, Paul came before her and was killed. The young man continued firing and pumped all the six bullets into them. Karmi

---

63   three-pronged spears

too was injured gravely, fell down, and almost lost consciousness. They were rushed to the hospital.

The fury of the mob was uncontrollable. The people started beating the young man, his head was smashed, his arms and legs were broken.

As Karmi was sinking, the subahdar tried to drop the holy water of Ganges in her mouth[64]. She could not speak but stared at him with anger as if she was saying "Keep *your* holy water away from me. *I*[65]have seen enough of *your*[66] meanness. *I* gave *you* life at every step, and you have given *me* death."

---

64 It is a custom among Hindus/Sikhs to pour Holi water of river Ganges into the mouth of the diseased person to purify the soul.

65 'I' stands for woman

66 You/ 'Your' stands for man

* 9 7 8 1 4 7 0 1 1 2 0 7 3 *